Evangelical Futures

Evangelical Futures

A Conversation on Theological Method

John G. Stackhouse, Jr., editor

Baker Books

A Division of Baker Book House Co
Grand Rapids, Michigan 49516

R
Regent College Publishing

© 2000 by Regent College

Published by Baker Books
a division of Baker Book House Company
P.O. Box 6287, Grand Rapids, MI 49516-6287

and

Inter-Varsity Press
38 De Montford Street
Leicester LE1 7GP
England

and

Regent College Publishing
an imprint of Regent College Bookstore
5800 University Boulevard
Vancouver, B.C. V6T 2E4 Canada

Printed in the United States of America

Library of Congress Cataloging-in-Publication Data

Evangelical futures : a conversation on theological method / John G. Stackhouse, Jr., editor.
    p.   cm.
Includes bibliographical references and index.
ISBN 0-8010-2246-0 (paper)
1. Evangelicalism. 2. Theology, Doctrinal. I. Stackhouse, John G., 1960–
BR1640.E855   2000
230'.04624'01—dc21   00-041470

Audio and video recordings of the conference from which this book is derived are available from the Regent College bookstore (1-800-334-3279; www.regentbookstore.com).

For current information about all releases from Baker Book House, visit our web site:
http://www.bakerbooks.com

Contents

Contributors

Stanley J. Grenz (D.Theol., University of Munich) is the Pioneer Mc-Donald Professor of Theology and Ethics at Carey Theological College and Regent College, Vancouver, Canada. Among his many books are *Renewing the Center: Evangelical Theology in a Post-Theological Era* (Baker, 2000); and *Theology for the Community of God* (Eerdmans and Regent College Publishing, 2000).

Trevor J. Hart (Ph.D., University of Aberdeen) is Professor of Divinity at the University of St. Andrews, Scotland. He is the author of *Faith Thinking* (SPCK/InterVarsity Press, 1995); and *Regarding Karl Barth* (Paternoster, 1999/InterVarsity Press, 2000).

Alister E. McGrath (D.Phil., Oxford University) is Professor of Historical Theology at Oxford University, and Principal of Wycliffe Hall, Oxford. He has authored many works, including *The Genesis of Doctrine* (Eerdmans, 1997); and *Iustitia Dei: A History of the Christian Doctrine of Justification* (Cambridge University Press, 2d ed., 1998).

Roger E. Olson (Ph.D., Rice University) is Professor of Theology at Truett Theological Seminary, Baylor University, Texas. His most recent book is *The Story of Christian Theology: Twenty Centuries of Tradition and Reform* (InterVarsity Press, 1999).

J. I. Packer (D.Phil., Oxford University) is the Board of Governors Professor of Theology at Regent College, Vancouver, Canada. Among his many books, the most widely read has been *Knowing God* (InterVarsity Press, 1973).

John G. Stackhouse, Jr. (Ph.D., University of Chicago) is the Sangwoo Youtong Chee Professor of Theology at Regent College, Vancouver, Canada. Among his writings is *Can God Be Trusted? Faith and the Challenge of Evil* (Oxford University Press, 1998).

Kevin J. Vanhoozer (Ph.D., Cambridge University) serves as Research Professor of Systematic Theology at Trinity International University, Illinois. His most recent book is *Is There a Meaning in This Text? The Bible, the Reader, and the Morality of Literary Knowledge* (Zondervan, 1998).

Stephen Williams (Ph.D., Yale University) is Professor of Systematic Theology at Union Theological College, Belfast, Northern Ireland. He is the author of *Revelation and Reconciliation: A Window on Modernity* (Cambridge University Press, 1995).

Preface

JOHN G. STACKHOUSE, JR.

"Say the one thing that you want to say to evangelical theologians about theological method. You've got one public address, and one article, to get across your personal message to your colleagues."

This was the invitation sent to the main contributors of this volume. They delivered their papers first to the annual Theology Conference at Regent College, Vancouver, in October 1999. Each speaker then fielded criticism from the other participants in turn. After the conference, I made further editorial suggestions, and the participants went back to work, refining their papers into the contributions you have before you now. Three observers from different points of the evangelical compass, Messrs. Hart, Olson, and Packer, then were invited to respond to the finished papers.

The fundamental conviction shared by all of those involved in this project is that evangelical theology needs to engage more fully in conversation about theological method. In the guild of academic theology, especially liberal, neo-orthodox, and postliberal, it has sometimes seemed that methodology is the *only* subject discussed. To date, however, when evangelicals have discussed methodology, we have generally preoccupied ourselves largely with the question of the nature and interpretation of the Bible. Clearly, however, evangelical theology is more than exegesis, so we need to attend to other dimensions of the theological task as well. (To be sure, the notes to these essays show that we recognize and appreciate the work of other evangelical theologians who have already made substantial contributions to this broader conversation.)

There are many such dimensions, and this book does not attempt to touch on them all, much less state programmatically what evangelical theological method now should look like in every detail. These essays are deliberately and only idiosyncratic: Each individual was invited because of his distinctive outlook and asked to offer his particular contribution to this conversation. We hope collectively simply to spur on our colleagues to further reflection regarding theological method, both for the benefit of other professional scholars of theology and for the blessing of the Christian church—the primary beneficiary of worthy theological effort.

Teachers and students who read this book will find it profitable, if I may so suggest, to trace both the commonalities and the differences in these essays. All of us are self-professed evangelicals, and all of us agree on the basics of evangelical identity as spelled out, for instance, in my own essay in this volume. True to historic evangelical diversity, however, we part ways on many other issues—sometimes straightforwardly, but in this collection much more often implicitly. As editor, it is not evident to me that each contributor shares exactly the same understanding of biblical inspiration and authority, for example, or the same understanding of the role in theological construction of tradition, or contemporary philosophy, or spiritual experience. It is not clear to me that everyone is "postconservative," as Roger Olson suggests in his interesting reflections on these essays. Indeed, if we were, it would be difficult to see why J. I. Packer—surely no one's idea of a "postconservative"—endorses these essays as he does in his own contribution. So an attentive reading to what is said, what is implied, and what is not said might well prove worthwhile for those wrestling with these questions.

It is obvious, however, that these essays are not all that diverse. They reflect the fact that the contributors do not vary much in age (all between forty and fifty-five years old, with Jim Packer the venerable exception), in training (all educated in some combination of the United Kingdom, Canada, and the United States—Stan Grenz is the exception, having studied with Wolfhart Pannenberg in Munich), and in race (all white). All of us, furthermore, are male. For this unhappy narrowness of field we can only plead in defense that the state of evangelical theology today is itself dominated by such demographics. In putting together both the conference and resulting volume, we did try to include a greater variety of participants, and failed. We promise, however, that our future conferences and volumes will succeed better in this important respect.

For now, then, we hope that these essays will be worthwhile in both affirming our evangelical common ground as a distinctive tradition in contemporary theology and provoking us all to develop that tradition more carefully and creatively to meet the needs of our time.

Our thanks as editor and contributors go to our partners at Baker Book House, especially editors Robert N. Hosack and Melinda Van Engen. We also are grateful to Peter Quek and Bill Reimer at Regent College for logistical assistance for the conference at the origin of this volume. Keith Grant prepared the index with characteristic competence. And the Social Sciences and Humanities Research Council of Canada provided the editor with valuable support.

Part 1
Setting the Stage

1

Evangelical Theological Method

The State of the Art

ALISTER E. MCGRATH

My task in this essay is to provide a survey of the current state of the art—in other words, to give an overview of the conversations that are presently taking place within evangelicalism over the issue of theological method. I think it will, therefore, be clear that my task is not to prescribe what evangelical theology ought to do in the future—or, indeed, what it ought to have done in the past!—but rather to attempt to establish what the current issues are in relation to evangelical theological method. In this way, we can at least have an idea of what the issues are perceived to be, what the proposed solutions might be, and who some of the individuals are who are making a significant contribution to its development.

There is widespread agreement within the evangelical theological community that evangelicals have not paid adequate attention to the issue of theological method, despite the fact that they have a generally high regard for theology. To some, this might seem curious or even unacceptable. How can one do theology without reflecting on the assumptions and methods that this involves? It is entirely possible that there may be at least some merit in this complaint.[1] Yet it must be noted from the outset that the contradiction may be more apparent than real. A poet may compose with an intuitive understanding of her art, just as an artist might be able to create works of brilliance without being able to set out precisely the method that was followed in their conception and production. We must allow for the fact that many evangelicals have grown up in an intellectual environment that shapes their thinking on how theology is done and have often absorbed this without feeling the need to give it formal expression in something as rigorous as "theological method."[2]

An appropriate point at which to begin our discussion is the question of whether evangelicalism continues to regard theology as important—in other words, has evangelicalism abandoned its former esteem for theology, on account of its preoccupation with pastoral, political, and evangelistic concerns?

Has Evangelicalism Lost Interest in Theology?

A major concern that has been expressed since roughly 1985 concerns the role allocated by evangelicalism to the discipline of systematic theology. The substance of this concern may be stated very simply: Evangelicalism has come to regard systematic theology as something that may be sidelined without any undue loss to the church, in that it is of limited relevance to the practical realities of powerful preaching, church growth, and effective pastoral techniques. In a number of recent works, David F. Wells has argued that evangelicalism has lost its way, primarily on account of its abandonment of an explicitly theological agenda.[3] Wells argues that evangelicalism is now currently characterized by a strongly pragmatic outlook, which leads to an emphasis on church growth and styles of ministry that are shaped largely by the insights of popular sector psychology. For Wells, theology no longer seems to have a foundational role for evangelicalism. It is not regarded as foundational for maintaining and nourishing evangelical identity, nor as an essential and seminal resource for Christian ministry. Evan-

1. See Richard Lints, *The Fabric of Theology: A Prolegomenon to Evangelical Theology* (Grand Rapids: Eerdmans, 1993).

2. See the useful survey in Clark Pinnock, "New Dimensions in Theological Method," in *New Dimensions in Evangelical Thought: Essays in Honor of Millard J. Erickson*, ed. D. S. Dockery (Downers Grove, Ill.: InterVarsity Press, 1998), 197–208.

3. See David F. Wells, *No Place for Truth, or, Whatever Happened to Evangelical Theology?* (Grand Rapids: Eerdmans, 1993). For some responses, see Alister McGrath, *A Passion for Truth: The Intellectual Coherence of Evangelicalism* (Downers Grove, Ill.: InterVarsity Press, 1996); John Stott, *Evangelical Truth* (Leicester: Inter-Varsity Press, 1999).

gelicalism, Wells argues, seems to prefer to draw on techniques rather than theology—and, to add insult to injury, these techniques often seem to be drawn from the worlds of business practice and popular psychology rather than the tried and tested resources of the Christian tradition. Theology once occupied the place of honor in evangelical seminaries; it is now being displaced by disciplines that focus on practice rather than theory, technique rather than theology.

Clearly there is much in Wells's analysis that merits close consideration. Wells appears to have identified a worrying trend in postwar evangelical Christianity. It is of considerable importance to attend to his criticisms and ensure that evangelicalism continues to be shaped by authentically Christian ideas and values, rather than just the latest techniques of popular business culture. Yet there is a question that must be raised at this point: Is Wells actually correct in his assessment? Do the facts support his analysis?

It is essential to emphasize that there are compelling reasons for suggesting that Wells has misread or misrepresented the situation on three different levels. In the first place, it is a simple and richly documented fact that evangelicalism continues to produce a substantial number of major theological works. The evidence available suggests that evangelicalism continues to regard theology both as a subject of essential importance to intellectual and spiritual formation and as an area of intellectual development that is of critical importance to the future of the movement. As Carl Braaten comments in the course of a 1996 review of recent works of systematic theology:

> The initiative in the writing of dogmatics has been seized by evangelical theologians in America. No doubt, German professors will continue to publish their summas to cap off their careers. But after Pannenberg, the interest in Germany in theology would seem to be on the wane. Most of what is being written there has the feel of having been recycled once too often. And in the United States, most mainline Protestant and progressive Catholic theology has landed in the graveyard of dogmatics, which is that mode of thinking George Lindbeck calls "experiential expressivism." Individuals and groups vent their own religious experience and call it theology.[4]

4. See Carl E. Braaten, "A Harvest of Evangelical Theology," *First Things* 61 (March 1996): 45–48. Braaten identifies the following works as pointing to evangelicalism's continuing concern with issues of theology: Donald G. Bloesch, *Holy Scripture: Revelation, Inspiration, and Interpretation* (Downers Grove, Ill.: InterVarsity Press, 1994); Stanley J. Grenz, *Theology for the Community of God* (Nashville: Broadman & Holman, 1994); Wayne Grudem, *Systematic Theology: An Introduction to Biblical Doctrine* (Leicester and Grand Rapids: Inter-Varsity Press, 1994); James William McClendon, Jr., *Systematic Theology: Doctrine*, vol. 2 (Nashville: Abingdon, 1994); Alister E. McGrath, *Christian Theology: An Introduction* (Oxford and Cambridge, Mass.: Blackwell, 1994).

Braaten points out that there are excellent reasons for suggesting that "the energy devoted to dogmatics by evangelicals today is far greater than among liberal or liberationist Protestants and Catholics." He traces awareness of this fact among non-evangelicals to the presidential address delivered in 1991 to the American Theological Society by Gabriel Fackre entitled "The State of Systematics: Research and Commentary." In addition to challenging the common opinion that dogmatics is dead or dying, Fackre called attention to a new generation of evangelical systematic theologians—which seems to have come as something of a surprise to his audience, which was mainly composed of theologians to whom the evangelical world was something of a mystery.

In the second place, it needs to be pointed out that one of the reasons why evangelicalism has been so successful in North America is its willingness to address the concerns of ordinary Americans, using both language and ideas that can readily be understood and appreciated by ordinary folk. Many studies of American intellectual culture have pointed out that it appears to be characterized by an aversion to theory and a preference for practice[5]—something that is by no means limited to the specific case of theology, but which finds application across a wide range of disciplines. This pragmatic orientation of American culture in general, and hence American evangelicalism in particular, inevitably leads to an emphasis on making sure that things work—that thinking is relevant, as much as right. It is not theology as such that is the subject of distrust within evangelicalism—it is a specific form of theology that fails to address pastoral issues and express itself in terms that can be understood by ordinary mortals. In short, it is theology that cannot be preached. It seems that Wells's criticisms reflect something of a misreading of the inbuilt assumptions of American culture, both popular and academic—assumptions that evangelicalism has actually been able to exploit in its recent growth and development.

Yet it is not merely the cast of American culture that Wells has misread; he also seems insensitive to the complexity of evangelicalism itself, not least the various intellectual and spiritual streams that converge to form its vortex. There has always been a tension within evangelicalism between what might be termed "scholasticism" and "pi-

5. Note the perceptive comment of John E. Smith, *The Spirit of American Philosophy* (New York: Oxford University Press, 1963), vii: "It is no exaggeration to say that in American intellectual life, irrelevant thinking has always been considered to be the cardinal sin." See also the excellent account of Cornel West, *The American Evasion of Philosophy: A Genealogy of Pragmatism* (Madison, Wis.: University of Wisconsin Press, 1989), 5.

etism," the former insisting on the importance of right thinking and the latter on the need for a personal transformative relationship with Jesus Christ. For the pietists, theology just gets in the way of that relationship, dulling it rather than sustaining it. J. I. Packer points out that those he terms "entrenched intellectualists" pose a serious problem. Packer here refers to "rigid, argumentative, critical Christians, champions for God's truth for whom orthodoxy is all." Their chief concern is the defense of "their own view of that truth." While they invest themselves unstintingly in this task, their total dedication to "winning the battle for mental correctness" often leads them to have "little warmth about them." Such "fixated Christian intellectualists" are "spiritually stunted, not in their zeal for the form of sound words, but in their lack of zeal for anything else." Having grasped the importance of the intellect, they undervalue everything else, including the importance of personal relationships. "Relationally, they are remote." Against this arid theological correctness, Packer urges a recovery of the Puritan vision of true religion as embracing the affections as well as the intellect. It is essential to move on from knowing about God to a relational acquaintance with God himself.[6]

None of these considerations can conceivably be taken as arguments against evangelicalism maintaining a commitment to systematic theology—but they do draw attention to the need for us to understand theology correctly if it is to have value to the community of faith. Wells seems to misread the situation and assumes that an aversion for what is actually a pastorally, apologetically, and spiritually irrelevant theology shows that evangelicalism has given up on its theological heritage. The truth is actually more disturbing for evangelical theologians, although more encouraging for everyone else—namely, that most evangelicals want their theologians to come down to earth and "talk real." We may like to ignore that challenge, but we dare not—for it is saturated with a plea for Christian sanity and authenticity. The early church made a firm distinction between *scientia* and *sapientia*—between "knowledge" and "wisdom." Most evangelicals feel that systematic theology has come to be about little more than head knowledge and lacks wisdom—a wisdom that can be supplied by those who live out the Christian life in churches and in the world rather than in the splendor of the seminaries. And what about the relational dimension of the Christian faith, which seems (at least, to its many critics) to be overlooked by many systematic theologies that seem to prefer the explora-

6. J. I. Packer, "An Introduction to Systematic Spirituality," *Crux* 26, no. 1 (March 1990): 2–8.

tion of the interplay of propositions to the impact of our knowledge of God on the quality of our Christian life?

There is also a third point that needs to be noted in rejecting Wells's analysis of the evangelical assessment of theology. One of the most distinguishing features of evangelicalism is its emphasis on the authority of Scripture. Scripture is to be seen not simply as a repository of Christian theology, but also as a God-given resource for nourishment in the Christian life. There can be little doubt that some evangelicals are nervous and anxious over the notion that systematic theology can somehow come between the believer and Scripture and somehow insulate or protect the believer from a direct engagement with the Bible. This concern can be seen throughout evangelical history, and it is important to acknowledge that it represents a serious concern that cannot easily be dismissed. The task to which evangelical theology must set itself is that of showing it is legitimate and helpful to use theology as a means of enhancing the quality of the believer's engagement with Scripture. This type of strategy can be seen in the preface to John Calvin's *Institutes of the Christian Religion* and in a host of significant works developing similar lines—namely, that at its best, systematic theology is to be viewed as an extended engagement with and commentary on the Bible. It is intended to assist the believer in this encounter rather than excuse him from that encounter or deny him access to the identity-giving and faith-enhancing Word of God.

I suspect that the jury is probably still out in relation to the question of evangelicalism's commitment to systematic theology. There are some signs that this commitment has become eroded—and here we need to heed David F. Wells's warnings, even if they seem to be unhelpfully overstated at points. Yet sometimes, to get a hearing for a case, it needs to be overstated; I am therefore reluctant to criticize the accuracy of Wells's analysis when he has managed to wake us up from our theological slumbers and shatter any complacency that might exist over this point. Against his view, however, we must note the substantial body of evidence pointing in precisely the opposite direction—namely, that evangelicalism is one of the conspicuously few constituencies within modern Christianity that continues to regard systematic theology as an important discipline, both in terms of its intellectual credentials and its pastoral and spiritual relevance.

The topic of this collection of essays, therefore, most definitely does not belong to the past. It is a present matter of importance and interest to evangelicalism as it faces the third millennium. This leads me to move on and consider what role systematic theology might have within contemporary evangelicalism.

Theology and the Spiritual Disciplines within Contemporary Evangelicalism

Our brief survey of the writings of evangelicals since the Second World War, both in North America and in Europe, gives us ample reason for affirming that theology is broadly seen as foundational to the Christian life within the evangelical constituency. It is certainly true that some evangelicals attach more importance to theology than others. Nevertheless, a recognition of the foundational role of theology can be discerned by even those who are more reticent in this respect. A right knowledge of God is seen as essential to every aspect of the Christian faith. Theological sloppiness can so easily degenerate into a heretical approach to the Christian life. Many examples can be given of this recognition of the importance of theology from evangelical history in the twentieth century. For example, it can be seen in J. I. Packer's 1955 critique of the "Keswick" teaching on sanctification, which had become popular within British evangelical circles during the first half of the twentieth century.[7] Packer argued that a theologically naïve pietism inevitably lapsed into precisely such a Pelagianism. "After all," he wrote, "Pelagianism is the natural heresy of zealous Christians who are not interested in theology." For Packer, good theology was thus the essential foundation of both Christian thought and life.

Yet it can be argued that evangelicalism's greatest contribution to systematic theology in the second half of the twentieth century relates to the interplay of theology with other spiritual disciplines. Having affirmed the foundational role of theology, evangelicals have gone on to explore the way in which theological foundations lead to the direction and development of various superstructures, particularly in the areas of pastoral care, preaching, spirituality, apologetics, and ethics. Space does not permit me to explore these matters in detail; I will note simply two of the areas in which the foundational role of theology has been acknowledged and fruitfully explored.

Spirituality

Although there remains resistance to the term within sections of evangelicalism, there is little doubt that the word *spirituality* has gained virtually universal acceptance as the best means of designating the group of spiritual disciplines that focus on deepening the believer's relationship with God and enhancing the life of the Spirit. Other terms are still used, of course, such as *piety, godliness,* and *spiritual theology.* Evangelical resistance to the word *spirituality* has rested partly on the

---

7. J. I. Packer, " 'Keswick' and the Reformed Doctrine of Sanctification," *Evangelical Quarterly* 27 (1955): 153–67.

fact that it is not a biblical term, which, of course, is an entirely correct observation. *Spirituality*—like the words *theology, Christology,* and *soteriology*—is not encountered in Scripture. Yet evangelicals have become used to employing non-biblical terms to refer to biblical concepts; the essential point is to ensure that they convey biblical insights. Evangelicals are perfectly free to use terms such as *theology, spirituality,* and *apologetics*—none of which are found in the Bible—so long as they are interpreted in a biblical manner and used to convey and articulate biblical insights.

So how does theology relate to spirituality? There is a substantial body of opinion within many sections of Christianity today that argues theology has no role to play. In effect, spirituality is an autonomous discipline, which is only hindered by allowing the dreary voice of the professional theologian to intrude. Evangelicalism, however, has tended to proceed in precisely the opposite direction, arguing that good theology provides the essential foundation for responsible and authentic Christian spirituality. Before exploring how evangelicals have understood this relationship, it is necessary to note that some legitimate concerns can be discerned as underlying a reluctance to allow a significant role for systematic theology in spirituality. In particular, the following points can easily be shown to constitute significant difficulties for many:

1. Theology is so academic and cerebral that it loses sight of the relational aspects of the Christian faith—aspects, of course, that are of central importance to spirituality.
2. Within the Western academic tradition, theology is seen as a disinterested and detached discipline, which inevitably leads to a weakening of the link between theology and prayer.

Both of these concerns can be addressed through challenging the assumptions concerning the nature and task of systematic theology. A false and deficient understanding of the nature of theology can be argued to lie behind these concerns, which can therefore be more properly met by rediscovering what theology is all about rather than excluding it from the field of spirituality!

But let us turn to consider how evangelicals have addressed the relation of theology and spirituality. As we were privileged to hold the conference on evangelical theological method at Regent College, Vancouver, I hope that I will not be too severely criticized for singling out the contribution of J. I. Packer to this debate. Two of his publications seem to me to be of especial importance here. One is his classic work

Knowing God, which articulates an essentially Puritan understanding of the interaction of Christian thinking and living.

> Knowing God is a matter of *personal involvement,* in mind, will and feeling. It would not, indeed, be a fully personal relationship otherwise. To get to know another person, you have to commit yourself to his company and interests, and be ready to identify with his concerns. Without this, your relationship with him can only be superficial and flavourless. . . . We must not lose sight of the fact that knowing God is an emotional relationship, as well as an intellectual and volitional one, and could not indeed be a deep relationship between persons were it not so. The believer is and must be emotionally involved in the victories and vicissitudes of God's cause in the world.[8]

We can see here a careful exploration of the emotional and affective aspects of theological knowledge, paralleling in important ways the emphasis on the "religious affections" of Jonathan Edwards. Knowledge of God is not an academic matter but a relational reality—and note, incidentally, how this answers one of the anxieties expressed above concerning the place of theology in spirituality.

Yet in my view, Packer's best treatment of this matter is in his 1989 inaugural lecture as Sangwoo Youtong Chee Professor of Theology at Regent College. The title he chose for his inaugural lecture, as much as its content, is highly significant: "An Introduction to Systematic Spirituality." In that lecture, Packer stressed the total impossibility of separating theology and spirituality:

> I question the adequacy of conceptualizing the subject-matter of systematic theology as simply revealed truths about God, and I challenge the assumption that has usually accompanied this form of statement, that the material, like other scientific data, is best studied in cool and clinical detachment. Detachment from what, you ask? Why, from the relational activity of trusting, loving, worshipping, obeying, serving and glorifying God: the activity that results from realizing that one is actually in God's presence, actually being addressed by him, every time one opens the Bible or reflects on any divine truth whatsoever. This . . . proceeds as if doctrinal study would only be muddled by introducing devotional concerns; it drives a wedge between . . . knowing true notions about God and knowing the true God himself.[9]

8. J. I. Packer, *Knowing God* (London: Hodder & Stoughton, 1975), 38–39. For details of the origins and development of this work, see Alister McGrath, *J. I. Packer: A Biography* (Grand Rapids: Baker, 1997), 186–95.

9. Packer, "An Introduction to Systematic Spirituality," 6. See also Packer's important article "Evangelical Foundations for Spirituality," in *Gott Lieben und seine Gebote halten,* ed. M. Bockmuehl and K. Burkhardt (Basel: Brunner Verlag, 1991), 149–62.

Packer's point is that a genuine experience of God makes the detached study of God an impossibility—a point appreciated by medieval mystical writers, who often spoke in rapturous terms of their experience and knowledge of God. It is like asking someone who is in love to be neutral about the person he or she loves! Theology needs to be taught in the context of a worshiping and prayerful community that is aware that to speak of God is potentially to end up adoring and worshiping him and proclaiming him to the world.

It will be clear from this discussion that evangelicalism has strongly contested the idea that theology may be undertaken by anyone, irrespective of whether he or she believes in God or not. The discipline of theology is seen to arise from the context of faith, in which obedience to God leads to all human faculties—reason, will, emotions, and imagination—being submitted to the claims of the gospel. Let me now turn to another area in which theology has implications: apologetics.

Apologetics

In recent years, there has been a renewed recognition of the importance of apologetics—that is, the defense and explanation of the Christian faith to those who have yet to come to faith.[10] The importance of theology to apologetics has long been recognized. The words of Cornelius van Til are an excellent example of an approach to apologetics that rests on rigorous theological foundations.[11] While some have raised doubts about the specifics of van Til's theological foundation, our concern here is to note his recognition of the importance of theology to this aspect of the ministry of the church to the world. Apologetics cannot be allowed to become a pragmatic discipline; it both rests on and reflects the intellectual integrity of the Christian faith to which it bears witness.

Theology may be thought of as essential to good apologetics in two ways. First, it provides the apologist with a network of beliefs and doctrines that enable him or her to detect weaknesses in alternative worldviews and to identify the strengths of the Christian proclama-

10. See Alister McGrath, *Bridge-Building: Effective Christian Apologetics* (Leicester: Inter-Varsity Press, 1992). North American edition published as *Intellectuals Don't Need God and Other Modern Myths* (Grand Rapids: Zondervan, 1993). Further works that merit close study here include Brian Allison, *Analytical Studies in Apologetics* (Unionville, Ontario: Brice & Bensa, 1990); C. Stephen Evans, *The Quest for Faith* (Downers Grove, Ill.: InterVarsity Press, 1986).

11. Cornelius van Til, *The Defense of the Faith* (Philadelphia: Presbyterian and Reformed, 1955). For further details, see William White, *Van Til: Defender of the Faith* (Nashville: Thomas Nelson, 1979).

tion. Thus, the doctrine of the final resurrection and eternal life is an essential component of any Christian apologetic response to the problem of suffering.

But theology is also important in a second manner. It provides an analytical framework by which the apologist may bring the full resources of the faith to bear on the situation in hand. Theological analysis allows the complex unity of the Christian faith to be broken down into its constituent parts in order that the apologist can decide which of its many aspects can be deployed to the best effect. The complex Christian proclamation of the death and resurrection of Christ can thus be analyzed in order that its various aspects can be identified and exploited.

I have often found it helpful to use the following analogy to clarify this important point. In 1666 the great British mathematician Isaac Newton noticed that a beam of white sunlight, entering through a narrow slit in the shutters of his darkened room, could be split into its constituent colors—red, orange, yellow, green, blue, indigo, and violet—by a glass prism.[12] The colors of the rainbow could be reproduced by a piece of glass in the laboratory, thus suggesting that raindrops act like glass prisms, diffracting the light of the sun and "decomposing" it into a brilliant spectrum of color.

The critical point here is that the glass prism did not *impose* these colors on the white light; it enabled them *to be discerned* within it. They were already there, although their distinctive identities remained unobserved. What had hitherto been taken to be a simple color—white—was now shown to be a complex unity of different colors. The prism split the white light into its constituent elements so that the colors, which were already there in the beam of white light, could be isolated and examined individually. The apparently white light of the sun was shown to be made up of many different colors of light in combination. In nature, all were combined; in the laboratory, they could be split up.

The same is true of responsible Christian theology, which breaks the message of the cross and resurrection down into its constituent parts so that they can be examined individually. The message of the cross is a unity—but it is a *complex* unity. It is by examining its individual components individually that the whole message can be better appreciated and understood. Theology does not invent these components; it merely uncovers them. They are not the product of some overactive theological imagination; they are already present, awaiting our analysis. All that the theologian has done is isolate them so that each can be studied

12. For details, see A. Rupert Hall, *Isaac Newton: Adventurer in Thought* (Cambridge: Cambridge University Press, 1996), 41–53.

individually. Theological analysis thus identifies apologetic possibilities. Apologetics is thus much more than the art of communication and persuasion; it is a theological science, undergirded by a rigorous analysis of the nature of the gospel on the one hand and the situation and nature of those to whom it is addressed on the other.

If space permitted, we could explore the ways in which evangelicals have affirmed the significance of theology for other spiritual disciplines, including ethics, pastoral care, and preaching.[13] Our concern, however, is to consider issues of debate within the evangelical constituency concerning questions of theological method. Some of these will be addressed in the course of this volume.

Evangelical Theological Method: Points of Debate

Evangelicalism is a broad term, embracing a complex network of individuals, seminaries, parachurch organizations, and journals, each with a distinctive "take" on what constitutes the essence of evangelical identity. Precisely because evangelicalism is a loose and contested concept, disputes regularly break out over who's in and who's out—disputes that generally achieve little in the way of clarification, apart from temporarily raising the temperature within the evangelical community and setting a long-term agenda of personal reconciliation between individuals who are alienated from each other as a consequence!

In the United States, if I might be permitted to make a critical observation as an outsider, the intrusion of a business culture appears to have led to new pressures in this matter. Seminaries compete for students and for endowments; it is tempting to bad-mouth other seminaries that might be competing for funds from the same donors, labeling them "liberal" or "apostate," if it helps secure funds. Individual ministries need donors, who are often unsure as to whom to give their hard-earned money. The intensely competitive business culture of the United States can easily reinforce the confrontationalism that lies not far beneath the surface of evangelicalism.

13. Helmut Thielicke, *Theological Ethics*, 3 vols. (Grand Rapids: Eerdmans, 1978); Stanley J. Grenz, *The Moral Quest: Foundations of Christian Ethics* (Downers Grove, Ill.: InterVarsity Press, 1997); O. M. T. O'Donovan, *Resurrection and Moral Order: An Outline of Evangelical Ethics* (Grand Rapids: Eerdmans, 1986); Alister McGrath, "Doctrine and Ethics," *Journal of the Evangelical Theological Society* 34 (1991): 145–56. Among other fascinating studies, see LeRoy Howe, *The Image of God: A Theology for Pastoral Care and Counseling* (Nashville: Abingdon, 1995); Thomas C. Oden, *Pastoral Theology: Essentials of Ministry* (San Francisco: HarperCollins, 1983); Peter Adam, *Speaking God's Words: A Practical Theology of Preaching* (Downers Grove, Ill.: InterVarsity Press, 1998).

Yet it is not my concern to explore this issue in any detail, save to note the point that concerns us in this conference—the diversity that exists within evangelicalism. The sources of this diversity are complex, and I shall note merely two:

1. Denominational issues. Evangelicals have denominational loy-alties, which often exercise a subtle influence over the assump-tions and agendas that are brought to the theological tasks. I suspect that evangelicals who are also Anglicans or Baptists, for example, might find that some of their divergences can be traced to specifically denominational loyalties. This is not something that should alarm us; it is merely a recognition of the complexities of the ecclesial world in which evangelicals live, worship, and think.

2. Cultural issues. Evangelicals grow up in certain cultures, which shape their thinking. For example, certain obvious differences exist between American and European evangelicalism, which reflect their different cultural backgrounds (and also help us understand the Canadian situation, which reflects concerns from each).[14] American evangelicalism often takes the form of specifically evangelical denominations or groupings; European evangelicalism generally takes the form of a reforming and re-newing movement within the mainline churches—an *ecclesiola in ecclesia,* to use the old way of speaking. Again, North Amer-ican evangelicalism is often right-wing and Republican; Euro-pean evangelicalism is far more diverse politically, reflecting a different historical and cultural heritage. Again, fundamental-ism was a major presence in North America, and many Ameri-can evangelicals consciously define themselves, both positively and negatively, with reference to its heritage. The movement had a strictly limited impact in Europe and thus plays a negli-gible part in shaping the identity of European evangelicals. And so on.

Yet these differences are to be seen as adding variety to the move-ment, not compromising its integrity. While it is a simple matter of evangelical family life that, sooner or later, members of that family take absolute stands on relative issues and demand that others follow them, history makes it clear that evangelicalism has always been a culturally,

14. See the helpful discussion of John G. Stackhouse, Jr., *Canadian Evangelicalism in the Twentieth Century: An Introduction to Its Character* (Toronto: University of Toronto Press, 1993).

theologically, and spiritually diverse movement. We do not need to feel anxious about this or worry in case it compromises the integrity of the term *evangelical.*

So what are the methodological issues debated within evangelicalism today? I offer in what follows a sketchy map of the terrain, which avoids fine detail in order to help us get an idea of the broad features of the complex landscape that lies before us.

Biblical Authority

There is no doubt that evangelicalism is characterized by its emphasis on the authority and sufficiency of Scripture. The Westminster Confession of Faith (1647) summarizes the evangelical consensus on this major issue:

> The whole counsel of God, concerning all things necessary for his own glory, man's salvation, faith and life, is either expressly set down in Scripture, or by good and necessary consequence may be deduced from Scripture; to which nothing at any time is to be added, whether by new revelations of the Spirit, or human traditions.[15]

Or perhaps we might cite from a leading Lutheran confessional document, the Formula of Concord (1577), which makes a similar point:

> We believe, teach and confess that there is only one rule and norm according to which all teachings *(dogmata)* and teachers are to be appraised and judged, which is none other than the prophetic and apostolic writings of the Old and New Testaments. . . . Other writings, whether of the fathers or more recent theologians, no matter what their names may be cannot be regarded as possessing equal status to Holy Scripture, but must all be considered to be subordinate to it, and to witness to the way in which the teaching of the prophets and apostles was preserved in postapostolic times and in different parts of the world. . . . Holy Scripture remains the only judge, rule and norm according to which all doctrines are to be understood and judged, as to which are good or evil, and which are true or truly false. Certain other creeds *(symbola)* and writings . . . do not themselves possess the authority of judges, as in the case of Holy Scripture, but are witnesses of our religion as to how [the Holy Scriptures] were explained and presented.[16]

15. Westminster Confession, I, 6, in *Die Bekenntnisschriften der reformierten Kirche,* ed. Ernst F. K. Müller (Leipzig: Böhme, 1903), 545.11–20.
16. Epitome, 1–8, in *Die Bekenntnisschriften der evangelisch-lutherischen Kirche,* 2d ed. (Göttingen: Vandenhoeck & Ruprecht, 1959), 767.14–769.34.

It is perhaps at this point that evangelicalism shows most clearly its theological and spiritual continuity with the Reformation and its concern to ensure that the life and thought of the Christian community was grounded in, and continually reevaluated in the light of, Scripture.[17]

Some such position would be widely acknowledged within evangelicalism today. Although differences of approach and vocabulary may be discerned, attended by the inevitable border disputes relating to these differences, there is nevertheless a shared emphasis on the total reliability and trustworthiness of Scripture as the ultimate foundation and criterion of our saving knowledge of God.[18] Yet the issue of how Scripture is to be interpreted cannot be ignored and constitutes one of the most important areas in which evangelicals are wresting with issues of method.[19] I shall note these divergences under two broad categories: hermeneutics and tradition.

Hermeneutics

How important is hermeneutics? The debate has become important within evangelicalism since about 1975. In the case of England, the importance of the issue became clear in 1977, when Tony Thiselton gave an address on the topic to the National Evangelical Anglican Congress at Nottingham. There is no doubt that, for many of those present, the interpretation and application of the Bible would never be quite the same again.[20] In North America, there has been wide acceptance of the importance of hermeneutical issues. Yet that acceptance has not been universal, and there is considerable disagreement over the methods and assumptions that are to be used.

17. For details of the various interpretations of the *sola scriptura* principle, see Alister E. McGrath, *Reformation Thought: An Introduction*, 2d ed. (Oxford and Cambridge, Mass.: Blackwell, 1993), 140–55. For the high view of Scripture associated with the Reformation heritage, see the excellent study of W. Robert Godfrey, "Biblical Authority in the Sixteenth and Seventeenth Centuries," in *Scripture and Truth*, ed. D. A. Carson and J. D. Woodbridge (Grand Rapids: Zondervan, 1983), 225–50.

18. In general terms, evangelicals agree that Scripture is inspired yet offer different understandings of what this means; most agree that Scripture is "inerrant," yet at least nine different understandings of what this means can be identified in recent evangelical writing. See David S. Dockery, "Variations in Inerrancy," *SBC Today* (May 1986): 10–11. For a full account, see Louis Igou Hodges, "New Dimensions in Scripture," in *New Dimensions in Evangelical Thought*, 209–34, esp. 211–13.

19. See the useful discussions in Robert K. Johnston, ed., *The Use of the Bible in Theology: Evangelical Options* (Atlanta: John Knox Press, 1985); Donald A. D. Thorsen, *The Wesley Quadrilateral: Scripture, Tradition, Reason, and Experience* (Grand Rapids: Zondervan, 1990).

20. Details in McGrath, *J. I. Packer*, 215–17.

For example, Wayne Grudem's *Systematic Theology: An Introduction to Biblical Doctrine* tends to imply that all that is required in the theological task is to assemble the biblical passages relevant to a particular topic. Interpretation takes the shape of reconciling apparently contradictory passages. Biblical passages are treated as timeless and culture-free statements that can be assembled to yield a timeless and culture-free theology that stands over and above the shifting sands of our postmodern culture. Yet a rather different approach is found in the writings of Grudem's colleague at Trinity Evangelical Divinity School, Kevin J. Vanhoozer. From the beginning, Vanhoozer has shown himself to be aware of the importance of hermeneutics and no mean student of the art. His study of Paul Ricoeur has been widely admired,[21] and he has explored the application of those ideas with considerable skill in his admirable study of "meaning" entitled *Is There a Meaning in This Text? The Bible, the Reader, and the Morality of Literary Knowledge.*[22]

Comparing and contrasting the approaches offered by these two distinguished evangelical writers, teaching within the same institution, is both fascinating and instructive. The divergences between Grudem and Vanhoozer illustrate both the importance of the issue of hermeneutics and the variety of responses found within contemporary evangelicalism. The questions that are of particular interest (at least, to me) are the following: Do these different approaches to hermeneutics yield significantly different approaches to theology? And which is to be preferred? A debate is taking place here, and it needs to be overheard by all of us who theologize.

Tradition

To what extent does the theological heritage of the past shape our thinking today? Are we obligated to take into account what past generations thought about theology, or the interpretation of Scripture, as we develop our theologies today? A strong tradition within evangelicalism argues that theology is about the direct engagement of the believer with Scripture. After all, is this not what people mean when they talk about *sola scriptura?* We do not need to take into account what past writers have to say on a given topic; we can derive a correct understanding simply by engaging directly with Scripture.

In reality, of course, it's not that simple, and it is arguably essential to explore why the debate is more complex than might at first appear. We can illustrate this by looking at the interesting debate that has bro-

21. Kevin J. Vanhoozer, *Biblical Narrative in the Philosophy of Paul Ricoeur: A Study in Hermeneutics and Theology* (Cambridge: Cambridge University Press, 1990).
22. Grand Rapids: Zondervan, 1998.

ken out within evangelicalism over N. T. Wright's views on Paul's theology of justification, particularly as he sets these out in his major work *Jesus and the Victory of God.*[23] In this study, Wright presents ideas that conflict with Martin Luther's interpretation of Paul, especially in relation to his theology of justification. Some evangelical critics of Wright argue that, because he disagrees with Luther, Wright is wrong—for that specific reason. Yet this raises an immensely important and difficult question. Are evangelical New Testament scholars under some kind of family obligation to repeat what their forebears affirmed? Or are they under an absolute obligation to determine what Scripture says, even if this may prove to be in tension with what the evangelical tradition held, and held dearly? There is no contradiction in speaking of an "evangelical tradition of Pauline interpretation," in that evangelicals have developed set patterns of thinking about the cross and resurrection of Christ. Wright's book challenges us to consider whether these are, as a matter of fact, quite as biblical as we would like to think. This is a deeply unsettling challenge.[24]

Some evangelicals respond to this by repeating what evangelicals of the sixteenth or eighteenth century affirmed, followed by comparing Wright's views to theirs. Where they are seen to differ, they conclude that Wright does not represent an evangelical perspective. While this may satisfy some, it is in fact deeply inadequate. It basically rests on the fallacious and indefensible assertion that evangelicals have always gotten things right in the past and are, for that reason, excused from critical examination or correction. It amounts to the affirmation of the inerrancy of the evangelical tradition, where evangelicals ought to be affirming the inerrancy of Scripture, while recognizing that we may, through weakness or sheer cussedness, get our interpretations wrong from time to time and need correction.

As the reformers affirmed so strenuously, we are under an obligation to constantly reexamine our ideas and values against Scripture and avoid the complacency and laziness of thinking that the parrot-like repetition of the past ensures orthodoxy. As J. I. Packer pointed out in a careful and wise study of the role of tradition within evangelicalism, we must be prepared to submit all our ideas to the court of Scripture and verify them on its basis.[25] Wright's challenge is to ensure that our

23. N. T. Wright, *Jesus and the Victory of God* (Minneapolis: Fortress Press, 1992).

24. For a serious engagement with the methodological and theological issues involved, see Carey C. Newman, ed., *Jesus and the Restoration of Israel: A Critical Assessment of N. T. Wright's Jesus and the Victory of God* (Downers Grove, Ill.: InterVarsity Press, 1999).

25. J. I. Packer, "The Comfort of Conservatism," in *Power Religion,* ed. M. Horton (Chicago: Moody, 1992), 283–99.

views do indeed represent a biblical perspective. Evangelicalism is principally about being biblical not about the uncritical repetition of past evangelical beliefs.

A related debate concerns the extent to which evangelicalism is obligated to repeat the views of writers such as Martin Luther and John Calvin. A number of evangelical writers, including Michael Scott Horton and R. C. Sproul, have argued for the need for the views and terminology of today's evangelicalism to be shaped by the Reformation heritage.[26] This has led to what might still eventually turn into a constructive and helpful debate over the complex interaction within evangelicalism between Scripture itself—as the supreme norm of evangelical thought—and confessional theological sources, such as Calvin's *Institutes* or the Westminster Confession of Faith.

The debate over whether, for example, an evangelical is necessarily Calvinist in her theology of grace has been met with a vigorous response from Wesleyan and other evangelicals who see such a development as an unacceptable restriction of the concept of "evangelical" and a failure to represent the diversity of the evangelical constituency. Wesleyans have appealed to the evangelical credentials of both John and Charles Wesley in this debate, thereby indicating the importance of tradition to both sides of this important debate. The role of tradition in evangelicalism is thus rather more complicated than might initially be thought, and I propose to explore this issue myself at a later point in this collection of essays.

Philosophy and Theology

A fourth area to which evangelicals are giving much thought is the relation of theology to philosophy. To what extent does theology rest on philosophical presuppositions? Or can it be conducted without entering into any kind of dialogue with philosophy? This is a long-standing debate that has assumed a new turn recently on account of the increasing recognition that much evangelical theology has been deeply influenced—apparently without being aware of it—by modern presuppositions. The modern assumption that there is only one rationality,[27] only one form of logic, and only one form of "common sense" has saturated much evangelical thought since roughly 1850 to 1950. It is perhaps unfair to critique this, in that those who adopted these assumptions believed they were self-evidently true. The rise of postmodernism has

---

26. See such works as R. C. Sproul, *Essential Truths of the Christian Faith* (Wheaton: Tyndale, 1997); Michael Scott Horton, *In the Face of God* (Waco: Word, 1996).

27. See the classic study of Alasdair MacIntyre, *Whose Justice? Which Rationality?* (London: Duckworth, 1988).

eroded that assumption and offered us a perspective that allows us to see these ideas as false claims to universality. Yet some earlier evangelicals, working on the assumption that these ideas were obviously true, appear to have hitched their theological wagons to the Enlightenment myth of a universal rationality and raced off into the sunset—the sunset, as it turned out, of the Enlightenment itself.

An interesting debate has broken out over who these evangelicals might be and whether it really makes much difference anyway. Donald G. Bloesch has argued that a strongly modernist or rationalist spirit can be discerned within the writings of such modern stalwart American evangelicals as Carl F. H. Henry, John Warwick Montgomery, Francis Schaeffer, and Norman Geisler.[28] For Bloesch, this opens the way to making the truth of divine revelation dependent on the judgments of fallen human reason. Now, let us agree that evangelicals, of all God's people, cannot allow revelation to be imprisoned within the flawed limits of sinful human reason. Whatever the extent to which the human mind is noetically compromised by sin, it is imperative that those finite and fallen human minds should not be permitted to be the judges of what is and what is not divine revelation on account of its supposed or perceived "rationality."

Clearly this is an important issue. It is not quite as simple as Bloesch suggests.[29] Nevertheless, Bloesch has done for evangelical approaches to reason what David F. Wells has done for its concern for theology in general—raise some uncomfortable questions and force us to ask whether all is well. Rather than worry about whether the great evangelical stalwarts of the past have accidentally made themselves dependent on fallen human reason—a debate that is likely to continue without final resolution—it is important to ensure that their evangelical successors do not. In other words, contemporary evangelical theology needs to examine its use of reason and ensure that it is employed in a ministerial, not a magisterial, role.

In any case, things have shifted since the 1960s, and evangelicals need to relate to the new issues that have accompanied the rise of postmodernism. In particular, we need to note two important developments that are being evaluated in evangelical discussions of theological method in relation to the "universal rationality" of the Enlightenment.

28. Donald G. Bloesch, *Essentials of Evangelical Theology,* vol. 2 (San Francisco: Harper & Row, 1979), 267–68.
29. See the excellent study of James Emery White, *What Is Truth? A Comparative Study of the Positions of Cornelius Van Til, Francis Schaeffer, Carl F. H. Henry, Donald Bloesch, Millard Erickson* (Grand Rapids: Baker, 1993).

1. The collapse of foundationalism has important consequences for the way in which we do theology. Stanley Grenz has been one of the evangelical pioneers in exploring the possibilities for evangelical theologizing in a postmodern age, and it is clear that he needs to be listened to, as carefully as critically.[30]
2. We have been liberated from the rationalist demand to set out "logical" and "rational" grounds for our beliefs. Belief systems possess their own integrities, which may not be evaluated by others as if there were some privileged position from which all may be judged.[31]

I have no doubt that the continuing exploration of these issues will be an important, legitimate, and controverted area of evangelical theological method in the next two decades.

Evangelicalism and the Great Tradition

The recent conversations between evangelicals, Roman Catholics, and those of the Eastern Orthodox faith have opened up a new debate within evangelicalism over the propriety and purpose of theological dialogue between evangelicals and those outside the evangelical community.[32] Can such dialogue ever lead to anything other than criticism and a call to repentance and conversion? The debate has been intense and has often degenerated into personal criticisms that do little to enhance the esteem in which evangelicalism is held. Yet with the passing of time, the temperature has cooled, and a more reflective approach is possible. Has evangelicalism something to gain from entering into discussion with theologically orthodox representatives of Roman Catholicism and Eastern Orthodoxy? Might not such a dialogue lead to enrichment all round?

Such thoughts are still at an early stage, and it is far too soon to make any kind of judgment on this one. Yet it is not too soon to consider the theological benefits that such a dialogue might bring. Perhaps one might be to help evangelicals realize that debate with medieval and patristic writers is a necessary part of the theological enterprise. Calvin, after all,

---

30. Useful evaluations and discussion may be found in David S. Dockery, ed., *Challenge of Postmodernism: An Evangelical Engagement* (Grand Rapids: Baker, 1995); Millard J. Erickson, *Postmodernizing the Faith: Evangelical Responses to the Challenge of Postmodernism* (Grand Rapids: Baker, 1998).

31. See Alvin Plantinga and Nicholas Wolterstorff, eds., *Faith and Rationality: Reason and Belief in God* (Notre Dame, Ind.: University of Notre Dame Press, 1983).

32. See, for example, the substantial and important article by J. I. Packer, "On from Orr: The Cultural Crisis, Rational Realism, and Incarnational Ontology," *Crux* 32, no. 3 (September 1996): 12–26.

serves as a role model to many evangelicals. Yet curiously, few share his interest in appropriating the patristic heritage in the service of the gospel.[33] Taking this issue seriously opens up new approaches to the debate and dialogue with other Christian traditions—such as Roman Catholicism and Orthodoxy—in which the interpretation of writers such as Athanasius and Augustine is an issue of major significance.

What risks might be associated with a dialogue between evangelicals and those outside the evangelical tradition? Most obviously, it could blur distinctions concerning major issues of Reformation theology, to which most evangelicals see themselves as heirs. The doctrine of justification by faith alone is a case in point, and recent ecumenical discussion here needs to be evaluated with care.[34] However, I would certainly argue that this is a dialogue to watch. It could lead evangelical theology in some very interesting directions. It might equally prove a dead end. Either way, it needs to feature on our theological radars.

Western Ways of Thinking? Challenges from Africa and Asia

Finally, I turn to an area of increasing importance, as evangelicalism advances further into Africa, Asia, and Latin America. Should evangelicals in these areas simply reproduce the evangelical theologies they learned in America or Europe? It is a simple fact of history that systematic theology has generally been developed in a Western context. As systematic theology is, at least to some extent, shaped by the audiences that it addresses and the issues that are debated within a culture, it is clearly open to being shaped by that culture. Wolfhart Pannenberg has argued that Western theology has been shaped by its engagement with the rise of the natural sciences and the secular critique of authority.[35] Yet these critiques are especially associated with—indeed, even limited to—the Western world. Might not very different styles of systematic theology arise when the engagement in question is not Western but rather reflects issues in the emerging world—such as an encounter with Hinduism rather than secularism?[36]

33. On this, see Luchesius Smits, *Saint Augustin dans l'oeuvre de Jean Calvin* (Assen: Van Gorcum, 1956); Alexandre Ganoczy, *Calvins handschriftliche Annotationen zu Chrysostomus: Ein Beitrag zur Hermeneutik Calvins* (Wiesbaden: Steiner, 1981); A. N. S. Lane, *John Calvin: Student of the Church Fathers* (Edinburgh: T & T Clark, 1999).

34. See Alister E. McGrath, *Iustitia Dei: A History of the Christian Doctrine of Justification,* 2d ed. (Cambridge: Cambridge University Press, 1998).

35. Wolfhart Pannenberg, *An Introduction to Systematic Theology* (Edinburgh: T & T Clark, 1991), 12–13.

36. This idea is pursued in an interesting study by Leonard Swidler, *After the Absolute: The Dialogical Future of Religious Reflection* (Minneapolis: Fortress Press, 1990).

This predominantly Western orientation of systematic theology thus raises some important questions for our theme. Why, for example, should an Asian feel in the slightest degree obligated to continue such a tradition? Is not the correct and obvious way ahead in the next century to develop theologies that arise out of her own engagement with the realities of the gospel, rather than accept what someone else—generally from a Western context—has bequeathed her?

It is here that evangelicalism has an important contribution to make to systematic theology, by insisting that theology arises from Scripture and is not derived from a series of philosophical presuppositions—presuppositions that, far from being universally valid and recognized, reflect the Western context in which they emerged. The history of evangelicalism suggests that the success of the movement rests on its willingness to correlate Scripture with the context in which it finds itself, rather than simply reaching backward into evangelical history to draw out past correlations, such as the way in which a text was applied by Calvin in his sixteenth-century Genevan context. Sixteenth-century Geneva bears little resemblance to today's Hong Kong or Singapore!

The issue is that of applying Scripture to our own contexts, rather than slavishly repeating interpretations of Scripture originally developed with a very different cultural context in mind.[37] David F. Wells argues as follows:

> It is the task of theology, then, to discover what God has said in and through Scripture and to clothe that in a conceptuality which is native to our own age. Scripture, at its *terminus a quo*, needs to be de-contextualized in order to grasp its transcultural content, and it needs to be re-contextualized in order that its content may be meshed with the cognitive assumptions and social patterns of our own time.[38]

Wells's words point to the need to see Scripture and our own context as two horizons—horizons that need to be related to each other.[39] For Calvin, the task was to relate Scripture to sixteenth-century Geneva; for others, it will be to relate that same Scripture to today's Buenos Aires,

37. For an excellent discussion of this point, see David J. Hesselgrave and Edward Rommen, *Contextualization: Meanings, Methods, and Models* (Grand Rapids: Baker; Leicester: Apollos, 1989).

38. David F. Wells, "The Nature and Function of Theology," in *The Use of the Bible in Theology: Evangelical Options*, ed. Robert K. Johnston (Atlanta: John Knox Press, 1985), 177.

39. This issue is explored in greater detail in Anthony Thiselton, *The Two Horizons: New Testament Hermeneutics and Philosophical Description* (Grand Rapids: Eerdmans, 1980).

Manila, or Nairobi. Calvin's approach and the results that it yields may be helpful as we undertake this task; yet his answers are not necessarily identical to ours. For instance, it is well known that Calvin was interested in—and, to some extent, influenced by—the language and concepts of the classical Roman philosophical and rhetorical tradition.[40] China has an older philosophical and rhetorical tradition. Why should Asian Christians use the same ideas that Calvin borrowed when they have a distinguished heritage of their own from which to draw?

Conclusion

In this paper, I have tried to set out some of the issues that confront evangelical thinkers as they seek to develop their ideas on theological method. Areas of difficulty and debate abound—but so, I trust, does a love of God, a patience with each other, and a longing to see the gospel faithfully and effectively communicated. I trust and pray that we will be guided as we seek to serve God and his church in the years that lie ahead.

---

40. See Charles Partee, *Calvin and the Classical Tradition* (Leiden: Brill, 1977).

2

Evangelical Theology Should Be Evangelical

John G. Stackhouse, Jr.

Evangelical theology is not a popular cause these days. In many evangelical churches, theology of any stripe is something for which apologies are rendered from the pulpit whenever an intrepid preacher ventures onto its turf. Among some evangelicals, theology is something to be held up for amusement or scorn, as the silly games of underemployed and slothful intellectuals. Or theology is something to be feared as an abyss of dangerous speculation in which one's traditional faith can be torn apart in the crosscurrents of divergent and even antagonistic streams of thought.

Having attended my share of professional theological conferences and read more than a few books of academic theology, I confess to some sympathy with these attitudes. But such antipathies hardly serve to encourage the work of evangelical theology.

The situation for evangelical theology is actually even worse than this, however, for trouble lies even within the ranks of the theologians. For nowadays evangelical theologians over here are enamored with Karl Barth, or over there by his latter-day saints, the postliberals. Some evangelicals currently explore intellectual trajectories farther, along which have traveled the theologians of process, while others seek wisdom from the ancient Eastern churches. Some evangelicals find both stimulation and stability in the first millennium, while others seek it in early modern Reformed scholasticism. And some few evangelicals work creatively in liberationist, feminist, and postmodern modes.

Evangelicals these days, then, seem to be looking interestedly at what almost everyone else is doing in theology. This openness to learn from other Christians is to be commended, particularly as one considers the confessional or fundamentalist blinkers many of these brothers and sisters have labored to shed. Still, however, the evangelical tradition itself stimulates precious little creative work within evangelicalism and virtually none, to my knowledge at least, from without. While evangelicals around the world rejoice as millions of people convert to their form of Christianity, there are few theologians of stature who have converted to evangelical theology from some other tradition and now work within it.[1] And even if I have overlooked a notable convert or two, to look for converts is to miss the larger point. Evangelicals can and do explore Ruether, or Hartshorne, or Zizioulas, or Gutiérrez in order to enrich their evangelicalism. But which liberals, neo-orthodox, Roman Catholics, or what-have-you take the evangelical tradition seriously as a theological resource even to enrich their own perspectives?

Whether or not anyone else takes notice, however, I suggest that the evangelical tradition itself continues to offer good gifts to evangelical theologians today. And I do not mean merely that this or that overlooked or forgotten evangelical theologian deserves greater attention— although it is gratifying to see attention paid to Jonathan Edwards and increasing attention paid to Adolf Schlatter, to mention just two worthy examples from the past. I mean that the evangelical tradition itself provides a stance in which theology can be ably and helpfully undertaken in our time. It is, I would now like to contend at some length, a stance that both guards against some of the dangers of contemporary theology and guides toward the benefit of all those who study the theology it produces.

What Is "Evangelical"?

It is an irony that in a tradition that prizes plain, clear speech, the very word *evangelical* is patient of at least half a dozen definitions, and

1. Among this small company might be numbered Alister McGrath, Royce Gruenler, and Tom Oden, depending on one's definition of *evangelical*. See Michael Bauman, "Alister McGrath," in *Handbook of Evangelical Theologians*, ed. Walter A. Elwell (Grand Rapids: Baker, 1993), 445–47; Royce Gordon Gruenler, *The Inexhaustible God: Biblical Faith and the Challenge of Process Theism* (Grand Rapids: Baker, 1983); and Thomas C. Oden, *Systematic Theology*, 3 vols. (San Francisco: HarperSanFrancisco, 1992, 1994).

some of those are hotly contested by interested parties within and without any particular form of evangelicalism. Recognizing that "evangelical" can indeed denote anything having to do with the gospel, evangelicalism as a distinct tradition in Christianity is generally traced to the eighteenth-century revivals on both sides of the Atlantic Ocean, led by eminences such as George Whitefield, John and Charles Wesley, and Jonathan Edwards. If we take this range of interconnected revivals as our benchmark for the evangelical tradition, we can induce a list of five characteristics. And such a list enjoys the approval of most historians and theologians who study evangelicalism.[2]

First, evangelicals believe and champion the gospel of God's work of salvation and particularly as it is focused in the person of Jesus Christ. Even more particularly, evangelicals teach and delight in the incarnation of the Lord and in his inauguration of the kingdom of God, but they pay special attention—as they believe the Bible itself does—to the death and resurrection of Christ as together constituting the central event of God's redemptive project. Christ, therefore, is worshiped as the Son of God, venerated as the center of history, followed as the model of righteousness, and looked for as the promised deliverer who will return someday in power to consummate salvation history.

Second, evangelicals believe and champion the Bible as the uniquely authoritative rendition of God's Word in words to us. Evangelicals appreciate that the Bible is a mysterious book in many ways and disagree on how to interpret it and thus what it says in each respect. But evangelicals agree that, while one can be puzzled by the Bible, the faithful Christian cannot disagree with it. As God's Spirit illuminates and commends it to God's people, their response to such teaching must be gratitude and obedience.

Third, evangelicals believe and champion conversion as the correct way to describe God's work of salvation in each Christian and as a reality to be experienced, not merely affirmed. Evangelicals, that is, believe that each person must be born again by the renewing power of the Holy Spirit—although evangelicals disagree on just how evident this renewal will be at any given time in the process. And then each Christian must go on to mature in growing conformity to the pattern of Christ's own devotion to God. Conversion, that is, denotes both the mo-

2. For more thorough discussion of definition, see D. W. Bebbington, *Evangelicalism in Modern Britain: A History from the 1730s to the 1980s* (London: Unwin Hyman, 1989), 1–19; George Marsden, "Introduction," in *Evangelicalism and Modern America*, ed. George Marsden (Grand Rapids: Eerdmans, 1984), viii–xvi; and John G. Stackhouse, Jr., *Canadian Evangelicalism in the Twentieth Century: An Introduction to Its Character* (Toronto: University of Toronto Press, 1993), 6–12.

ment of new birth and the lifetime of transformation that follows as the Holy Spirit prepares us for eternity with God.

Fourth, evangelicals believe and champion mission as the chief goal of Christian life on earth. At times, such activism in seeking to bring to others both the message of salvation and the charity of Christ has meant that evangelicals have paid relatively less attention to worship, or theology, or the cultivation of the earth, and other expressions of the well-rounded Christian life. Still, evangelicals affirm that Christ has built the church on earth and maintains it here not merely, or even primarily, to praise, or to think, or to garden, but to make disciples.

Fifth, evangelicals believe and champion these four elements of the generic Christian tradition in ways that other traditions do not. To be sure, all branches of the orthodox Christian faith affirm the story of salvation centering on Christ; the authority of the Bible as God's written Word (even as some place other authorities alongside it); the necessity of conversion; and the call to mission. There is nothing peculiarly evangelical in any of these four convictions. But evangelicals place special emphasis on this constellation of four and do so in such a way as to relativize every other conviction. There is nothing in the generic evangelical impulse that militates directly against denominational distinctives and divisions, but there is an important ecumenical dynamic to the elevating of these four convictions above the faultlines of denominational division. Evangelicals see these four convictions as nonnegotiable elements of Christian profession and practice, and therefore are willing to negotiate, or even simply leave to each Christian community, decisions regarding all other issues of dispute, which are seen as secondary and nonessential. This transdenominationalism, therefore, is the fifth evangelical quality to round out our list.[3]

So what? That was then, this is now, and tomorrow will be yet another new context. Why should the convictions of two hundred years ago guide us in contemporary theology? Indeed, these convictions might have been helpful then, as they are today, for providing a basis for cooperative evangelistic ministry. But how useful are they theologically?

Bold and exciting it would be, indeed, to call all Christian theologians to adopt evangelical principles. I shall aim, however, at a more modest objective: to encourage evangelical theologians—that is, theologians who already take these five principles seriously for their Christian identity—to be guided by these convictions in their theological work. And as fellow Christians watch evangelicals doing so, one might

---

3. Evangelical statesman John R. W. Stott demonstrates this quality vividly in the conclusion to his *Evangelical Truth: A Personal Plea for Unity, Integrity, and Faithfulness* (Downers Grove, Ill.: InterVarsity Press, 1999), 115–19.

entertain the hope that such Christians will find it sufficiently interesting and (more important by far) edifying so as to learn what they can from it, even as we evangelicals already are learning from them.

Evangelical Convictions and Evangelical Theology

Christ and Salvation

Evangelical theology ought to focus on Jesus Christ both epistemologically and substantively. Thus, evangelical theology ought to be both Christological and Christocentric.

In the epistemological sense, evangelicals traditionally have interpreted the Bible and gone on to construct theology primarily in the light of the revelation of God in Christ. Historical-critical exegesis of the Old Testament properly considers the process by which God's revelation of himself and his work on earth emerges in human, and particularly in Israelite, history. But evangelicals unapologetically not only move forward from beginning to end of so-called progressive revelation in the Old Testament but also freely move backward from the New Testament to see the Old Testament illuminated in the light of God's definitive revelation in Jesus. Similarly, as evangelicals encounter later developments in Christian thought and practice—whether the formulation of the doctrine of God as Trinity, or the understanding of the status and role of Mary and the saints, or the direction of Christian mission in the world—they properly, even reflexively, refer back always to what God has revealed of himself during the earthly career of Jesus of Nazareth.

In the substantive sense, evangelical theology views Christ as the center of God's story—the most important thing God has ever done or said. The person and work of Christ do not merely crown God's work of revelation and redemption as a sort of splendid ornament or even as the best example of God's activity in the world. The person and work of Christ constitute the defining chapter of the whole narrative, the hinge of history, the basis upon which everything else in creation makes sense.

One might think that a religion that is content to be called "Christianity" would not need evangelicals (or any others) to champion the importance of a "Christ-ian" focus to its theology. Yet in contemporary theology, as in the history of Christian thought, theologians have called theology away from its Christological and Christocentric focus.

A couple of decades ago, James Gustafson wrote his well-known ethics that calls for a "theocentric" perspective, stating straightforwardly in the title what most liberal theology has taught since Schleiermacher—himself perhaps the first and last liberal to see the Redeemer as essential, and not just helpful, in salvation history.[4]

Process theology interprets the world through the scheme of A. N. Whitehead and his theological epigones, not through any important Christological lens. And the "salvation history" celebrated by process theology has no central role for Jesus to play. His witness to the truth of God and his example to his followers in realizing that truth constitute a considerable gift to humanity. But the actual scheme of God "luring" the world to its highest end does not in any important sense *require* the career of Jesus of Nazareth, as the orthodox gospel does.[5]

It is this reduction of the importance of Jesus that, not coincidentally, links liberals such as Gustafson and process theologians such as John Cobb to a third form of contemporary Christian thought that also is determinedly non-Christological and non-Christocentric, namely, pluralism in the encounter with world religions. In the pluralism espoused by John Hick, Wilfred Cantwell Smith, Hans Küng, and many others, Jesus is one prophet among many, an admirable man who gestured instructively toward Ultimate Reality and provided a model for relating appropriately to that reality—just as Lao Tzu, Moses, Confucius, Krishna, Zoroaster, Gautama Buddha, and Muhammad did. Evangelical theology rightly maintains the "scandal of particularity" in this conversation, even as evangelicals themselves debate just how best to understand the work of Christ toward non-Christians and the relationship of the Christian faith and other faiths.[6]

Liberal theology of various stripes is not the only sort of theology needing correction from an evangelical focus on Christ, particularly in his cross and resurrection. Recently, evangelical theologians have encountered, and some embraced, Orthodox theology—perhaps epito-

4. James M. Gustafson, *Ethics from a Theocentric Perspective* (Chicago: University of Chicago Press, 1983); cf. Friedrich D. E. Schleiermacher, *The Christian Faith*, English translation of the 2d German ed., ed. H. R. Mackintosh and J. S. Stewart (Philadelphia: Fortress Press, 1928).

5. John B. Cobb, Jr., and David Ray Griffin, *Process Theology: An Introductory Exposition* (Philadelphia: Westminster, 1976).

6. Sir Norman Anderson, *Christianity and World Religions: The Challenge of Pluralism* (Leicester and Downers Grove, Ill.: InterVarsity Press, 1980 [1970]); Harold A. Netland, *Dissonant Voices: Religious Pluralism and the Question of Truth* (Grand Rapids: Eerdmans, 1991); Clark H. Pinnock, *A Wideness in God's Mercy: The Finality of Jesus Christ in a World of Religions* (Grand Rapids: Zondervan, 1992); John Sanders, *No Other Name: An Investigation into the Destiny of the Unevangelized* (Grand Rapids: Eerdmans, 1992); Gerald D. McDermott, *Can Evangelicals Learn from the Buddha?* (Downers Grove, Ill.: InterVarsity Press, forthcoming).

mized best in John Zizioulas's work.[7] There is much in both Orthodoxy's piety and theology to complement and even correct Roman Catholic and Protestant Christianity. But evangelicals who appreciate their tradition's emphasis on the cross and resurrection of Jesus, and see such an emphasis as emergent from the New Testament itself, will be cautious about a too hasty and too enthusiastic embrace of a theological tradition that does not share this emphasis.

Indeed, non-Orthodox Christians have long been chary of Orthodoxy's focus on ontological categories of divinity and humanity, eternal and temporal, spirit and matter, when it comes to salvation. In the light of these concerns (which doubtless reflect Orthodoxy's cultural cradle in the Hellenistic East), Orthodoxy focuses more on the incarnation itself as the basis of salvation—as God bridges the various ontic divides—and the impartation of God's divine nature to the human soul as the central mechanism of this salvation. However much Catholic and Protestant Christians can profit from such a theological model (and I believe we can profit a great deal), evangelicals do well not to throw over their model in their excitement over the riches of the Eastern traditions. Instead, evangelicals ought to recognize that Orthodoxy's model—Christ-centered as it is, in its way—also does not fully account for the biblical portrait of Christ.

Within evangelical theology itself, finally, a Christological and Christocentric reminder perhaps needs to be issued to those who currently pursue trinitarianism as a sort of key to unlock a wide range of theological puzzles. We can learn about the one true God, yes, from Old Testament revelation that only hints at God's trinitarian nature, but we know what we know about the Trinity per se mostly because of God's revelation in Christ. It was, after all, the disciples' encounter with Christ that led to their worship of him and conceptualizing of him as the divine Lord—thus leading to a binitarian understanding of God that became trinitarian only as Christian thought matured (indeed, one would say, only as the Holy Spirit himself guided the church to this insight).[8] And the Holy Spirit remains—despite some impressive expositions by evangelicals of late—a relatively minor, shadowy figure in the New Testament compared with the center stage, fully lit person of

7. For examples, see John Zizioulas, *Being as Communion: Studies in Personhood and the Church* (New York: St. Vladimir's Seminary Press, 1997); cf. John Meyendorff, *Byzantine Theology: Historical Trends and Doctrinal Themes*, 2d ed. (New York: Fordham University Press, 1979 [1974]).

8. Larry W. Hurtado, *One God, One Lord: Early Christian Devotion and Ancient Jewish Monotheism* (Philadelphia: Fortress Press, 1988).

Jesus.[9] For all we know, to put the point more provocatively than it perhaps should be put, God might actually be "quadritarian"—or more complex still. Christian theology, after all, has inferred the triune nature of God from what we see in God's revelation in Christ.

Of course evangelicals should be trinitarian (for we have no evidence that God is more than a trinity and lots of evidence that he is), and of course we should plumb what depths we can of God's revelation of himself as triune in order to know and enjoy and serve him best. My concern here is simply to emphasize that evangelicals ought to maintain our Christological approach and Christocentric emphasis in all doctrine, including the doctrine of God. This tradition will keep us from presuming to know more about, and emphasizing more than we should about, the Holy Spirit, or God the Father, or the Triune God in Godself. God the Holy Spirit points us to Christ, and Christ is the one who shows us God the Father.

The Bible

Evangelicals have always been "Bible people." Evangelicalism typically has championed excellent preaching, personal Bible study, general biblical literacy—all in the name of the unique authority of the Bible for our belief and practice. Evangelicals have symbolized this regard for the Bible typically by erecting impressive pulpits in the center of church platforms, by lionizing great preachers, and by observing rituals of everyday piety, such as never letting a Bible rest on the floor or be covered by another book.

Indeed, among the criticisms most frequently leveled against evangelicals is that we are *too* focused on the Bible at the expense of not taking other God-given theological resources as seriously as we should, whether tradition, reason, or experience. A similar criticism runs that evangelicals are simplistic in their interpretation of the Bible and use of it in theology—seeing the Bible as a two-dimensional plane of proof-texts that can be applied directly to matters of doctrine or ethics without recognizing the realities of progressive revelation, genre differences, and other important qualifications of the "voice" of the Bible. These attitudes combine to a syndrome that places the text of the Bible at the center of evangelical life and in fact displaces the Holy Spirit's role as primary teacher, thus amounting to a bibliolatry.

Evangelical theologians, aided especially by the findings of our colleagues in the historical study of evangelicalism, can wince and agree

9. Gordon D. Fee, *God's Empowering Presence: The Holy Spirit in the Letters of Paul* (Peabody, Mass.: Hendrickson, 1994); Clark H. Pinnock, *Flame of Love: A Theology of the Holy Spirit* (Downers Grove, Ill.: InterVarsity Press, 1996).

with many aspects of these charges.[10] In our embarrassment over our overuse, misuse, and abuse of the Bible, however, we might yield to the temptation to surrender the kernel in the midst of so much husk. That kernel remains the unique and supreme authority of the Bible as both itself the Word of God written and as an unequaled tool in the hands of the Spirit of God to render God's Word to us today.

To be sure, the renewed interest in the historical theology of the church and the postmodern critique of epistemology have combined to warn contemporary evangelical theologians not to confuse any particular interpretation of the Bible with the Bible itself. The Bible is God's Word written, but our interpretations of it are not. And our interpretations of the Bible may well need to be adjusted in the light of our interpretations of God's other means of revelation, whether science, history, tradition, spiritual experience, and so on—just as, nonetheless, our interpretations of those phenomena also ought to be in respectful dialogue with our understanding of Scripture. Indeed, truly evangelical thinking about any subject will always privilege scriptural interpretation and never willfully contradict what the Scripture at least *seems* to say—however much tension we must live with while we try to sort out apparent contradictions.[11]

Our own generation has been blessed by some first-rate wrestling with matters of the nature of the Bible, its authority, its interpretation, and its application to our lives: Books by Anthony Thiselton, Kevin Vanhoozer, Nicholas Wolterstorff, and Tom Wright shine among other luminaries in a constellation of scholarship.[12] No one supposes, however, that we have sorted out all of the pertinent issues.

Indeed, few have ventured to respond to postmodernism with a theology that takes it seriously from the inside and responds to it with biblical truth: Richard Middleton and Brian Walsh's pioneering *Truth Is Stranger than It Used to Be* is a lonely effort in this vein.[13] Evangelical-

10. Mark A. Noll, *Between Faith and Criticism: Evangelicals, Scholarship, and the Bible in America* (San Francisco: Harper & Row, 1986).

11. For quite different, but complementary, statements of this point, see Donald A. D. Thorsen, *The Wesleyan Quadrilateral: Scripture, Tradition, Reason, and Experience as a Model of Evangelical Theology* (Grand Rapids: Zondervan, 1990); and Nicholas Wolterstorff, *Reason within the Bounds of Religion*, rev. ed. (Grand Rapids: Eerdmans, 1979 [1976]).

12. See several successive books by Anthony C. Thiselton, beginning with *The Two Horizons: New Testament Hermeneutics and Philosophical Description* (Grand Rapids: Eerdmans, 1980); Kevin J. Vanhoozer, *Is There a Meaning in This Text? The Bible, the Reader, and the Morality of Literary Knowledge* (Grand Rapids: Zondervan, 1998); Nicholas Wolterstorff, *Divine Discourse: Philosophical Reflections on the Claim That God Speaks* (Cambridge: Cambridge University Press, 1995); and the series begun by N. T. Wright with *The New Testament and the People of God* (Minneapolis: Fortress Press, 1992).

13. J. Richard Middleton and Brian J. Walsh, *Truth Is Stranger than It Used to Be: Biblical Faith in a Postmodern Age* (Downers Grove, Ill.: InterVarsity Press, 1995).

ism has yet to produce a substantial theology written from a feminist perspective. On this score, we continue to spend our limited theological resources arguing about, among other things, whether women can be theologians at all. But where is the theology—or even the sustained biblical study as resource for such theology—that starts with evangelical premises and pays attention to gender, to power, to women, and to other subjects overlooked by male-dominated theology, and in modes unexplored by such theology heretofore? And formal evangelical theology written from the perspective of the Third World is relayed to us mostly by informed Americans (such as William Dyrness) and expatriates (such as Lamin Sanneh)—even as informal theology, especially in Pentecostal and charistmatic modes from Argentina and Korea, flows powerfully into "sending" countries such as ours.[14]

Evangelical respect for the Bible continues, however, to be needed in theology today. Resistance to the full affirmation of homosexuality—especially in the face of the collapse of the psychological and psychiatric community's recognition of its pathology—can be justified only on the basis of something like an evangelical Scripture principle. Anything short of a clear divine word can be dismissed as mere human convention or invention and thus simply "homophobic." What is true of this particular debate is true of other ethical debates as well: Discussion of the legitimacy of war, capital punishment, care for the poor, and so on is crucially shaped in each case by whether we believe we have authoritative guidance from God in Scripture.

Evangelicals properly distance themselves from a liberal methodology that feels "free" to ignore, and even contradict, express teachings of Scripture in the name of the putative superiority of current opinion. And evangelicals continue properly to wonder just how "postliberal" postliberals really are in this respect. Do they stand under the authority of the Bible—even the awkward parts, even the parts that seem sexist, or fantastic, or wrong—or are they still working with too much liberal freedom?[15]

A sound allegiance to the authority of the Bible, furthermore, speaks to at least three dangerous trends within evangelicalism itself. One trend has evangelicals engaged in theological speculation, particularly

14. Lamin Sanneh, *Translating the Message: The Missionary Impact on Culture* (Maryknoll, N.Y.: Orbis Books, 1994); William A. Dyrness, *Learning about Theology from the Third World* (Grand Rapids: Zondervan, 1990). See also William A. Dyrness, gen. ed., *Emerging Voices in Global Christian Theology* (Grand Rapids: Zondervan, 1994).

15. See the engagement of evangelicals and postliberals on some of these questions in Timothy R. Phillips and Dennis L. Okholm, eds., *The Nature of Confession: Evangelicals and Postliberals in Conversation* (Downers Grove, Ill.: InterVarsity Press, 1996); see also William C. Placher's candid recognition of precisely this issue in *Narratives of a Vulnerable God: Christ, Theology, and Scripture* (Louisville: Westminster/John Knox, 1994), 126–27.

associated with the doctrine of the Trinity, in ways that would be profitably chastened by a closer tethering to the scriptural text. Indeed, it is
becoming common to hear an evangelical theologian simply make the
following syllogistic move without recourse to Scripture itself: "God,
the Holy Trinity, is X; we are created in God's image; therefore, we are
X."[16] Martin Luther and John Calvin, who wrote a great deal about
God, nonetheless would chide us for repeating the scholastic mistake
of presuming to venture much beyond the scriptural text into the abyss
of Godself.[17]

A second dangerous trend is heading in the other direction, toward
a traditionalism, even a credalism, that is satisfied that God has broken
forth all the light from his holy Word that he is ever going to break. If
the previous danger is that of speculation, we now encounter the danger of formalism. It arises in evangelicalism nowadays with certain
devotees of certain brands of Reformed orthodoxy, often dubbed the
"Truly Reformed" by those who have felt the sting of their criticism.
These warriors not only claim to speak authoritatively and univocally
for what is in fact a multistranded Reformed tradition, but presume
then to go on to speak for all evangelicals (as in the Alliance of Confess-
ing Evangelicals).[18]

16. Colin Gunton is arguably the most important theologian of this type. His writing
honestly attests at times to his own ambivalence about using the doctrine of the Trinity
as a kind of "control" or "way into" other theological issues. When it comes to the nature
of the church, for instance, he acknowledges that "different theologies of the Trinity generate correspondingly different ecclesiologies" (Colin E. Gunton, *The Promise of Trinitarian Theology* [Edinburgh: T & T Clark, 1991], 74; see also Miroslav Volf, *After Our
Likeness: The Church as the Image of the Trinity* [Grand Rapids: Eerdmans, 1998], esp.
214–20). Indeed, when it comes to the particular question of gender in the church, egal-
itarians (such as Gunton) appeal to the "perichoretic dance" of the Trinity, while hierar-
chalists appeal to the eternal subordination of the Son to the Father (e.g., Michael
Harper, *Equal and Different: Male and Female in the Church and Family* [London: Hodder
& Stoughton], 153–63). Space here does not permit an adequate discussion of this issue.
But one perhaps can fairly raise the question of just how truly illuminative and directive
the mystery of the Trinity can be in this respect, and how much we should instead look
at more explicit biblical guidance in considering this or that theological issue. (For a recent attempt to set out a trinitarian guide to hermeneutics from a conservative Reformed
American point of view, see Vern S. Poythress, *God-Centered Biblical Interpretation* [Phil-
lipsburg, N.J.: Presbyterian & Reformed, 1999].)

17. See B. A. Gerrish, " 'To the Unknown God': Luther and Calvin on the Hiddenness
of God," in *The Old Protestantism and the New* (Chicago: University of Chicago Press; Edinburgh: T & T Clark, 1982), 131–49.

18. So several books by David F. Wells beginning with *No Place for Truth, or, Whatever
Happened to Evangelical Theology?* (Grand Rapids: Eerdmans, 1993); for the ACE, see
www.AllianceNet.org.

Evangelical allegiance to the Bible would instead, however, take all of us to the place of John Calvin, who revised his own summary of doctrine (the *Institutes of the Christian Religion*) several times—without, to my knowledge, ever claiming infallibility for it. Or perhaps to the place of Martin Luther, who never felt it urgent to systematize his theology. Or to Jonathan Edwards and John Wesley, who wrote much theology in their different ways but always to meet the needs of their contemporaries, not presuming to speak for generations past or to generations in the future. The Bible, they each recognized, was inexhaustibly rich, complicated, and mysterious—just as one would expect from a divine Author.

The "Truly Reformed" formalists are joined, of course, by those other credalists who are willing to put their own tradition's statements of faith above any fresh reading of Scripture, whether the Canons and Decrees of the Council of Trent, the Canons of Dort, the Westminster Confession, the Formula of Concord, the Thirty-Nine Articles, or the Lausanne Covenant. Such doctrinaire theologians parallel those Christians who rigorously defend traditional liturgies (whether traditional Anglican, traditional Mennonite, or traditional Pentecostal!), traditional hierarchies (whether ecclesiastical or domestic), or traditional devotional practices (whether saying a rosary or having a "daily quiet time") without continual openness to scriptural investigation to "see if these things be true" (Acts 17:11). Evangelical biblicism at its best, then, is not only a conservative force but also a radical dynamic. It frees theology from automatic conformity to any such human approximations of God's truth—wonderful gifts to the church as many of these traditions may be.

A third danger is the danger of mysticism, of spiritual experience trumping all other claims to knowledge. Evangelicalism has always gloried in spiritual experience. One of its chief characteristics, I am in fact arguing in this paper, is its emphasis on personal conversion. "You ask me how I know he lives," evangelicals still like to sing, "he lives within my heart." And recent Christian work in epistemology (one thinks of William Alston especially) has been reclaiming spiritual experience as cognitively important not merely personally moving.[19]

The worthiness of spiritual experience as a theological resource is not in question here, however. My question concerns *mysticism* as a cognitive style. "I believe God is saying . . ." can function dangerously

19. William P. Alston, *Perceiving God: The Epistemology of Religious Experience* (Ithaca, N.Y., and London: Cornell University Press, 1991); cf. the unusual argument in Phillip H. Wiebe, *Visions of Jesus: Direct Encounters from the New Testament to Today* (New York and Oxford: Oxford University Press, 1997).

as "Thus saith the Lord . . ." unless everyone agrees to place priority on God's written Word as supreme guide to those who exercise discernment over such prophecy. Failure to truly give such priority to the Bible is at the root of many oddities in contemporary mystical movements, whether charismatic (as in the Toronto Blessing) or devotees of particular mystical writers (such as Madame Guyon or Thomas Merton).[20] And such extremes point to the importance for evangelical theology of keeping together in right balance all five of these evangelical convictions.

One of the earliest practitioners of historical or "higher" criticism of the Bible was the zealous Roman Catholic Roger Simon. His agenda in the face of the rise of Protestantism was transparent: to so undermine the Bible's authority that any sensible and devout Christian would flee from the broken reed of *sola scriptura* to the strong, wise guidance of Mother Church. In our own day, ironically, the Jesus Seminar and certain other higher critics seek to undermine the Bible's authority in order to encourage a move in the opposite direction, toward a religious pluralism that glorifies no one particular religion or leader or scripture as divinely authoritative. Centuries ago, Roger Simon recognized the crucial importance of a "high" doctrine of Scripture. So today does Robert Funk. Evangelicals must not forget it.

Conversion

Princeton Seminary's Ellen Charry has been bringing a widely noted message to academic theology of late. In her book, *By the Renewing of Your Minds*, she reminds us that once upon a time—indeed, in most times until our own—Christians pursued theology in the cause of spiritual transformation.[21] Theology, that is, was no mere intellectual exercise, let alone a full-time profession that even unbelievers could undertake (*pace* Paul Tillich and David Tracy).[22] Theology always served the fundamental Christian concern for conversion.

When Professor Charry graced our theology conference at Regent College in 1998, however, she found (to her express delight) that she was bringing coals to Newcastle. For all of evangelicalism's many faults both theological and spiritual, evangelicals at least have kept theology and piety together as an ideal, and often as a reality as well.

---

20. James A. Beverley, *Holy Laughter and the Toronto Blessing: An Investigative Report* (Grand Rapids: Zondervan, 1995); I know of no scholarly study of the widespread evangelical interest in Madame Guyon, Thomas Merton, and other non-evangelical mystics.

21. Ellen T. Charry, *By the Renewing of Your Minds: The Pastoral Function of Christian Doctrine* (New York and Oxford: Oxford University Press, 1999).

22. For Tracy, following Tillich, see David Tracy, *Blessed Rage for Order: The New Pluralism in Theology* (Minneapolis: Winston/Seabury Press, 1975), esp. 57 n. 3.

Theology is doxology, as J. I. Packer likes to put it, and it is properly (to borrow a phrase from Andrew Murray) an "aid to devotion." Certainly Calvin intended his "handbook" (or *Institutio*) to serve in this way. Whether one considers John Wesley or Jonathan Edwards, Charles Finney or Charles Hodge, Donald Barnhouse or Donald Bloesch, John Wimber or John Stott, evangelicals characteristically view theology as fundamentally concerned with the new birth and the subsequent life of discipleship.

Beyond the academic theology indicted by Charry, some other forms of contemporary theology, and particularly those with a clear political focus, also have neglected the spiritual dimension of the Christian message. If we turn to feminist theology, we find that some exponents—not all of them, of course—preoccupy themselves with secular matters: who occupies which position in the ecclesiastical hierarchy or domestic economy, and more general questions of how women are to function and be treated in a just society. Some forms of liberation theology—again, not all of them—similarly have been criticized for focusing on the amelioration of economic and social oppression to the exclusion of spiritual deliverance.

In such programs of social concern, one can sympathize with activists who fear that any promise of "pie in the sky by and by" will cut the nerve of the political revolutions they see to be mandated by Christian compassion and justice. They hear Marx's warning about religion's narcotic powers, and they also are inspired by the New Testament, which denounces those who intone good wishes for the needy without lifting a finger to help them (James 2:16).

Still, an evangelical will prefer the wholistic agenda of a Gustavo Gutiérrez, and particularly of our own Ron Sider.[23] These theologians have established irreproachable records of advocacy for the needy while steadfastly proclaiming the "whole counsel of God." This counsel demands care for the poor that includes the good news of God's offer of conversion in Christ as the heart of his plan to restore all of creation to shalom—indeed, his plan of cosmic conversion.[24]

Evangelical theologians, furthermore, will beware the lure of strictly academic theology. To be sure, it seems rather odd to warn evangeli-

23. Gustavo Gutiérrez, *A Theology of Liberation: History, Politics, and Salvation*, rev. ed., trans. Caridad Inda and John Eagleson (Maryknoll, N.Y.: Orbis Books, 1988); Ronald J. Sider, *Living like Jesus: Eleven Essentials for Growing a Genuine Faith* (Grand Rapids: Baker, 1999).

24. So William A. Dyrness, *The Earth Is God's: A Theology of American Culture* (Maryknoll, N.Y.: Orbis Books, 1997); Nicholas Wolterstorff, *Until Justice and Peace Embrace* (Grand Rapids: Eerdmans, 1983).

cals of excessive intellectualism: The "scandal of the evangelical mind" seems not to lie in overindulgence in arcana.[25]

But as evangelicals continue to graduate from prestigious research universities and enter the professional guilds of the Society for Biblical Literature, American Academy of Religion, and other such high-altitude organizations, we do well to maintain the life-giving linkage between the science of theology and the *scientia* that begins with the "fear of the LORD," the vital connection of head, heart, and hands that characterized so many of our evangelical forebears.

Mission

Therefore, in the light of this our faith and our resolve, we enter into a solemn covenant with God and with each other, to pray, to plan and to work together for the evangelization of the whole world. We call upon others to join us. May God help us by his grace and for his glory to be faithful to this our covenant! Amen, Alleluia![26]

Thus ends the Lausanne Covenant (1974), perhaps the definitive statement of international evangelical commitment in the twentieth century. The Covenant places mission, and particularly evangelistic mission, at the center of the church's role in the world. It recognizes worship, compassionate ministry of various sorts, and the edification of the church as key responsibilities for all Christians. But it affirms that evangelism is the central call of God on the church in this epoch.

Not all evangelicals—and certainly not all Christians—endorse this priority.[27] Some take their cues from what they read in other traditions, notably Roman Catholic or Orthodox Christianity, and declare worship to be the church's main task, now and ever. Others see the church's primary responsibility to lie in care for the needy, and while such service will involve spiritual counsel at times, such counsel is only a part of a full-orbed representation of God's purposes in the world. And many evangelicals act as if the kingdom of God consists entirely of the steady expansion of congregations, church buildings, and parachurch agencies.

Even if for the sake of argument, however, we leave aside the knotty question of just which of the good things Lausanne says the church is

25. Mark A. Noll, *The Scandal of the Evangelical Mind* (Grand Rapids: Eerdmans, 1994).

26. Lausanne Covenant, 1974; http://www.lausanne.org/statements/covenant.html.

27. It is more than a little ironic that just as some evangelicals are disputing the priority of evangelism, some mainline and Anabaptist Protestants are reaffirming it: see Darrell L. Guder, ed., *Missional Church: A Vision for the Sending of the Church in North America* (Grand Rapids: Eerdmans, 1998).

to do deserves priority, evangelicals cannot be evangelicals without endorsing the importance of evangelism. And even this less controversial affirmation—which, one might think, would be endorsed by every Christian—sets evangelical theology over against some trends in contemporary Christian thought.

For one thing, it keeps evangelical theology from falling into the respective ditches of liberal and postliberal theology. The liberal tendency is to echo the culture—or, at least, to echo certain elites in that culture. This liberal "evangelism," perhaps exemplified best today in the proselytizing efforts of the Jesus Seminar, John Spong, and Hans Küng, says very little to the culture that the culture is not already saying. Indeed, its fundamental message seems not to be directed toward the culture at all but to traditional Christians in the kerygmatic formulation of Bishop Spong, "Change or die!"[28]

Postliberalism, for its part, retains a commitment to the gospel as traditionally understood in many respects, but its tendency, reacting as it does to the liberalism that is its constant foil, is to sectarianism and even unintelligibility. An evangelical will fear that postliberalism's stout insistence on retaining the church's own language and subsuming the contemporary world (somehow) into the biblical world can entail (as it did for Barth) a denial of sufficient common ground with the world upon which to proclaim the faith—despite the evident cultural sophistication of scholars in this school. Apologetics, therefore, is, at best, an ad hoc enterprise (as Hans Frei and William Werpehowsi put it) and perhaps at worst a simply dubious one (as Barth thought it was). It is not at all clear, as William Placher himself candidly puts it, how postliberals can suggest that what they themselves have found in Christianity to be true can be proclaimed as "just plain true" for everyone.[29]

And therefore evangelism becomes deeply problematic.

In fairness to the postliberals, however, the postmodern critique of knowledge does render problematic the proclamation of a universal gospel. Indeed, a cutting edge for evangelical theology today—as it is for any form of Christian theology that takes evangelism seriously—is to work out the epistemological grounds upon which we can then compose the most appropriate forms of evangelistic address to our neighbors. Analyses of some fundamental problems have been undertaken by an impressive group of scholars, ranging from sociologists such as

28. John Shelby Spong, *Why Christianity Must Change or Die: A Bishop Speaks to Believers in Exile* (San Francisco: HarperSanFrancisco, 1998).

29. William C. Placher, *Unapologetic Theology: A Christian Voice in a Pluralistic Conversation* (Louisville: Westminster/John Knox, 1989), 163–66.

Craig Gay and David Lyon to theologians such as Richard Middleton and Brian Walsh to philosophers such as Alvin Plantinga and Nicholas Wolterstorff.[30]

What has yet to emerge clearly is a posture and a rhetoric appropriate to evangelism in such conditions.[31] Indeed, if evangelicals are to continue to prize evangelism, then more of us must engage, and engage in, apologetics—both working out its theory for this cultural moment and actually undertaking conversation with thoughtful "others" in our culture. We must not confine, as we currently do, the great preponderance of our theological efforts to addressing either the church or the religious studies academy.

By extension, of course, it is evangelicalism's commitment not only to our neighbors but also to world evangelization that should prompt evangelical theology's investigation of perhaps the greatest theological question of our time: the plurality of the world's religions. The state of the art, alas, consists of evangelicals disputing over whether anyone who has not heard an authentic presentation of the gospel by the Holy Spirit can somehow be saved. Only elementary work, and not much of it, has been done so far toward constructing a thorough theology of religions that can explain world religions under the providence of God, and then suggest how Christian evangelism should be carried out in the light of such a theological understanding. It is a paradox, and perhaps an indictment, of evangelical theology that theological liberals have been working on this question in detail for years while evangelicals—whose missionaries continue to have the most actual contact with people of other faiths—lag conceptually far behind.

Indeed, one of the greatest scandals of evangelical theology in our time—and of academic theology in general—is the almost complete disinterest such theology has for the experience and reflection of missionaries and missiologists. Yet theologians today would do well to link

30. Craig M. Gay, *The Way of the (Modern) World: Or, Why It's Tempting to Live as If God Doesn't Exist* (Grand Rapids: Eerdmans; Cumbria, U.K.: Paternoster; Vancouver: Regent College, 1998); David Lyon, *Postmodernity* (Minneapolis: University of Minnesota Press, 1994); Middleton and Walsh, *Truth Is Stranger than It Used to Be*; Alvin Plantinga, the three-volume series on warrant that begins with *Warrant: The Current Debate* (New York and Oxford: Oxford University Press, 1993); and Wolterstorff, *Reason;* and *Divine Discourse.*

31. A good beginning is made in David Clark, *Dialogical Apologetics: A Person-Centered Approach to Christian Defense* (Grand Rapids: Baker, 1993). For examples of a change in tone from the common evidentialist and rationalist forms of evangelical apologetics, see Kelly James Clark, *When Faith Is Not Enough* (Grand Rapids and Cambridge, U.K.: Eerdmans, 1997); Thomas V. Morris, *Making Sense of It All: Pascal and the Meaning of Life* (Grand Rapids: Eerdmans, 1992); and my *Can God Be Trusted? Faith and the Challenge of Evil* (New York and Oxford: Oxford University Press, 1998).

up the ivory tower and the mission field, to draw together *Theology Today* and the *International Bulletin of Missionary Research*. What historian David Bebbington calls the "activistic" quality of evangelicalism has often militated against the sedentary work of theology, as action takes precedence over reflection. But if one looks at the theology written by Paul the missionary in the New Testament; the work of the early Greek apologists; Thomas Aquinas's missionary handbook, the *Summa Contra Gentiles;* or the musings of Jonathan Edwards on the missionary frontier of colonial Massachusetts, one sees that the evangelistic impulse has galvanized Christian theology many times, and wonderfully, throughout church history. Evangelical theologians should joyfully seek its energy today.

Transdenominationalism

Evangelicalism's elevating of the previous four concerns above all others has allowed evangelicals to band together on a variety of Christian projects: relief and development, publishing and broadcasting, education from preschool to graduate school, music, and evangelism both domestic and international, among many others.

When it comes to theology, this transdenominational openness has positioned evangelicals also to engage in dialogue with Roman Catholics, with postliberals, and with the Eastern Orthodox.[32]

Evangelicals also have increasingly contributed to mainline theological inquiry, notably in the pages of both academic journals and middlebrow periodicals such as *Theology Today* and *The Christian Century*. Each of these is a dramatic development when viewed from the perspective of just a generation or two ago, whether one's perspective is British, American, or Canadian.

But one can ask for more—and less. For more, we could ask that evangelicals capitalize on their transdenominationalism beyond affirming their lowest common denominator of theology or acknowledging respectfully their various differences (so the genre of books that offer "four views" on this or that area of disagreement). Could evangelicals profitably seek to read each other, as well as reading liberals of various stripes, postliberals, Catholics, and others, in order to refine

32. For the Evangelicals and Catholics Together document and evangelical commentary, see *Christianity Today* 41 (8 December 1997): 34; or www2.christianity.net/ct/7TE/7TE034.html. For evangelicals and postliberals, see Phillips and Okholm, *Nature of Confession.* For an example of evangelical-Orthodox theological exchange, see the articles by J. I. Packer and Bradley Nassif in *Crux* 32 (September 1996): 12–32; see also the magazine *Touchstone,* which brings together certain conservatives of Catholic, Protestant, and Orthodox traditions.

their own views precisely on the secondary, but still important, matters on which evangelicals disagree?

It seems to me that an evangelical transdenominationalism might dispose an evangelical Calvinist toward considering more seriously than he might the merits of Arminian or Pentecostal theology since such a Calvinist already recognizes and affirms his Arminian brother or Pentecostal sister as not only a fellow Christian but a fellow evangelical. Mennonites are sometimes read with profit by evangelicals—John Howard Yoder is exhibit A—but do Anabaptist evangelicals read other evangelicals in order to refine (I do not say "desert") their outlook? Such a perspective—that starts from a given tradition but is inclined to appreciate, not merely guard against, other evangelical traditions—might lift us beyond inherited impasses and draw on fresh light regarding perennial mysteries such as original sin, the relation of human will and divine providence, and the nature and scope of the atonement.

Evangelicals hold conferences to learn from each other regarding worship, preaching, church growth, social action, and other areas of joint concern. Will we support conferences that also bring together different viewpoints on gender, salvation, polity, the fate of the unevangelized, God's redemption of creation, and so on that help each of us become at least better versions of ourselves? Wheaton College's theology conference is a good step in this direction, and I hope Regent's conference will be another. When the *Journal of the Evangelical Theological Society* has avoided mere diatribes to concentrate on constructive work, it has offered useful fruit. In this regard, I believe that our British counterparts have much to show us, particularly in the ongoing example of the Tyndale Fellowship and the journal *Themelios*—which regrettably have no exact parallels in either Canada or the United States, as they have fostered evangelical theological excellence for more than a generation.[33]

We can also ask for less, however. We can ask for less arrogance and energy devoted to sorting out who are the true evangelicals and who are the pretenders, deviants, or apostates.[34]

We can ask for definitions of evangelicalism that are truly as broad as historic evangelicalism has been, and then move on to the interesting and important work that theology has to do in our time. Indeed, as

33. For an appreciative American account, see Noll, *Between Faith and Criticism*, chap. 4 and passim.

34. At this particular juncture, I have deliberately avoided the scholarly convention of providing examples of the genre in question precisely because I do not want to fight fire with fire, denunciation with denunciation. Readers who are not already familiar with such diatribes can count themselves blessed.

a Canadian with some familiarity with the American scene, I wonder if British and Canadian evangelicals have less inclination to specify sharp boundaries of authentic evangelicalism, not because we are morally or spiritually or intellectually superior to our American cousins, but because we simply can't afford the luxury of continual heresy hunting and the division that it produces. Indeed, the logic of my argument today is that such intra-evangelical wars are actually anti-evangelical.[35]

A robust transdenominationalism, finally, should promote respect for difference in secondary matters and devotion to the central importance of Jesus Christ and his gospel. Such an attitude fosters related theological virtues of zeal tempered by reserve, of confidence qualified by humility. Evangelicalism at its best keeps these pairs in play and, by God's grace, in balance.

Conclusion

Evangelical theology has profited in the past as it has attended to the voices of other Christians and, indeed, people of other faiths and philosophies. Evangelical theology according to the sketch I have set out here does not, and cannot, answer every question and solve every problem. Still, I have found it to be a good stance from which to consider theological challenges. I see no compelling reason to abandon it for another. I recommend it to theologians of other stripes as a resource well worth exploring for their own enrichment. Most centrally, I encourage my fellow evangelical theologians to engage unapologetically in theology from this perspective and to maintain this historic balancing of evangelical convictions as they do.

35. Thus when Gary Dorrien suggests that evangelicalism "has been poorly suited to affirm pluralism of any kind" and that "the evangelical impulse is to insist that only one religious tradition can be true," he overlooks the transdenominational dimension of evangelical conviction and focuses instead on the dogmatic and sectarian dimensions only (*The Remaking of Evangelical Theology* [Louisville: Westminster/John Knox, 1998], 3).

Part 2
Programmatic Proposals

3

The Voice and the Actor

A Dramatic Proposal about the Ministry and Minstrelsy of Theology

Kevin J. Vanhoozer

Evangelical Theology Should Be a Theology of the Gospel

When Bernard Ramm was once asked to define American evangelical theology, he reports having experienced inward panic: "Like a drowning man who sees parts of his life pass before him at great speed . . . so my theology passed before my eyes. I saw my theology as a series of doctrines picked up here and there, like a rag-bag collection."[1] Is Ramm perhaps alluding to Isaiah's comment that our righteous deeds (and doctrines) are as "filthy rags" (Isa. 64:6 KJV)? Probably not, though he would doubtless agree with Martin Luther's conviction that even the best humanly devised doctrines—which together comprise what he termed the "theology of glory"—are as filthy rags when compared to God's truth revealed in Jesus Christ and the "theology of the Cross."

---

1. Bernard Ramm, *After Fundamentalism: The Future of Evangelical Theology* (San Francisco: Harper & Row, 1983), 1.

Ramm later makes it clear that his real worry was a perceived lack of coherence or integrity to his theological "system."[2] The several doctrinal truths that made up Ramm's evangelical theology lacked, by his own admission, an overall cohesion—the unity not of a haphazard set of truths but the unity of *truth*.

Now one might think that Ramm protests too much. *Of course* evangelical theology is more than a miscellaneous collection of truths and teachings. Are not its doctrines all derived from the Bible? Is there not a correlation between the "system" of ideas in evangelical theology and the "system" of ideas in Scripture? Wayne Grudem, in his recent presidential address to the Evangelical Theological Society, suggests that the main task of evangelical theology is to determine what the "whole Bible" says about particular topics of special concern and importance.[3] The way forward would seem to be a "whole Bible exegesis" in which biblical scholars could determine what the whole Bible teaches about a given subject.

Grudem is surely right to call our attention to the centrality and authority of the whole Bible: *sola scriptura* and *tota scriptura*. Yet his call for a "whole Bible" approach may not alleviate Ramm's problem; indeed, it may exacerbate it. For it seems rather arbitrary to set about doing theology by asking, "What does the whole Bible say about x, about y, about z?" If theology is to be more than a rag-bag collection, it must demonstrate the deeper connections *among* x, y, and z. Theologians need not begin from scratch every time they confront a new problem. One's understanding of specific issues should rather emerge from one's cumulative understanding of the nature of God and of his ways with human beings. Rather than asking what the relevant parts of the whole Bible say about such and such an issue, evangelical theologians must seek to understand all the parts in light of the Bible as a unified whole. Moreover, is it really the case that one can come to an appropriately theological understanding of birth control and gun control (to cite two of Grudem's dozen or so pressing problems) by exegeting the relevant portions of Scripture? Studying biblical words and concepts takes us only so far. It is one thing to know how a biblical author spoke

2. Ramm came to see himself, and evangelical theology in general, as a product of the orthodox-liberal debate that dominated much of the twentieth-century theological discussion in North America. In Ramm's view, that debate has "warped" evangelical theology to the extent that the doctrines that evangelicals tend to stress are the ones that need to be defended at the time. Yet being reactionary is not the essence of evangelical theology.

3. Wayne Grudem, "Do We Act as If We Really Believe That 'the Bible Alone, and the Bible in Its Entirety, Is the Word of God Written'?" *Journal of the Evangelical Theological Society* (forthcoming).

or thought about a particular issue in the context of ancient Israel or the early church, quite another to relate those words and thoughts about a particular issue to the message of the Bible as a whole and to the significance of the Bible's teaching for us today.

So what is evangelical theology? How would I have answered Ramm's nightmare question? With Grudem, I affirm that evangelical theology is, or should be, biblical. To be precise, it should be a canonical-linguistic theology, that is, a theology whose speech about God is ruled by the testimony of the two testaments. But *why*, and *how?*

Why I Am Still an Evangelical: The Gospel and the Drama of Redemption

Why be biblical? Because the Bible communicates the gospel of Jesus Christ—the account of what God has said and done as sovereign Lord and as suffering servant for our salvation. "Evangelical" designates theology that seeks to know the "God of the gospel," the God who revealed himself in the prehistory and history of Jesus Christ as well as through the apocalyptic vision of his future coming.[4] I am an evangelical theologian because I believe the "good news" of what God has done in Jesus Christ and because I believe that theology—indeed, all of life—ought to be conformed to this reality, for ultimately there is no other reality, just as there is no other gospel (Gal. 1:7).

According to Ramm, "Evangelical Christianity refers to that version of Christianity which places the priority of the Word and Act of God over the faith, response, or experiences of men. Concretely this means the supremacy and authority of the Word of God (as a synonym for all the revelation of God, written and unwritten) over all human philosophies or religions."[5] Theology done in accord with the *euangelion* highlights two divine initiatives that together make up God's good news about God. First, God acting: There is only news if something has been done. Second, God speaking: There is only news if someone reports what has been done. Evangelicals accept these divine initiatives—the divine acts and their inspired reports—as the two givens with which theology begins.

The Bible not only reports what God has done but puts it in perspective. What God has done in Jesus Christ makes sense only because the

4. See my "Exploring the World; Following the Word: The Credibility of Evangelical Theology in an Incredulous Age," *Trinity Journal* 16 (1995): 3–27, where I develop this point. The essay also proposes a five-point summary of the essentials of evangelical theology with the aid of the acronym "DAISY": divine initiatives; amazing grace; imputed righteousness; scriptural authority; yesterday and today.

5. Bernard Ramm, *The Evangelical Heritage: A Study in Historical Theology* (Grand Rapids: Baker, 1973), 13.

biblical account places the person and work of Jesus Christ in the Old Testament context of the divine creation and the divine covenant. There is a cosmic stage and a covenantal plot; there is conflict; there is a climax; there is a resolution. Evangelical theology deals not with disparate bits of ideas and information but with an all-embracing narrative that relates the unified action of God. What the evangelical theologian ultimately wants to say about x, y, and z stems not from isolated word studies but from a sustained reflection on the meaning of what God has done through Christ to create and recreate the world. The Bible is not a theological dictionary but a theological drama, and should be used as such. The gospel is, in the words of Dorothy Sayers, "the greatest drama ever staged . . . a terrifying drama of which God is the victim and the hero."[6]

Evangelical theology, to the extent that it is a theology of the gospel, is therefore no rag-bag collection of teachings but rather a dramatic "from rags to riches" tale in which God the Son makes himself nothing in order that his human followers gain everything. The Bible, to repeat, is therefore not a collection of unrelated dicta on diverse subjects but an integrated drama concerning the unfolding of the covenant of grace. The Triune God is the principal actor throughout, uniting even the drama of creation with the drama of redemption.[7]

A theology of the gospel will focus on both the covenant and the canon, for the two are integrally linked. The Christian canon, Old and New Testaments together, is the book of the covenant that reaches its fullest expression in Jesus Christ. It is therefore proper to speak of a canonical covenant and of a covenantal canon. Moreover, both the covenant and the canon are species of communicative action, a notion that will loom large in what follows. The crucial point is that neither the covenant nor the canon can be reduced to a set of concepts.[8] On the contrary, both covenant and canon are, like the gospel, essentially dra-

6. Dorothy Sayers, *Creed or Chaos?* (New York: Harcourt, Brace, 1949), chap. 1. I am grateful to John G. Stackhouse, Jr., for calling my attention to Sayers's remarks on dogma and drama.

7. For a very helpful attempt to develop an evangelical biblical theology based on the gospel, see the collection of essays in R. J. Gibson, ed., *Interpreting God's Plan: Biblical Theology and the Pastor* (Carlisle: Paternoster, 1998).

8. I here assume that the nature of theology partakes of the nature of its covenantal subject matter and canonical form. All three—canon, covenant, theology—involve cognitive and relational dimensions alike. I therefore resist any and all attempts to reduce theology (and revelation) to something exclusively "propositional" or exclusively "personal." The proposal, to be more fully argued below, that theology is "phronetic" is an attempt at an enriched or expansionist account of what it is to interpret the Bible theologically.

matic in nature—a matter of God engaging his creatures, covenant-breakers and covenant-keepers alike, in dialogical action.

How to Be Biblical: The Gospel and the Drama of Reading

Theology done in the proper way is interpretation.[9]

How can we be appropriately "biblical" in our theology? How ought the method and form of theology do justice to its matter and content? How would I answer Ramm's nightmare question? Let me define evangelical theology as a "higher form" of biblical interpretation in which one reads the gospel in the context of the whole of authoritative Scripture and responds to the gospel in the context of the contemporary situation. What is "higher" about this interpretation is that it is not satisfied with word studies or even detailed commentary but rather requires the reader personally to engage with the central matter of the text. A theology of the gospel thus highlights both the redemptive-historical *substance* of the biblical text (e.g., the matter it relates) and what we may call its "redemptive-hermeneutical" *form* (e.g., the manner in which the word is addressed to and appropriated by the hearer/reader). The action in evangelical theology thus takes place on two levels, as it were: the historical unfolding of the covenant recorded in the canon and the reader's personal confrontation of and with this recorded history.

The Bible depicts the drama of redemption, but Meir Sternberg is right to speak about the "drama of reading" the biblical text as well. The "drama," for Sternberg, concerns the struggle between the worldview set forth in Scripture on the one hand, and the heart and mind of the reader on the other.[10] In a similar vein, a number of recent studies of biblical interpretation employ the metaphor of "performance" to describe how readers "make something" of a script. According to Stephen Barton, the idea of "performing" the Scriptures invites us "to locate our work as exegetes in a wider context of divine and human action."[11] Indeed, as John Webster rightly points out, the drama of reading is located in the broader drama of redemption, for God's speaking to readers in and through the biblical text, and the readers' subsequent responses, is itself part of the drama of sin and

9. Ramm, *Evangelical Heritage*, 159.

10. Meir Sternberg, *The Poetics of Biblical Narrative: Ideological Literature and the Drama of Reading* (Bloomington, Ind.: Indiana University Press, 1985).

11. Stephen C. Barton, "New Testament Interpretation as Performance," *Scottish Journal of Theology* 52 (1999): 179–208. Barton examines the approaches of Nicholas Lash, Rowan Williams, Frances Young, and Tom Wright (but, strangely, not Hans Urs von Balthasar).

its overcoming: "Reading the Bible is an event in this history. . . . Each reading act is also bound up with the dynamic of idolatry, repentance, and resolute turning from sin which takes place when God's Word addresses humanity."[12]

If theology is a higher order form of biblical interpretation, then the current crisis in biblical interpretation is *ipso facto* a crisis in theological method as well. This clearly seems to be the case. The present-day evangelical disputes over the nature of theology stem, more or less directly, I believe, from the current hermeneutical crisis. It is, to be precise, a legitimation crisis, a crisis over the principles by which one recognizes any particular interpretation as more valid than another. Whose reading—whose voice—counts, and why? That is what postmoderns insist upon knowing. It is also one of the most common arguments against the superiority, if not the very possibility, of evangelical theology. Daniel Raul Alvarez, for example, accuses evangelical theologians of illegitimately privileging seventeenth-century interpretations of Scripture over other interpretative traditions (not to mention over the text itself) and of mistakenly identifying these culturally conditioned, time-bound interpretations with the very essence of Christianity.[13]

Modern biblical scholars read the Bible "like any other book," using historical tools to dig up the historical meaning. Postmoderns, by contrast, read the Bible suspicious of any interpretation that claims to have gotten it right. For moderns, reading the Bible is valuable for what it tells us about what lies *behind* the text (history). For postmoderns, reading the Bible is valuable for what it tells us about the reader in front of the text (ideology). The question that both ask is whether it is possible to read the Bible as God's Word, and if so, how.

In brief, theology construed as a higher form of biblical interpretation must answer the above as well as the following questions: Does theology's use of concepts make systematic theology idolatrous? Does biblical authority stifle the work of the Spirit in the church today? Does systematic theology encourage the rote memorization of dogmatic formulae, an uncritical repetition I shall later refer to as "dead theatre"? The present-day confusion about how to do theology—within evangelicalism and without—is thus directly related to the contemporary crisis in biblical interpretation. At the same time, I believe

12. John Webster, "Hermeneutics in Modern Theology: Some Doctrinal Reflections," *Scottish Journal of Theology* 51 (1998): 336.

13. Daniel Raul Alvarez, "On the Possibility of an Evangelical Theology," *Theology Today* 55 (1998): 175–94.

that this latter methodological crisis—about how to interpret the Bible—is, at root, theological.[14]

The Contribution of Bernard Ramm

I began this essay by recounting Ramm's panic at having to give a reasonable account of the evangelical theology that was within him. It would be misleading not to point out that Ramm himself made considerable headway in his published works toward responding to that unanswered question. And, though he nowhere explicitly addressed the problems of postmodernity, Ramm did make several programmatic suggestions about the future, and not only the past, of evangelical theology. The present essay is indebted at several points to his foresight and insight into the pattern or "structure" of evangelical theology vis-à-vis God's special revelation.[15]

In the first place, Ramm rightly perceived that evangelical theology must be a theology of the gospel, and hence, that it must be a form of interpretation. In Ramm's view, evangelical interpretation is in ethos quite different from the obscurantist, literalistic, and absolutistic style that often characterized fundamentalism's opposition to modernity. Evangelicals ought not presume that a final statement of theology has already been achieved. Nor is it of the essence of evangelicalism to believe that revelation is solely propositional or only the conveying of information.[16] On the contrary, Ramm called for a renaissance of the evangelical imagination, for a literate handling of the literary forms of Scripture: "There is appeal to imagination in Scripture as well as to mind, and we certainly know that imagination far more powerfully affects the self than conceptual thinking."[17]

Ramm's instincts concerning theological hermeneutics are worth recalling. First and foremost is his Christocentric emphasis. All of Scripture testifies, in diverse ways and on different levels, to the reality mediated by the story of God in Jesus Christ. It follows that the "test of truth in Christianity is conformity to the Word of God."[18] We might call

14. This is the fundamental premise of my *Is There a Meaning in This Text? The Bible, the Reader, and the Morality of Literary Knowledge* (Grand Rapids: Zondervan, 1998).

15. This is not the place for a full-blown analysis of Ramm's own theology, apologetics, and hermeneutics. See my chapter on Ramm in *Handbook of Evangelical Theologians*, ed. Walter A. Elwell (Grand Rapids: Baker, 1993), 290–306. Suffice it to say that I find the "middle" Ramm more satisfying on these points than the "later" more Barthian Ramm of *After Fundamentalism*. At the same time, the present essay, like Ramm, does try to make evangelical peace with Barth on the relation of Scripture and revelation.

16. Ramm, *Evangelical Heritage*, 129.

17. Ibid., 131.

18. Ibid., 144.

this the "material principle" of a theology of the gospel. Second, Ramm insists that "Christianity is one and not many and is not capable of continuous radical interpretation."[19] Simply put, we must not exchange the apostolic gospel concerning Jesus Christ for some other gospel, which is really no gospel at all. Christian theology is disciplined inquiry into the one truth of the one gospel, defined by the apostolic witness. Such is the "formal principle" of Ramm's theological hermeneutics.

In the concluding chapter of his book *The Evangelical Heritage,* "The Future of Evangelical Theology," Ramm makes the following five recommendations:

1. Evangelicals must be students of Scripture. "To be truly biblical is one of the most difficult achievements."[20] The revelation of God in Scripture is "foundational."
2. Evangelicals must know the inner structure of evangelical theology. We must not, like sects or heresies, major on the minors.[21]
3. Evangelicals must know their cultural climate: first, because culture affects exegesis, and second, because we want to communicate the gospel to our culture. Ramm calls for evangelicals to know the art, literature, science, and philosophy of their times; this means understanding the culture of late modernity and postmodernity.
4. Evangelicals must rethink the God-world relation.[22]
5. Evangelicals must be students of linguistics, philosophy of language, and communications. "It is my conviction that the next impetus to rethink our evangelical doctrines of inspiration and revelation is going to come from the modern communications theory."[23]

The Dramatic Proposal: A Synopsis of the Plot

The present essay, a sequel of sorts to my *Is There a Meaning in This Text?*[24] sets forth an approach to theology that takes up, at least implic-

19. Ibid., 140.
20. Ibid., 152.
21. Ramm explores this in greater detail in *The Pattern of Religious Authority* (Grand Rapids: Eerdmans, 1957), a book that, though somewhat out of date, still contains much wisdom.
22. Assumptions about the way in which God relates to the world lie behind virtually every doctrine in theology. For a critical engagement with contemporary panentheistic ways of conceiving this relation, see my "The Case Remains Unproven: Two Types of Systematic Theology," *Dialog* 38 (1999): 281–85. The present essay rethinks divine agency in terms of communication rather than causality.
23. Ramm, *Evangelical Heritage,* 163. Ramm mentions, among others, Wittgenstein, Ricoeur, Chomsky, and McLuhan.
24. See n. 14 above.

itly, Ramm's five recommendations. My book explored the last of Ramm's above-mentioned suggestions, developing an understanding of God's special revelation in terms of "communicative acts." Whereas the book brought Christian doctrine to bear on interpretation theory, the present work examines how biblical interpretation eventuates in Christian doctrine. The goal is not a theological hermeneutics but a hermeneutical theology.

My aim in what follows is to propose what an evangelical theology with a postpropositionalist Scripture principle, and with one ear cocked to the postmodern condition, should look like. I argue that evangelical theology is able both to face up to the postmodern challenge to hermeneutics and to affirm the authority of the Christian Scriptures. The hallmarks of such a theology include performative understanding and creative fidelity. Evangelical theology is a matter of "joyful faith seeking creative understanding" of the Word and Act of God.

The present paper is made up of three "acts" and a conclusion. Act 1 offers a reformulation of the Scripture principle in terms of communicative action. Act 2 sets forth a canonical-linguistic approach for doing theology in accordance with my reinvigorated Scripture principle. Act 3 considers the nature of doctrine that is the desired outcome of the canonical-linguistic approach. The conclusion offers some reflections with regard to the ministry of theology in the church and suggests that our identity as persons and Christians is linked to how well we practice the doctrines we profess. At each stage of my analysis, I draw upon analogies from the world of theatre in order to underline the importance of thinking through these matters in terms of communicative action.

Act 1. The Voice and the Actor: Divine Revelation, Human Response, and "First Theology"

My emphasis on the voice and the actor derives both from my understanding of the gospel and from how we ought to respond to it. The form of theology is "dramatic" inasmuch as it concerns a word addressed by God to man and a response from man to God. The substance of theology is dramatic because it concerns what God has done in Jesus Christ. The task of theology, therefore, is to enable hearers and doers of the gospel to respond and to correspond to the prior Word and Act of God. The Triune God is the primary speaker and actor, but the people of God have been given the privilege and responsibility not only of thinking God's thoughts after him but of speaking God's words and of acting God's acts after him as well.

The Voice: The Word of God and Theological Speech

Word of God

What is the nature of the Word of God? Some evangelicals, reacting to mid-twentieth-century movements that denied the verbal and cognitive nature of divine revelation, tended to identify God's Word with the revealed propositions found in Scripture. Carl Henry, for instance, argues that revelation in Scripture is a matter of objective truths stated in conceptual and verbal form. The task of theology thus becomes the systematization of the information conveyed through biblical propositions.[25] Karl Barth, on the other hand, claims that the Word is first and foremost Jesus Christ: God in his self-revelation. Yet Barth does not want his "personalizing" of the concept Word of God to lead to its "deverbalizing."[26] Indeed, in one place he refers to revelation as a divine "speech act" or *"Rede-Tat"*[27] and insists that God's speech is not a mere symbol.[28] Nevertheless, Barth does tend to "deverbalize" the Word of God, just as some evangelicals tend, in their doctrine of Scripture, to "depersonalize" it.

Here, then, is a first doctrine for which evangelicals need to exercise "joyful faith seeking creative understanding." I have already stated that evangelicals assert the primacy of God's Word. The question here concerns its nature. The gospel is a word *about* God in Jesus Christ *from* God the Holy Spirit. Revelation is thus not merely the disclosure of information about God but an act of God himself. I shall argue below that we need to think of biblical revelation in such a way that we transcend the older "propositional" versus "personal" models. The operative concept for doing so, as we shall see, is communicative action: God does things in speaking and *thereby* reveals himself.

Theology as Speech about God

The voice or words of the theologian should correspond to the Word of God. As Barth famously put it: "As ministers we ought to speak of God. We

25. See Carl F. H. Henry, *God, Revelation, and Authority,* vol. 3 (Waco: Word, 1979), chap. 27, "The Bible as Propositional Revelation," esp. 477–78. Henry thinks that the primary concern of revelation is "the communication of truth." Even divine commands, such as "Thou shalt not murder," can be "translated into propositions" (e.g., "murder is wrong") (477). This example of Henry's is instructive; in my view, the primary purpose of a command is not to state a universal truth (though I would agree that such a statement is implicit) but to direct human behavior. The question, then, is whether evangelical theology can correspond to the primary concerns of Scripture, whether this be the communication of truth or the regulation of action.

26. Karl Barth, *Church Dogmatics* I/1, trans. Geoffrey Bromiley (Edinburgh: T & T Clark, 1975), 138.

27. Ibid., 162.

28. Ibid., 150.

are human, however, and so cannot speak of God."[29] This encapsulates the theologian's challenge too. Barth's worry about orthodox theology is that it substitutes its human statements for God's own speech. Right doctrine, like the child promised to Abraham, cannot be conceived through human effort alone. On the contrary, human speech about God is true insofar as it corresponds to and participates in God's prior speech.

In a 1923 address to the General Assembly of the Union of Reformed Churches in Germany, Barth noted that "doctrine" is considered something less worthy and less important than "life."[30] Little has changed in this regard over the intervening years. Yet the question of doctrine is nothing less than the question of the content of Christian preaching. The crisis in doctrine is therefore symptomatic of a deeper crisis in the church. In Barth's words: "The question of right doctrine introduces us to the vacuum *inside* our churches and *inside* Christianity."[31] Simply put, what does the church have to say that no other institution can say or do?[32] Any answer to this important question will finally have to do with our doctrine.

John Webster has recently called attention to the eclipse of Christian doctrine in discussions about biblical hermeneutics. By and large, the modern (and postmodern) "hermeneutical situation" theorizes about what it is to read and interpret texts in general, and the Bible in particular, with little or no sustained theological reflection on the reading process.[33] Evangelical exegetes and theologians have sometimes shown themselves to be as prone as their liberal counterparts to adopt nontheological accounts of meaning and truth. Indeed, what lies behind the all-too-frequent charge that evangelicals are "propositionalists" is the perception that some biblical interpreters may be working with a concept of truth that owes more to nineteenth- and twentieth-century views of language and science than, say, to incarnational theology.

From a theological perspective, the most important fact about the Bible is that it is the voice of God addressing the people of God. From this theological indicative follows the prime hermeneutical imperative: Let God's Word accomplish the purpose for which it was sent (see Isa. 55:11). The point is that God interacts with contemporary readers through the Scriptures. The Bible—the Word of God—is simultaneously an instrument of divine *action*.

29. Karl Barth, *The Word of God and the Word of Man* (Gloucester, Mass.: Peter Smith, 1978), 186.

30. Barth, "The Doctrinal Task of the Reformed Churches," in *Word of God and the Word of Man*, 219.

31. Ibid., 221.

32. See John Leith, *The Reformed Imperative: What the Church Has to Say That No One Else Can Say* (Philadelphia: Westminster, 1988), chap. 1.

33. Webster, "Hermeneutics in Modern Theology," 307–41.

The Actor: The Act of God and Theologian as Agent

Act of God

While "Word" describes the verbal form of the gospel, we need another category—"act"—to describe the gospel's subject matter. The good news implies that something was *done;* it can neither be contemplated in a pure aesthetic nor proved in a pure logic.[34] The gospel refers to the act of God in Jesus Christ in, and for, and upon the world. "Both tragedy and the Passion have the same basic nature: they are act. Reality is action, not theory."[35] What God performs on the stage of world history is *covenant,* and when this drama reaches its climax—the cross—the curtain separating the historical "already" and the eschatological "not yet" is not only raised but torn in two (Matt. 27:51).

Balthasar admired Goethe's translation of John 1:1, "Am Anfang war die Tat" ("In the beginning was the deed"). By placing Goethe's translation in tension with John, Balthasar produces the notion of the *Tatwort.* Whereas Barth writes of speech-acts, Balthasar thinks in terms of deed-words. (He was also fond of quoting Ignatius of Antioch on the three "speeches" of God: creation, Scripture, and incarnation.) The crucial point is that God reveals himself by what he does. We can integrate the respective approaches of Barth and Balthasar, I believe, under the rubric of communicative action. God's Word *does* things, and what God does also *communicates.* Divine revelation, we may conclude, is God in communicative action.

Evangelical theology arises from a faithful and understanding response to the divine communicative action that is both the form and the subject matter of the gospel. The gospel is both something done and something said and hence presupposes both a voice and an actor. It is important to recall that the Bible itself, and not just the events it recounts, is one of God's communicative acts too.[36]

34. Hans Urs von Balthasar states that divine revelation is not so much an object to be looked at as it is God's action in and upon the world. He devotes a chapter to examining trends in contemporary theology. Though they each seek to get beyond rationalistic abstraction, none is as rich as the notion of theodrama. See *Theodrama,* vol. 1, trans. Graham Harrison (San Francisco: Ignatius Press, 1988), 25–50. Cf. Raymund Schwager, *Jesus in the Drama of Salvation: Towards a Biblical Doctrine of Redemption* (New York: Crossroad, 1999).

35. Balthasar, *Theodrama,* vol. 1, 66.

36. Balthasar is aware of the dangers of the analogy. He speaks of the "twin abysses of a systematics in which God, absolute Being, is only the Unmoved before whom the moving world plays out its drama, and a mythology which absorbs God into the world and makes him to be one of the warring parties of world process" (*Theodrama,* vol. 1, 131).

Theology as Action

Revelation is thus God's initiative, his communicative act in and upon the world; the world, says Balthasar, "can only respond, and hence 'understand,' through action on *its* part."[37] If revelation is not only speech but action, it follows that theology, if it is to correspond to revelation, must take the form of speech and action too. Indeed, Balthasar goes further, suggesting that intellectual apprehension alone is not yet a sufficient condition for understanding the gospel—"even the demons believe" (James 2:19). Perhaps the most appropriate response to *euangelion* is *eucharisto:* thanksgiving. The *Tatwort* of the theologian should correspond to the *Tatwort* of God as gratitude corresponds to gift.[38]

"First Theology"

Evangelical theology need not choose between God as speaker and God as actor. Nor should we choose between theology as solely propositional or solely personal. As we have seen, both Barth and Balthasar hint at ways to overcome this distinction: *Rede-Tat, Tatwort*. Interestingly, the great discovery in twentieth-century philosophy of language is the "speech act" or "illocution," the notion that we do something in speaking. Philosophers have learned what playwrights have known for centuries, namely, "Parler c'est agir" ("To speak is to act").[39] How does this insight better help us to think about the Word of God as authority for theology?

David Kelsey, in his celebrated work, *Proving Doctrine: The Uses of Scripture in Modern Theology*, demonstrates that theologians appeal to biblical authority in several different ways.[40] The great merit of David Kelsey's analysis is that he identifies a, perhaps *the*, crucial point over which theologians disagree, their methodological parting of the ways. What Kelsey discovered is that we typically formulate our doctrines of God and Scripture *together*. When we decide in what way the Bible is authoritative—as doctrine, as history, as narrative, and so forth—we

37. Ibid., 15.

38. Barth would no doubt agree. He stressed in his Tambach lecture that human action must participate in the prior action of God. The Christian "is that within us which is not ourselves but Christ in us" (*Word of God and the Word of Man*, 273). We shall explore just how we "understand" God's communicative action through action on our part in the section "Dramatic Theology: 'The Doctrine Is the Drama'" below.

39. Abbé d'Aubignac, *La Pratique du théâtre* (Paris, 1657).

40. David H. Kelsey, *Proving Doctrine: The Uses of Scripture in Modern Theology* (Harrisburg, Pa.: Trinity Press International, 1999), formerly published as *The Uses of Scripture in Recent Theology* (Philadelphia: Fortress Press, 1975).

are simultaneously making a judgment as to the way in which God is involved with Scripture and with the believing community.

I have come to believe that, with regard to method, we have to construe or configure *three* factors together: God, Scripture, *and* the nature of theology. We have to enter into a biblical-theological variant of the hermeneutic circle. Decisions taken here affect what we might call, after the philosophers, "first theology"—the principles that, methodologically speaking, come first.

I disagree with Kelsey's analysis at two important points: First, each of the views he examines tends to see the authoritative function of Scripture in terms of a single model only, and Kelsey accepts this as normal, if not normative. Typically, theologians tend to gravitate to one particular aspect or portion of Scripture (e.g., doctrine, narrative, history, apocalyptic) and then interpret the whole of Scripture in light of that part. The problem with this one-size-fits-all approach is its reductionism; we should not read all of Scripture as myth, or history, or doctrine, or as any one thing only.

My second problem with Kelsey is that the imaginative decision about the God/Scripture relation is, according to him, pre-text. The *sensus fidelium*—the impression of what Christianity is all about—is shaped by participating in the Christian community not by exegeting the text. It follows that the decisive authority—the authority deciding how to construe both God and Scripture—lies with the community rather than with the text. In my view, there is a better alternative.

The point to note is that theology begins neither with a *sensus divinitatis,* nor a *sensus literalis,* nor even a *sensus fidelium,* but with a *sensus scripturalis* (e.g., a sense of the Bible as a unified Scripture, as divine communicative action). Theology has to do with God in self-communicative action (incarnation) and with Scripture as God's self-communicative act (inspiration). Authority in theology, I believe, is a matter of the Triune God in self-communicative action. Hence, God is a communicative agent, Scripture is a human/divine communicative action, and theology, as we shall see, is a matter not only of responding to but of participating in divine communicative action.

Act 2. The Canonical-Linguistic Approach: Toward a Five-Point Sapiential Systematics

What would a theology that corresponded to the gospel—to the voice and act of God—look like? To the extent that theology fosters the love of God with all our mind, heart, and strength, we need not only propositional information but also poetic imaginations and practical initiatives in order to correspond to the *Tatwort* of the gospel. We need a theology that is oriented toward wisdom, for wisdom integrates cognition (mind), imagination (heart), and action (strength).

What I here call the canonical-linguistic approach is my shorthand term for an approach that could also be described as postpropositionalist, pluralistic, phronetic, Protestant, and postfoundational. The first two points concern the voice (of God, of the theologian), the third concerns the theologian as actor, while the final two points relate my proposal to the theology of the Reformation and to recent disputes about epistemology respectively.

Postpropositionalist Theology

It is not of the essence of evangelicalism to believe that revelation is solely propositional or only the conveying of information.[41]

It is one thing to speak of propositions as a component of speech acts, quite another to affirm propositionalism. The propositionalist theologian holds that what is of value in Scripture are the statements or truth content conveyed by its language. It would seem to follow that assertions, insofar as they convey cognitive information, hold pride of theological place on this model. I am a postpropositionalist theologian because, though I begin with the Scriptures as special revelation and affirm their truthfulness, I do not conceive either revelation or truth in a narrowly propositionalist fashion. Biblical authority is not simply a matter of its conveying information.

Language

According to Nancey Murphy, both conservative and liberal theology assumed a pictorial-referential theory of language, according to which words either refer to the external world (e.g., to history), as conservatives maintained, or express the inner world of human subjectivity, as liberals were wont to say.[42] In either case, however, the assumption is that language is essentially a matter of *picturing* (e.g., objective referentialism, subjective expressivism). In brief, the propositions conveyed by language are thought to be pictures of states of affairs. The canonical-linguistic approach is postpropositionalist because it rejects the picture theory of meaning. Instead, it insists with speech act theory that language is a form of action and that propositions may be used to do more than picture the world. Referring to history and expressing human subjectivity are only two of the things speakers can do with words.

41. Ramm, *Evangelical Heritage,* 129.
42. See Nancey Murphy, *Beyond Liberalism and Fundamentalism: How Modern and Postmodern Philosophy Set the Theological Agenda* (Valley Forge, Pa.: Trinity Press International, 1996).

Scripture

The present approach is *post*conservative theology because it transcends the debilitating dichotomies between referring and expressing, between propositional and personal revelation, between God saying and God doing, precisely by focusing on the Bible as a set of divine communicative acts. God in Scripture is doing many things with words, not simply conveying information, nor even revealing himself. The approach is post*conservative* in that it maintains there is something in the text that is both indispensable and authoritative, namely, the divinely intended meaning.

John Goldingay makes a valid point when he says that no one model—neither authority, nor witness, nor inspiration, nor revelation—enjoys the status of being the biblical way of framing the doctrine of Scripture.[43] I am therefore inclined to maintain the Scripture principle—the notion that the Bible is the Word of God—on the basis of communicative action. The Bible is not so much a handbook of revealed propositions as it is a set of divine communicative acts, of which statements and assertions—propositions that convey information about God—are an important subset.[44] The concept of communicative action functions as a unifying model for all of Scripture yet recognizes the several ways in which the Bible exerts its authority: Its assertions are to be believed, its promises trusted, its commands obeyed, and its songs sung. Scripture not only relates divine action but is itself one of its forms. The Bible is communicative action—action that initiates, sustains, and nourishes covenantal relations.

What happens to propositions in this view? The demise of propositionalist theology—of propositionalism—does not entail the loss of propositions, for every speech act has a propositional component. Every sentence propounds something for our consideration, though not everything proposed for our consideration has assertive force, nor do all assertions picture states of affairs.[45] Everything depends on what authors do with their words. Indeed, perhaps the most important deci-

43. John Goldingay, *Models for Scripture* (Grand Rapids: Eerdmans, 1994).

44. From Scripture being divine communicative action, it follows that the Bible is indeed revelatory, in the sense that all communicative action discloses, at the very least, something about the will and intention of the author. Goldingay, as well as Nicholas Wolterstorff, may be working with an overly narrow concept of revelation—the unveiling of what would otherwise remain a mystery (cf. Nicholas Wolterstorff, *Divine Discourse: Philosophical Reflections on the Claim That God Speaks* [Cambridge: Cambridge University Press, 1995], 19).

45. See my "The Semantics of Biblical Literature," in *Hermeneutics, Authority, and Canon*, ed. D. A. Carson and John D. Woodbridge (Grand Rapids: Baker, 1995), 53–104, esp. 87–88.

sion an interpreter makes concerns illocutionary force; in deciding what the author has done, the interpreter also decides how the propositions are to be taken.

Whose Voice? Which Practice?

A number of evangelical theologians have discarded propositionalist theology only to take up the cause of "postliberal" theology.[46] In this view, the meaning and truth of Christian faith are to be found neither in the cognitive information conveyed by Scripture (as theological conservatives maintain), nor in personal disclosures or religious experience behind the text (as theological liberals maintain), but rather in the life and language—the practices—of the believing community. After all, as the philosopher Ludwig Wittgenstein advised, if you want the meaning, look to the term's use.

Alister McGrath identifies what, in my opinion, is a crucial weakness of George Lindbeck's cultural-linguistic or postliberal approach.[47] The problem concerns the origin of the cultural-linguistic tradition, the "genesis of doctrine." What norms a communal practice of speaking of God in such and such a way? Lindbeck takes the tradition as a given, a potentially dangerous assumption given the postmodern predilection for deconstruction through genealogy. The serious point, however, concerns the legitimacy of this particular linguistic-cultural practice. It is not clear whether its ultimate genesis lies in divine revelation or in human corporate insight, namely, religion.[48]

The postpropositionalist theology advocated in this chapter is better described as postconservative rather than postliberal. What finally distinguishes the two qualifiers is the insistence of the former on the communicative practices of the canon, rather than those of the interpreting community, as the primary locus of the meaning and truth of Christian faith. While meaning may well be a matter of use rather than reference, the authoritative uses of terms such as *God, grace,* and *salvation* are those of the biblical authors, not its readers.

46. See the collection of essays in Timothy R. Phillips and Dennis L. Okholm, eds., *The Nature of Confession: Evangelicals and Postliberals in Conversation* (Downers Grove, Ill.: InterVarsity Press, 1996).

47. Alister E. McGrath, *The Genesis of Doctrine: A Study in the Foundations of Doctrinal Criticism* (Grand Rapids: Eerdmans, 1997), chap. 2.

48. This is where I feel I must register a demurral with regard to Nicholas Lash's otherwise very helpful contribution to theological method with regard to "performing" the Scriptures. See Gale Z. Heide, "The Nascent Noeticism of Narrative Theology: An Examination of the Relationship between Narrative and Metaphysics in Nicholas Lash," *Modern Theology* 12 (1996): 459–81.

Pluralistic Theology

What stance does the canonical-linguistic approach take with regard both to the plurality of biblical texts and biblical theologies on the one hand and the plurality of biblical interpretations and interpretative traditions on the other? It seems that theology must take the form of a hermeneutic. Because theology is "enmeshed in texts,"[49] interpretation is, in the words of Werner Jeanrond, "the soul of theology."[50] The canon is our interpretative framework, but it is not a unified conceptual scheme with ready-made universal categories.

Emmanuel Lévinas has a name for that kind of systematic mind whose thoughts are restless until they find their rest in a totalizing conceptual framework. Lévinas calls this mentality "Greek" think, and suggests that it is fundamentally violent and unethical. A totalizing system acknowledges only what conforms to its conceptual scheme; it therefore absorbs the "other" into the "same" (i.e., into my categories). In Lévinas's terms: "The labor of thought wins out over the otherness of things and men" (and we might add, texts).[51] Exegetes have no problem recognizing their systematic theological colleagues in this description. Indeed, the cynic might say that Lévinas has written the perfect job description for the systematic theologian!

A Plurality of Biblical Voices

A certain plurality would seem to be biblical. At the very least, there is a recognizable plurality of communicative acts in Scripture.[52] As we have already seen, the language and literature of the Bible do not engage reality in one way only. We need to be sensitive to *the way the words go.*

While the truth about what God has done in Christ may transcend the particular interpretative perspectives, interpreters cannot. While it is true "that God was in Christ reconciling the world to Himself" (2 Cor. 5:19 NASB), we may need more than one interpretative framework to articulate fully its meaning and significance, just as it took four Gospels to articulate the truth of Jesus Christ. There may therefore be several normative points of view in the Bible that are all authoritative because they disclose *aspects* of the truth. It is therefore possible simulta-

49. Werner G. Jeanrond, *Text and Interpretation as Categories of Theological Thinking* (New York: Crossroad, 1988), xv.

50. Ibid., 153.

51. Emmanuel Lévinas, "Ethics as First Philosophy," in *The Lévinas Reader*, ed. Seán Hand (Oxford: Basil Blackwell, 1989), 78.

52. See S. E. Gillingham, *One Bible, Many Voices: Different Approaches to Biblical Studies* (London: S. P. C. K., 1998).

neously to admit a multiplicity of perspectives and to maintain an "as-pectival" realism.

A Plurality of Interpretative Traditions

Plurality is even more apparent when we turn from text to interpre-tative traditions. Church history confronts us with a plethora of bibli-cal interpretations. A theological tradition refers to a certain trajectory of biblical interpretation, or as Alasdair MacIntyre puts it, a socially embodied argument about the meaning and significance of a founda-tional text.[53]

Postmoderns have fueled the crisis in biblical interpretation by in-sisting that social formations—of race, gender, and class—exert more influence on our interpretations than does the text itself. One's inter-pretations generally reveal more about the ideology of the interpreter than they do about the text. The postmoderns are right to caution against thinking we can master the text. At the same time, the mere fact of plurality does not legitimate the ideology of pluralism.

While not going so far as the postmoderns, I believe it is important to recover a way to do justice to the "catholicity" of the canon as well as to the catholicity of church interpretation. But how? I know of at least one book in which contributors from a number of different cul-tures came together to interpret the Bible, not with the intent of explor-ing how this or that group read the text for themselves, but rather with the goal of providing a richer appreciation of the historical meaning of the text.[54]

A Pluralistic Systematic Theology?

Might both of the above-mentioned pluralities stand on properly theological ground? Perhaps the richness of the gospel is such that it required four written Gospels adequately to articulate it (a fourfold or plural sufficiency of Scripture). The richness (or to use a favorite post-modern term, the "excess") of the event of Jesus Christ calls for multi-ple *perspectives* to do justice to the many *aspects* of its truth.[55] It is the many voices taken together that correspond adequately, though not necessarily exhaustively, to the reality of Jesus Christ. If this is true of the canon, might the same hold for theological traditions?

---

53. In this respect, tradition is biblical interpretation of a higher order too. See Alas-dair MacIntyre, *Whose Justice? Which Rationality?* (Notre Dame, Ind.: University of Notre Dame Press, 1988).

54. See my *Is There a Meaning in This Text?* 172, 415–24.

55. As I am here using the terms, *perspective* is an epistemic notion, *aspect* a meta-physical one.

Let's remember what is at stake. Authority lies with the Triune God in self-communicative action, but the operative question is, Who speaks for God? Whose interpretation of God's Word is the legitimate one?

One option is to recall Vincent of Lerin's definition of orthodoxy: "that which is believed everywhere, by everyone, at all times." This "rule of faith" is not bad as a rule of thumb, but we should resist locating interpretative authority in community consensus, for even believing communities, as we know from the Old Testament narratives, often get it badly wrong, and to locate authority in the community itself is to forgo the possibility of prophetic critique.

Another approach is to think about the possibility of a plural unity. Here we are helped by the Russian literary critic Mikhail Bakhtin. Bakhtin's notion of "plural unity" echoes a thought of Pascal: "A plurality that cannot be integrated into unity is chaos; unity unrelated to plurality is tyranny."[56] Like Lévinas, Bakhtin resists the absolutization of a particular point of view. Bakhtin questions whether any single voice—any single perspective, any single genre—is able to articulate the truth. The dialogue's the thing. One of the defining characteristics of dialogue is its "unfinalizability." The moral for Christian theology is clear: "Final" or absolute biblical interpretations are properly eschatological. For the moment, we must cast our doctrines not in the language of heaven but in the time-bound, culture-bound languages of earth, governed, of course, by the dialogue we find in Scripture itself.[57]

I for one would be sorry if everyone thought just like me. I would deeply regret it if there were no Mennonite, or Lutheran, or Greek Orthodox voices in the world. Why? Because I think that truth would be better served by their continuing presence. To some, this may be a shocking way of thinking about truth. Is not truth one? Must not our confessions of faith contain not only affirmations but also denials? Yes. Yes! But my question concerns whether a systematics that employs only a single conceptual system can fully articulate the truth.[58]

56. Blaise Pascal, *Pensées*, #809.

57. As Cyril O'Regan points out, the hope for unity remains the horizon of dialogue. See his "Balthasar: Between Tübingen and Postmodernity," *Modern Theology* 14 (1998): 349.

58. Interestingly, Mary Potter Engel argues that no less a systematic theologian than Calvin required a "dynamic perspectival structure" with which to articulate the whole counsel of God. For example, Calvin considers human beings from the perspective of time and from the perspective of eternity. See her *John Calvin's Perspectival Anthropology*, AAR Academy Series, no. 52 (Atlanta: Scholars Press, 1988).

Obviously some restriction must be put on plurality, otherwise there would be no way of setting parameters on the content of the gospel. I have already indicated that, for me, it is the Scripture principle that sets these critical parameters, this "fence around the gospel." The Scripture principle asserts that the various authorial voices in the Old and New Testaments, taken together in their canonical context, constitute the Word of God written. What is authoritative about Scripture is the whole canonical dialogue; the dialogue of diverse biblical voices is itself the measuring rod for Christian theology. But just how does the Scripture principle, construed as canonical communicative action, actually work?

Phronetic Theology

Given the necessity of a certain legitimate plurality, how can we judge which interpretative traditions correspond, and are genuinely responsive, to the text? We come now to the third point, one that is both structurally and materially at the heart of the canonical-linguistic approach.

Reasoning in a Canonical Situation

Theology is biblical interpretation that aims at knowledge of God. Well and good, but what kind of knowledge? We can distinguish, using Aristotle's categories, *theoria* (a knowledge of true propositions, as in Euclidean geometry) from *technem* (a product of instrumental reason, or in the case of biblical interpretation, of biblical criticism). Neither is entirely appropriate, however, for a theological interpretation of Scripture. Could it be that *two* pictures of rationality have held us captive?

There is a third voice of reason, neither theoretical nor instrumental: it is *phronesis*, practical reason, prudence. This was Aristotle's term for moral reasoning in concrete situations. It is more deliberative than deductive, more a matter of consideration than of a moral calculus. In deciding on the rightness of a particular action in a specific situation, *phronesis* considers both principles and particulars.[59] To deliberate well one needs both a general principle and an accurate grasp of the particular situation one happens to be in. Phronesis is the ability to exercise good judgment in specific contexts. In short, it is wisdom: the ability (which includes know-

59. The intellectual roots of this idea may be traced back to Aristotle's *Nicomachean Ethics*, though his insights were made into a general theory of understanding in the twentieth century by philosophical hermeneutics, especially Hans-Georg Gadamer and Paul Ricoeur. See Richard J. Bernstein, *Beyond Objectivism and Relativism: Science, Hermeneutics, and Praxis* (Oxford: Basil Blackwell, 1983).

ing but is not limited to knowing) to say or do the right thing in a specific situation.[60]

The canonical-linguistic approach seeks to appropriate the insights of, among others, Paul Ricoeur and Martha Nussbaum, that "literary form is not separable from philosophical content, but is, itself, a part of content—an integral part, then, of the search for and the statement of truth."[61] Whereas *theoria* encourages us to look *beyond* the text (at revealed propositions as building blocks of a system of absolute truth), and *technem* encourages us to look *at* or *behind* the text (e.g., at the history of its composition or at a reconstructed history for which the text is evidence), *phronesis* asks us to look *along* the text. This is not the postmodern's historically or culturally situated reason (this does not get us beyond relativism) but rather the evangelical's *canonically situated reason*. What we have in the biblical texts is theological *phronesis:* right reason *in action;* reason leading to *right* action.[62] The Bible exhibits *phronesis* in a variety of literary situations; wisdom is embedded in narrative, law, prophecy, epistle, and apocalyptic.

We learn language by participating in practices; that is by now a common postmodern insight. What is postconservative about the present proposal, however, is its claim that the practices that teach us to respond, and correspond, to God rightly are *canonical* practices: the sum total of the diverse communicative practices that make up the biblical text. My thesis is that theological wisdom and understanding are formed through an apprenticeship to the biblical texts. The practices that should inform and transform evangelical theology are therefore those of what we might call the "society of biblical literature."

Theological Judgments

Theology yields instructions for deliberating well about the gospel— for deliberating well about what God has done in Christ, for deliberat-

60. It has been widely recognized that prudence fills the gap between moral rules and specific situations (see Daniel Westburg, *Right Practical Reason: Aristotle, Action, and Prudence in Aquinas* [Oxford: Clarendon, 1994], chap. 1). For an attempt to articulate a theological method that relies on *phronesis,* see Linda Zagzebski, *"Phronesis* in the Methodology of Theology," in *Philosophy and Theological Discourse,* ed. Stephen T. Davis (New York: St. Martin's Press, 1997), 204–23.

61. Martha C. Nussbaum, *Love's Knowledge: Essays on Philosophy and Literature* (New York: Oxford University Press, 1990), 3. Cf. Paul Ricoeur, *Figuring the Sacred: Religion, Narrative, and Imagination* (Minneapolis: Fortress Press, 1995), part 3.

62. And not reason only. Nussbaum argues persuasively that *phronesis* is nurtured by feelings and the imagination as well. See Nussbaum, *Love's Knowledge,* chap. 2.

ing well about what the church is to say about God and do in the name of God in particular situations, for deliberating well about how we can live well, as individuals and as communities, in light of the gospel. This is what I mean by describing theology as biblical interpretation of a higher order. Normally this is understood to mean that theology conceptualizes the biblical text, puts its house in good logical order. This only gets as far as *theoria*. What difference does a phronetic approach make? To answer this I must draw upon an excellent article by David Yeago on theological exegesis.[63] When Paul in Philippians 2:5–11 speaks of Jesus' "equality with God," asks Yeago, does he mean the same thing the fathers at Nicea mean when they speak of Jesus' being *homoousios* with God? Yeago believes that it is essential "to distinguish between *judgements* and the *conceptual terms* in which those judgements are rendered."[64] His point is that the same judgment can be rendered in a variety of conceptual terms. The moral is that we look to Scripture for the judgments that must govern whatever set of concepts we happen to use to speak of God.

Now, "the only way to uncover the judgements made in a text is to pay close attention to what is said and implied, to the specific, contingent ways in which its conceptual resources are deployed: to attend, in short, to the *circumstantia litterarum* [the ways the words go]."[65] But this is precisely what *phronesis* is: the display of good judgment, the grasp of what is required in a particular literary situation.

Forming judgments is an activity of discrimination, of distinguishing between what is and what is not appropriate in a given situation. Making a judgment is a matter of deciding between right and wrong—between right and wrong beliefs, right and wrong interpretations, right and wrong actions. Judgments are neither expressions of private feelings nor are they universal statements of theoretical truths.[66] As often as not, we are called upon to make theological judgments in the absence of clear and distinct propositions. What we have instead to guide us are some broad principles, a number of biblical examples, and a host of canonical judgments, formulated for specific situations, on what is appropriate to say and do in the light of the gospel of Jesus Christ. The Bible does not

63. David S. Yeago, "The NT and the Nicene Dogma: A Contribution to the Recovery of Theological Exegesis," in *Theological Interpretation of Scripture*, ed. Stephen Fowl (Oxford: Blackwell, 1998), 87–100.

64. Ibid., 93.

65. Ibid., 96.

66. Cf. my remarks on "lyric" and "epic" systematic theology below. For a concise introduction to and defense of the rationality of "interpretative judgments," see C. Stephen Evans, *Philosophy of Religion: Thinking about Faith* (Downers Grove, Ill.: InterVarsity Press, 1985), chap. 8, esp. 166–71.

give us the axioms for a theological calculus so much as a variety of narratives, laws, prophecies, letters, and songs that cultivate the evangelical heart, mind, and imagination. Evangelical theology, at its best, is a matter of deliberating well (e.g., canonically) about the gospel in non-canonical (e.g., contemporary) situations.

The Prosaics of Biblical Literature

The biblical texts, in their literary diversity and their canonical unity, are the normative means for forming right theological judgments. But we have to attend to the way the words go. We need to look *along* the biblical texts. For the diverse literary genres in the Bible are of more than aesthetic interest. Mikhail Bakhtin speaks for a number of literary critics when he asserts that genres are cognitive strategies, modes of cognition, ways of thinking about and experiencing the world. Each genre "is adapted to conceptualizing some aspects of reality better than others."[67] Balthasar concurs: A genre is a "mode of seeing."

Yet if the canonical practices and biblical genres are to nurture our judgment, then we must learn not only the language but the literature of the Bible. We must cultivate what Bakhtin calls "prosaics": the practical reasoning that governs a particular communicative practice. We must achieve a practical know-how—the know-how that allows us to follow apocalyptic, narrative, prophecy, and so forth.

Wisdom and understanding involve not only propositional knowledge but "ways of seeing" as well. In this respect, the imagination plays a vital role. The imagination is not merely the faculty of fantasy—the ability to see things not there—but rather a means for seeing what *is* there (e.g., the meaning of the whole) that the senses alone are unable to observe (and that the propositional alone is unable to state). The imagination is our port of entry into other modes of experience, into other modes of seeing and thinking, and as such is the unique and indispensable condition of participating in the communicative action of others.[68]

Canonical Competence

Transported from its home in moral theory to literary theory, then, *phronesis* becomes a matter of canonical competence, of practical, hermeneutical know-how in specific literary situations. Again, the goal is to learn right theological judgments through an apprenticeship to biblical texts. We need to understand how the biblical authors thought

67. Gary Morson and Caryl Emerson, eds., *Mikhail Bakhtin: Creation of a Prosaics* (Palo Alto, Calif.: Stanford University Press, 1990), 276.

68. For an expanded treatment of these points, see my chapters in *The One, the Two, and the Many: Unity and Diversity in the Relation of Biblical and Systematic Theology*, ed. D. A. Carson and Kevin J. Vanhoozer (Grand Rapids: Eerdmans, forthcoming).

about God, the world, and themselves—not necessarily to use their concepts in our situation but to transfer the wisdom behind their judgments to our situation, different though it be.

"Phronetic" theology is thus a matter of cultivating canonical competence. Again, this is less a technical skill than it is a matter of practical wisdom. It is not enough to have mastered an eight-step exegetical technique; it is equally a matter of one's spirituality. Biblical interpreters have to be willing apprentices, students who are willing to *live* as well as to look "along the text," according to the Scriptures. It would therefore be incorrect to associate this position with "commonsense realism." The biblical interpreter is not an autonomous knower but an apprentice to biblical literature. It is therefore more accurate to speak in terms of "canon-sense realism," for the thrust of my proposal is that reality is mediated, in various ways, by the ensemble of texts that comprise the canon.[69] Right theological judgment is the product of human cognitive action that has been nurtured by divine canonical action concerning right covenantal relations. The canon is nothing less than a unique and indispensable framework—the spectacles of faith, as Calvin put it—that enables us faithfully to imagine (to see and to taste) the world as it is in Christ, the "wisdom of God" (1 Cor. 1:24), or in other words, as it really is.

Protestant Theology

My proposal for a canonical-linguistic approach to theology reclaims two characteristically, and equally controversial, Protestant insights, albeit in a slightly different key.

Sola Scriptura

First, *sola scriptura*. The final authority over matters of faith and life, including biblical interpretation itself, must be Scripture. Alister McGrath's remark about the origin of doctrine is apt: "The *sola scriptura* principle is ultimately an assertion of the primacy of the foundational scriptural narrative over any framework of conceptualities which it may generate."[70] In other words, the Word written is the critical principle for everything we say and do as theologians. Divine communicative action, embedded in the canonical texts, is the final criterion for the church's communicative action.

---

69. For a similar account, see Francis Watson's remarks on "intratextual realism" in his *Text, Church, and World: Biblical Interpretation in Theological Perspective* (Grand Rapids: Eerdmans, 1994), 223–25.
70. McGrath, *Genesis of Doctrine,* 64.

The Priesthood of All Believers

Second, the priesthood of all believers. Ultimately it is the privilege and responsibility of all believers to interpret the Bible, both as church and as individuals. Schleiermacher was right at least in this—the believer is not first related to the church which in turn relates her to Christ, but is instead first related to Christ who in turn relates her to the church. Interestingly, Balthasar too lays a great emphasis on the individual, not as an autonomous knowing subject but rather as a responsible responsive agent. This is the aspect I wish to underline as well. God calls individuals; it is as individuals that we are united to Christ. We do not enter the church of Jesus Christ by being born into it so much as by answering a personal call. "Communion with God in Christ comes first, communion with others second."[71] Let's not forget the lesson that Kierkegaard sought to convey to his age, namely, that persons cannot hide behind or surrender their individual responsibility to the collective, even if that collective is the Christian community.[72]

Postfoundationalist Theology

Is Protestant theology therefore foundationalist? Does everything ultimately boil down to "the Bible and me," to the individual's commonsense interpretation of the Word of God? Not quite. Can we take the canon as our theological foundation without succumbing to epistemological foundationalism? Indeed we can.

The Epistemology of My Mother

Does Mother Church alone have the right to judge the true sense of Scripture, as an increasing number of Protestant as well as Roman Catholic voices would have it, or does my mother have a similar right? For the record, my mother came to Christian faith through reading the Bible on her own. If a single counterinstance amounts to the falsification of a theory, then my mother's conversion counts as a falsification of strong non-foundationalism. Not only did she come to believe the gospel of Jesus Christ on her own but she also assessed local congregations on the basis of how well they corresponded to what she took to be

71. Thomas G. Dalzell, "Lack of Social Drama in Balthasar's Theological Dramatics," *Theological Studies* 60 (1999): 462.
72. The community is not a theological panacea. As Niebuhr pointed out, corporate sin is worse than individual sin. We find examples of how communities go wrong in the Old Testament—the nation of Israel, for much if not most of its history, and the German national church during the 1930s. At the same time, I shall argue below that the community has a special role and responsibility of enshrining "great performances" of the drama of redemption as a model for new members and as a witness for outsiders.

the biblical message (again, for the record, a number of them did not fare well by this measure). It is no part of my claim to suggest that such a lonely itinerary be the normative one for every Christian. On the other hand, that the text can be used as a critical principle against an interpretative community (as Martin Luther was to show) does seem to be a correct inference from the priesthood of all believers.

A Three-Stranded Epistemological Cord Is Not Easily Broken

I turn now to a postfoundationalist account of the knowledge of God we may hope to receive through biblical interpretation. Note that the knowledge of God is a matter of right cognitive contact *and* of right covenantal relation, and not of mere information only. The three-stranded epistemological cord described below is loosely informed by the biblical-theological categories of creation, fall, and redemption respectively.

1. Right Cognitive Functioning: Reliabilism

The first strand of my epistemological cord derives from the doctrine of creation, from what Alvin Plantinga calls the "design plan" of the human mind, to be exact.[73] This neo-Reformed reliabilism holds that we are justified in holding a belief, or an interpretation, if it is the product of reliable belief- or interpretation-forming cognitive faculties, when they are functioning rightly in the right kind of cognitive environment. God designed us to believe on the basis of testimony. We do not need first to ground our belief in biblical testimony in something more sure and certain; we are within our epistemic rights if we simply believe what we are told unless there is good reason to question the source.[74]

2. Right Spiritual Relations: The Virtues

Of course, as postmoderns never tire of telling us, our interpretative faculties are not working properly, nor do they function in a clean interpretative environment. On the contrary, I am a man of unclean interpretation dwelling in the midst of a people of unclean hermeneutics. In short, our interpretations are always biased, always partial, always ideological. It is because of this epistemic corruption that I need a second stage in my epistemology. Because our cognitive and interpretative faculties are not functioning properly, we must work to regain right

73. See Alvin Plantinga, *Warrant and Proper Function* (New York: Oxford University Press, 1993).

74. I have applied, and somewhat amended, Plantinga's account in order to stretch his insight to human interpretative faculties in my *Is There a Meaning in This Text?* 288–90.

functioning. In short, we need to cultivate the intellectual, and more particularly the interpretative, virtues.

An interpretative virtue is a disposition of mind and heart that arises from the motivation for understanding, that is, for establishing cognitive contact with the meaning of the text.[75] Recognizing our tendency to distort the text, to read *against* the textual grain, we need to confess our willfulness and pray for the interpretative virtues, both intellectual and spiritual. This is a correlate of my overall emphasis on practical wisdom, on becoming a certain type of person, a certain type of knower.[76] We may therefore add the "drama of epistemology" as a further ingredient, or sub-plot, to the broader "drama of redemption." An emphasis on intellectual virtue serves as a crucial mediating step that allows us to connect our cognitive acts with the rest of our character, thereby integrating doctrine and life.

3. Sanctification and Scholarship: On Fallibilism and Other Fruits

Given the ever present conflict of interpretations, it is not enough to claim that one's cognitive faculties are functioning properly, or even that one is reading with the full array of interpretative virtues. We need a further stage in our epistemology. The third strand of my epistemic cord follows from the previous emphasis on virtue. The prime Christian virtue, one that did not even figure on the lists of the ancient Greeks, is humility. I believe that rationality is largely a matter of humility, or to be precise, of the willingness to put one's beliefs (and one's biblical interpretations) to the critical test.

The procedure with which the theologian works is less a matter of building one's interpretation on some solid foundation (e.g., proof texts) as it is of reasoning to the best explanation. The rationality proper to systematic theology is neither a matter of making deductions from solid starting points nor of arriving at general principles from an inductive survey of biblical data. It is rather a hermeneutic rationality, involving what C. S. Peirce termed "abduction," or "inference to the best explanation."[77] Those who lay their interpretations open to be criticized (e.g., by experience, by other disciplines, by other interpretative traditions) are rational; those who are unwilling to entertain criticism

75. I am slightly modifying the definition of an intellectual virtue found in Linda Zagzebski, *Virtues of the Mind* (New York: Cambridge University Press, 1996), esp. 270.

76. It should be noted that my emphasis on the authority of canonical practices responds to one of the common objections to virtue theory, namely, that there is no test for *phronesis* that is not tradition-bound. Those who profess Christian faith, I contend, must treat biblical *phronesis* as the final authority in matters moral and theological. Such is the implication of *sola scriptura* for virtue epistemology.

77. See also, Peter Lipton, *Inference to the Best Explanation* (London: Routledge, 1991).

of their interpretations are not. I have already suggested that such willingness to be tested is part and parcel of the Protestant ethos.

Among the various kinds of critical tests (e.g., for clarity, logical consistency, coherence) two types stand out. One tests for faithfulness to the text (e.g., does it give a comprehensive explanation in light of the gospel?), the other for fruitfulness in life (e.g., does it transform the reader and thus demonstrate the power of the gospel?). These are the two criteria by which we measure progress in biblical interpretation. Indeed, the criteria for the critical test and the inferential best are the same: fidelity to the text and fruitfulness in the Spirit—rightness and righteousness.

In sum, all three strands of this epistemology are informed by Christian doctrine. Creation is the ground of our confidence in the reliability of our cognitive functions; the fall into noetic sin implies that our knowing is corrupt, thus necessitating the countermeasure of epistemic virtue; and sanctification implies the cultivation of one virtue in particular—humility—for "redeeming" one's interpretative claims.[78]

Toward a Sapiential *Systematics*

The epistemology I have just set out is merely a more sophisticated version, and perhaps an unnecessarily complicated one at that, of Jesus' teaching on wisdom in Luke 6. The wise man builds upon a solid foundation. It is not, however, a merely intellectual foundation. For wisdom is like hearing *and doing* Jesus' words. A simple assent to his words is not enough to protect one from the flood, the ultimate "defeater." Is Jesus thus a foundationalist or a non-foundationalist? Neither. The dominical parable, like my three-stranded epistemological cord, is rather an attempt to transcend this unfortunate dichotomy.[79]

What results from the canonical-linguistic approach is not a single system of propositional truths, all couched and coordinated in the same conceptual scheme. Such a system, were it to exist, would probably not be of much pastoral help when it comes to making concrete decisions in particular contexts. As Martha Nussbaum observes, "A doctor whose only resource, confronted with a new configuration of symptoms, was to turn to the textbook would be a poor doctor."[80] This is as true of the doctor of theology as of the doctor of medicine. The canonical-linguistic approach, while rational, is not a science in the

78. Note that this epistemology is not an attempt to sneak a universal point of view in through the back door. We do not yet have a "God's eye point-of-view," if this means an absolute or unrevisable interpretation.

79. If Jesus is teaching foundationalism in this parable, it is of a very peculiar kind—call it "*sapiential* foundationalism."

80. Nussbaum, *Love's Knowledge*, 71.

mathematical sense of the term. It may qualify, however, as what Jürgen Habermas calls a reconstructive science, in which the aim is to render theoretically explicit the implicit know-how underlying a particular
kind of communicative action.[81] It is a matter not simply of counting
propositions and calculating their laws but of achieving competence in
the canonical practices in which propositions are put to various kinds
of communicative work (e.g., in assertions, promises, warnings, commands, doxologies, etc.).

In the final analysis, however, the systematic task is oriented
more to *sapientia* than *scientia:* to renewing the mind and the imagination for the sake of making right theological judgments. Scripture is profitable "for training in righteousness" (2 Tim. 3:16), and
theology is an extension of this task: the training of right (that is, canonically competent) judgment. The particular excellence of systematic theology lies in its distinct contribution to the formation
of Christian wisdom through its explicit reconstructions of the
phronesis embodied in the diverse canonical practices. The canonical-linguistic approach is thus a concrete program for developing
the seminal suggestions made by Ellen Charry concerning the pastoral function of Christian doctrine, namely, to promote spiritual
and social flourishing.[82] It also partakes of the spirit of the opening
lines of Calvin's *Institutes* concerning "the whole sum of our wisdom."[83] Christian wisdom, I suggest, is the real aim of evangelical
theology. What remains to be developed is the properly dramatic
nature of the wisdom of Christ.

Act 3. Dramatic Theology: "The Doctrine Is the Drama"

What Has Broadway to Do with Jerusalem?

What follows for an understanding of the nature of doctrine
from the canonical-linguistic approach and its focus on wisdom?
The emphasis on hearing and doing the Word suggests a parallel of
sorts with dramatic interpretation. Why draw upon analogies with
drama when the only incident recorded in the Bible as taking place
in a theatre is a riot that Demetrius, an idol maker, incited against

81. See Jürgen Habermas, "Philosophy as Stand-In and Interpreter," in *After Philosophy: End or Transformation?* ed. Kenneth Baynes, James Bohman, and Thomas McCar-
thy (Cambridge, Mass.: MIT Press, 1987), 296–315.

82. See Ellen T. Charry, *By the Renewing of Your Minds: The Pastoral Function of
Christian Doctrine* (New York: Oxford University Press, 1997).

83. T. H. L. Parker notes that in his first edition, Calvin spoke more narrowly of "sacred doctrine" (*Calvin: An Introduction to His Thought* [Louisville: Westminster/John
Knox, 1995], 13).

Paul in Ephesus (Acts 19:29, 31)? This is hardly an auspicious beginning for a new model of theology! Nevertheless, there are several compelling reasons for exploring this analogy. For the moment, let me state five reasons for bringing the two fields into conversation with one another.

First, doctrine emerges from the drama of redemption. The history of Jesus is the generative event of Christian doctrine.[84] Theology is an attempt to understand all of reality in light of the gospel and, as I have already mentioned, the gospel involves both the voice (a verbal report) and the actor (what God has done). Theology both emerges from drama (as critical reflection) and, in a manner yet to be specified, continues the drama (as faithful witness).

Second, dialogue is at the heart not only of drama but also of the covenant relation between God and humanity. While the essence of drama is the interplay of personal relationships, its form is communicative action.

Third, drama reinvigorates the anemic imagination of our contemporary culture. Instrumental reason results in the atrophy of the cultural imagination and a loss of contact with ultimate reality. Our modern and postmodern lives are suffering from spiritual malnutrition. We need more imagination, not less, for the best imaginative literature does not remove us from the real but allows it to take residence in it: "The play's the thing."[85] Dorothy Sayers laments the amount of "slipshod thinking and trashy sentiment" that has taken the place of the divine drama and calls the church to "set it on an open stage to startle the world into some sort of vigorous reaction."[86]

Fourth, the theatrical metaphor encourages us to look upon our daily life as replete with tension and urgency. Something of great importance is at stake in our day-to-day decisions. The Word of God is something to be spoken, something to be *done*. Knowing how to act in new and complex situations requires wisdom, the formation of heart, mind, and imagination. It may also require the ability to improvise. Indeed, improvisation is needed whenever new problems are faced. The trained actor, however, knows how to improvise in a way that is fitting to the occasion.[87] Like the drama critic, the theologian reviews the ef-

---

84. McGrath, *Genesis of Doctrine*, 1.
85. William Shakespeare, *Hamlet*, 2.2.
86. Sayers, *Creed or Chaos?* 24.
87. See Frances Young, *The Art of Performance: Towards a Theology of Holy Scripture* (London: Darton, Longman and Todd, 1990), esp. chap. 8.

fectiveness of our ministry and the integrity of our witness—our biblical *phronesis*.[88]

Finally, the dramatic model enriches our appreciation of what is involved in biblical authority and the doing of theology by providing us with a model for conceiving the relation between text and interpretation: *performance*. The famous contest between Cicero and the actor Quintus Roscius as to which of the two could better portray a particular emotion—the one in words, the other in gestures—is resolved on stage by uniting both. A dramatic performance thus accomplishes what C. S. Lewis ascribes to story, namely, the ability to integrate two modes of knowledge: seeing (abstract theory) and tasting (concrete experience).[89]

The most impressive attempt to bring theology and drama together, however, is surely Balthasar's five-volume tour de force, *Theodrama*. God is the author-producer who as creator undertakes the divine project, the play of the world. God is the actor, the one who through word and deed—especially through the words and work of Jesus Christ—carries the action toward the completion of the plot. The whole existence of Jesus Christ is an "interpretation" of the Father. And God is the director, the one who, as Holy Spirit, mediates between text and actors. It is the director's job to bring about a performance marked by creative fidelity, a performance that does justice both to the author's vision and to the abilities of the actors. The theologian, as interpreter of the gospel, has a speaking and acting part too. The theologian's role is to bear witness to the meaning and significance of God's communicative action, to the wisdom of Jesus Christ. "And when the Spirit proceeds from the Father and the Son and is breathed into the Church of Christ, something of God himself speaks in the mouths of the actors."[90]

---

88. Is theology, to use a familiar distinction, first- or second-order religious discourse? Is it a statement of faith or about faith? My dramatic model, based as it is in a "faith seeking understanding" approach, asks the theologian to speak on both levels. The theologian is both actor and critic (or to change metaphors, a player-coach). On the one hand, the theologian is part of the action. On the other hand, the theologian seeks to distance himself somewhat in order to pose the question of the integrity of the church's performance of its authoritative script. Doctrine is instruction in how to participate fittingly in the drama of redemption; as such, it is instruction in how to act understandingly. Insofar as the theologian gains understanding through participating in the canonical practices of Scripture, theology may be said to proceed "from faith to faith" (Rom. 1:17 NASB). In short, we gain theological understanding as we do wisdom—by reflecting on our experience and by acting on the basis of our reflections.

89. See C. S. Lewis, "Myth Became Fact," in *God in the Dock: Essays on Theology and Ethics* (Grand Rapids: Eerdmans, 1970), 63–67. Lewis in this article is reflecting on the nature of theological truth, in particular, the "myth become fact" of the incarnation. "Drama of salvation" is, in my view, another way of speaking about "myth become fact."

90. Balthasar, *Theodrama*, vol. 1, 319.

The Nature of Doctrine

Doctrine: A Dramatic Definition

If the dogma is the drama, just what is the nature of doctrine, and theology? Theology remains "faith seeking understanding": Theology is critical reflection on the meaning and significance of the dramatic action of the gospel. "Critical reflection" does not fully capture the performative dimension of theology, however. We may recall that the goal is *phronesis:* the practical wisdom that acts rightly—in a way that corresponds to the drama of salvation—in specific situations. The nature of doctrine is, therefore, directional: Doctrine is instruction ("direction") concerning one's fitting participation in the drama of redemption.[91] Theology, like the Scriptures themselves, aims to communicate "the wisdom that leads to salvation" (2 Tim. 3:15 NASB). And salvation itself may helpfully be viewed as the process of being incorporated into the divine life of the Triune God. The dramatic action includes both a "going out" (incarnation) and a "coming back" (resurrection). The ultimate aim of doctrine, then, is not simply to "picture" the divine drama but to incorporate more players into it.

This, I submit, is the best way to conceive doctrine if it is to correspond to my rethinking of the Scripture principle in terms of communicative action and to my rethinking of theology as canonical-linguistic.[92] For if we explain the Scripture principle in terms of divine communicative action rather than revealed propositions, then it follows that theology must do more than seize upon the Bible's propositional component. At the same time, the intent behind the canonical-linguistic approach is not to exchange one restricted view for another, nor to lose any important element of the truth, but rather to gain something richer.

Right theological judgment involves, as we have seen, more than culling out propositions. *Phronesis* puts the emphasis on the right or wise response to particular situations. To see doctrine as dramatic direction is to think in terms of concrete Christian wisdom. Yet there is a sense in which doctrine as dramatic direction requires us to speak of propositions. Any direction about what to say or do presupposes some-

---

91. In what follows, I unpack this definition in terms of the missions of God the Son and God the Spirit.

92. I do not know whether or not this is what Curtis Freeman has in mind when he says "the church is more than simply the people who tell the gospel story. The church is the story" ("Toward a *Sensus Fidelium* for an Evangelical Church," in *Nature of Confession,* ed. Phillips and Okholm, 164). My own analysis of biblical authority would incline me rather to say that the church is the performance of the story. The story—the gospel in its canonical context—is always prior to its retelling or performance.

thing about the concrete situation. If theology is a matter of under-standing how to participate rightly/correctly/fittingly in the dra-matic action, then doctrine is a statement of what is, of what has already been done (by God), and of what remains to be done (by God and by me/us).

Many philosophers contend that action too has propositional con-tent. The propositional content of my kicking, for example, may be a soccer ball or a broken down TV. There is a similar propositional com-ponent in doctrine. Let us therefore define doctrine as a *propositional project:* something to be believed-by-me, done-by-me, hoped-by-me, sung-by-me. We demonstrate that we know and understand God, at least in part, through right action. God, as Duns Scotus put it, is the "doable knowable."[93]

Doctrine as Direction for Learning One's Role: Stanislavski's "System"

What has London or Broadway to do with Jerusalem, theological method with method acting, systematic theology with the Stanislavski sys-tem? Why read books on the theory and practice of drama in connection with issues concerning theological method? Why indeed? Sir John Giel-gud's list of lessons that one learns in the theatre provides a clue: concen-tration, self-discipline, the use of the voice and the body, observation, imagination, application, self-criticism.[94] These are qualities of theolo-gians with interpretative virtue. I can think of four further reasons for bringing together the discourses of drama and doctrine.

First, doing so helps us recover the role of the (dramatic) imagina-tion in the doing of theology. "Art establishes the basic human truths which must serve as the touchstone of our judgement."[95] The problem: Evangelicals for the most part have the right doctrine—the right prop-ositional knowledge—yet correct doctrine too often stops short of hav-ing a decisive impact on our lives. The doctrines are not transformative truths. For truths to transform us we must keep company with them. Theatre can be an institution of cultural and moral education. In Stanislavski's words, "Theatre is a pulpit."[96] Conversely, there may be a theatrical element to Christian proclamation: One form of Christian witness is to perform biblical narrative and "put on" Christian doctrine.

Second, theology also is about training actors to interpret texts (hermeneutics). The Stanislavski method is, according to its propo-

93. Cited in David H. Kelsey, *To Understand God Truly: What's Theological about a Theological School* (Louisville: Westminster/John Knox, 1992), 45.

94. Cited in Sonia Moore, *The Stanislavski System: The Professional Training of an Ac-tor* (London: Penguin, 1974), x.

95. John F. Kennedy, address at Amherst College, October 1963.

96. Cited in Moore, *Stanislavski System*, 3.

nents, "the solution to spontaneous behavior on stage."[97] What better evidence of the measure of our faith than spontaneous behavior on the stage of life? The method "consists in a total dedication—encompassing body, mind, and soul—to the role."[98] Through discipline and interpretation the actor embodies the role and "substantiates" its truth. The goal of the actor-interpreter, however, is to project the main idea of the play through words and actions. Each action should have some purpose, some justification. Stanislavski insisted that everything that happened on stage should be related to the idea of the play. The ultimate point of a performance is to communicate what he called the play's main idea or "super-objective." As in the theatre, so in theology: The communicative action's the thing.

Third, the analogy with drama reminds us that action is itself a form of interpretation, with genuine performance serving as the goal. Theological interpretation of Scripture involves both behavior and belief, theory and practice. Indeed, Stanislavski held that "verbal action depends on the physical action."[99] Actors need to study thoroughly the author's intention. The actor is to embody the meaning behind the words—the subtext. We can think of this in terms of witnessing. "Spectators come to the theatre to hear the subtext," said Stanislavski. "They can read the text at home."[100] And again: "The actor must know his mission in the chain of events of the play, his responsibility to make the main idea live."[101]

Stanislavski himself was part of the "realist" tradition, which was a reaction against artificial styles in which the characters delivered their speeches in conventional poses and in an exaggerated style. His system rejects overacting, clichés, and mannerisms—in short, theatrical hypocrisy (a perennial problem in the church as well). Before Stanislavski, drama schools taught the externals—fencing, dancing, diction—but not how to communicate the *inner man* (cf. the Pauline language). The goal of our dramaturgy, the telos of the voice and the actor, is spiritual communication. In good theatre, the actor creates the inner experiences of his character, incarnates them, and communicates them to the audience. "A gesture," it has been said, "is a movement not of a body but of a soul."[102] In short, psychology is expressed through phys-

97. Ibid., vii. This book, in the words of its author, is a "précis of [Stanislavski's] practical wisdom" (xi).

98. Balthasar, *Theodrama*, vol. 1, 288.

99. Cited in Moore, *Stanislavski System*, 20.

100. Cited in ibid., 28.

101. Ibid., 59.

102. Cited in ibid., 13.

ical action—perhaps the theatrical way of saying that faith without works is dead.

Finally, drama teaches us how to assume and play the roles we have been given in a genuine and compelling fashion. Here the vocation of the actor shades into the vocation of the Christian disciple.

Stanislavski believed that actors had to strive to answer the question of what they would do *if* they were a certain character. He encouraged his actors to explore their characters' backgrounds, to invent details if need be, in order to have as full a conception of their role as possible. This "magic *if*" transforms the character's aim into the actor's. Christians, of course, should think in terms not of the magic but the *mystic* "if": "*Since* you are in Christ, what should you do?"

Stanislavski believed that ultimately "the actor is given not only the 'task' of the role, but also the 'higher task' of entering into the horizon of meaning that encompasses the role, for the latter is the author's final goal."[103] Everything the actor does helps define his role. Stanislavski encouraged actors to think about the "through line of actions," that is, the way to embody the role so as to project the main idea of the play's action: "It is the consecutive incarnation of the super-objective in scenic action"[104]—an intriguing description of the Christian life.

Stanislavski's "system"—the means by which actors assimilate the role of their character—bears more than a passing resemblance to the Christian doctrine of sanctification. And sanctification, in turn, is an implication of our dramatic proposal about the nature of doctrine, for doctrine is not something inert but rather the dynamic ability to understand—to think and to imagine one's role in the drama of redemption—so as to participate fittingly in the action.[105]

And now an objection. Is there not a danger that the canonical-linguistic approach to theology I have been advocating only relocates the "picture theory" of reference that was considered and discarded earlier, the difference being that community practices rather than canonical propositions now picture or refer to the gospel? In this case (so goes the objection), doctrine trains disciples to illustrate theological truth, but not to the extent that this truth becomes transformative.

The danger is real. It is possible to "playact" the Christian life. The New Testament authors have a special term for this phenomenon: hypocrisy. The dramatic nature of doctrine as I have here presented it has nothing to do with *pretending*, however, but everything to do with *par-*

103. Balthasar, *Theodrama*, vol. 1, 279.

104. Moore, *Stanislavski System*, 50.

105. Theatre is a collective work, and Stanislavski believed it was essential that each actor work for the benefit of the whole performance and not solely for himself (ibid., 4).

ticipation. The purpose of theology is to train disciples to participate in the once-for-all mission of Jesus Christ and the Holy Spirit. Participation is neither playacting on the one hand nor a Platonic, ontological category on the other. On the contrary, we participate in Christ's mission only through loving obedience. The purpose of corresponding to Jesus Christ with our voice and with our actions, then, is not pictorial reference but catalytic catechesis. To have a speaking part in the drama of redemption is to be a catalyst in drawing others into the action, into the self-communicative life of the Triune God.

According to Balthasar, only in Jesus Christ does the "I" and the "role" become one. The identity of Jesus Christ is identical with his role, with his mission. "Thomas Aquinas describes this identity by saying that in Christ the *processio* within the godhead, which constitutes the Son as the Father's dialogue partner, is identical . . . with the *missio*, the sending of the Son to mankind."[106] Our theology and our witness must participate in the missions of the Son and the Spirit of God. To participate in Jesus' mission is to share in his yes to his Father. And this sharing in Jesus' yes—the Son's obedience—is really "a participation in the eternal yes-saying of the Son in the original drama of the immanent Trinity."[107] It is also to participate in the mission of the Spirit of adoption. Christian doctrine enables the people of God to participate in the missions of Son and Spirit in a fitting or appropriate manner.

Stanislavski's system helps me deal with another objection. Does my directional model of doctrine really account for doctrines such as the impeccability of Jesus or of traducianism? How do these doctrines, apparently far removed from the Christian life, help me fit into the drama of redemption? Reply: by helping us to understand the primary actors better and by helping me to understand my role better. Even when a doctrine does not direct my action, it almost invariably provides some help in determining my attitudinal response. Doctrine either guides our action or helps us strike the right attitude.[108]

A Dramatic Proposal about Doctrinal Realism and Theological Truth

Evangelical theology thus seeks the fitting response to the gospel, to the prior Word and Act—the communicative action—of God. The appropriate theological response should be equally dramatic: *Tatwort*, a saying-doing, a

106. Balthasar, *Theodrama*, vol. 1, 646.
107. Dalzell, "Lack of Social Drama in Balthasar's Theological Dramatics," 465.
108. I take some comfort from what my *Oxford English Dictionary* tells me about the origin of the word *attitude,* from Lat. aptus "fit." Doctrine provides instruction on right thinking and the behavior that exhibits this or, in short, instruction on right attitude.

matter of biblical interpretation in which one performs one's role—as a human creature, a man or woman, a disciple—in ever new situations. Faith seeks textual understanding, and understanding is displayed in the performance. If theology is to remain dramatic, however, it must resist the temptation to perform doctrine in either an epic or a lyric style.

Systematic Theology as Epic: Monological, Metaphysical, Objective

Epic unfolds history from one absolute perspective, with a stylistic *gravitas* that approximates the grandly religious, giving to the events recounted a sense of inevitability. Nevertheless, only a very small portion of Scripture could rightly be classified as "epic." The world projected by epic, though highly unified within itself, is remote and disconnected from the reader. It invites admiration rather than action. Erich Auerbach rightly captures the difference between Greek epic and biblical narrative: "Far from seeking, like Homer, merely to make us forget our own reality for a few hours, it [Scripture] seeks to overcome our reality: we are to fit our own life into its world, feel ourselves to be elements in its structure of universal history."[109]

"Epic" theology, similarly, unfolds its story from an absolute perspective, with categories that feel impersonal and inevitable. As such, epic theology has the feel of a monological metanarrative. Natural theology is perhaps the most notable example of such epic style. Epic celebrates the heroic past (e.g., of Being) and gives it the solemn weight of inevitability (e.g., Hegel's philosophy reads like an epic history of Reason). Epic is not particularly good at evoking a sense of urgency about the present or at arousing a passion for the possible. Neither is systematic theology when done in the epic style. Epic prefers to rehearse the past. Applied to theology, this approach results in a highly stylized repetition of past thought forms that remain unchanging over the centuries.

We have already encountered Lévinas's objection to such a totalizing approach. It is one thing to affirm the history of Jesus Christ as the definitive revelation of God, quite another to enshrine any one telling or interpretation of that event as the definitive interpretation. Alister McGrath has rightly warned of the danger of "uncritical repetition" in Christian theology. Furthermore, even an inerrant epic is theologically inert unless it is performed. And this is the fundamental weakness of theology done in epic style: There is no place for the eschatological, for the already/not-yet, for the reader's ongoing participation in the events of the narrative.

---

109. Erich Auerbach, *Mimesis: The Representation of Reality in Western Literature* (Princeton, N.J.: Princeton University Press, 1968), 15. See also Leland Ryken, *Words of Delight: A Literary Introduction to the Bible* (Grand Rapids: Baker, 1987), chap. 5, for the relation of epic and biblical narrative.

Systematic Theology as Lyric: Monological, Experiential, Subjective

Whereas epic theology leaves no room for the present participation of the theologian in the subject matter, lyric theology, typical of the nineteenth and twentieth centuries, swings to the opposite extreme, virtually identifying the subject matter of theology with the interpreter's experience.[110] In Schleiermacher, for example, theology is a matter of describing the contents of religious consciousness. The doctrines of creation, sin, and salvation, for example, are for Schleiermacher higher-order descriptions of the consciousness of absolute dependence, guilt, and grace respectively.[111]

Against the ultimacy of subjective experience or consciousness, however, it may be argued that our feelings are themselves properly subject to theological judgment. The question is whether our religious feelings are *fitting*, and this is determined in part by the way the world is. One can read theology neither off the cosmos (as in epic) nor off consciousness (as in lyric). That is because the Word of God is primarily located neither in our experience nor in the world, but rather in the *communicative action* that initiates the history of the covenant and that culminates in Jesus Christ.

Systematic Theology as Dramatic: Dialogical, Communicative, Intersubjective

As opposed to lyric and epic, then, dramatic theology projects a world in which various subjects (e.g., God and human beings) interact through dialogue and communicative action.[112] "Drama" comes from the Greek *drao* ("doings"), and theology is concerned both with what God has said and done and with how it engages human beings today. As we have seen, there seem to be two leading candidates for the rubric "dramatic theology": the postliberal and the postconservative.

1. The Cultural-Linguistic Approach: Lindbeck's Misdirected Drama

There is much for evangelicals to admire in George Lindbeck's postliberal account of doctrine. Its critique of experiential-expressivist theology is especially welcome and insightful. However, Lindbeck fails to pay the same attention, or respect, to theology that is cognitive and proposi-

110. George A. Lindbeck, in *The Nature of Doctrine: Religion and Theology in a Postliberal Age* (Philadelphia: Westminster, 1984), calls this approach to theology the "experiential-expressivist."

111. See Friedrich Schleiermacher, *The Christian Faith*, trans. H. R. Mackintosh and J. S. Stewart (Edinburgh: T & T Clark, 1928), 76–78.

112. Bakhtin himself feels that the drama, compared with the novel, is too coherent and not dialogical enough, despite the fact that the action is carried along largely through dialogue. More work needs to be done in this area. See O'Regan, "Balthasar," 325–53, esp. 347–48.

tional. And the travail of postliberalism itself over the issues of realism and truth is well documented.[113] My own concern with postliberal theology is that it represents a version of inconsistent or abbreviated intratextuality. For on the crucial issue of truth in theology, Lindbeck falters, locating authority, not to mention meaning and reference, in the linguistic practices of the community rather than in those of the canon.

2. The Canonical-Linguistic Approach: Reprise

I believe the canonical-linguistic approach integrates the best of all three approaches to doctrine, including Lindbeck's own, yet in such a way as to avoid their respective weaknesses. If doctrine is direction on how to participate fittingly in the drama of redemption, then it is imperative that one do justice to the dramatic indicatives. We are to fit into something that is already there: There is both structured stage (creation) and determinate plot (the history of salvation). "Fittingness" makes sense only on the assumption that there is a state of affairs— God's action in the world, the drama of redemption—against which one can measure the rightness or wrongness of a course of action.[114]

Doctrinal claims about what is to be done by me (the imperative, propositional *direction*) thus rest on claims about what God has done for me (the indicative, propositional *statement*). This is the propositional aspect of a directional model of doctrine. Lindbeck's cultural-linguistic model, by seeing theology's task as describing the grammar of the community's culture and language, ultimately runs the risk of reducing theology to cultural anthropology, in which talk about God *just is* talk about the community. Such a reduction amounts to a failure to speak of God (Barth's impossible requirement), and hence to a failure to preserve the reality of God, together with his divine initiatives. Failure to refer to the divine initiatives results, in turn, in the loss of the central point of the good news, which is to say, in the loss of the gospel itself.

The strength of Lindbeck's model is its emphasis on the necessity of performing or practicing doctrine, though what regulates Christian practice is not the form of ecclesial life in the first instance, but the authoritative script of Scripture. Yet the canon's primary role is to culti-

---

113. See the essays in Phillips and Okholm, *The Nature of Confession;* and Bruce D. Marshall, ed., *Theology and Dialogue: Essays in Conversation with George Lindbeck* (Notre Dame, Ind.: University of Notre Dame Press, 1990).

114. Gale Heide describes "impure systematics" as theology that believes in eternal truth but recognizes the historical-conditionedness of its interpretations, and we might add, of its performances. The point is that the modest systematician works with the notion that it is possible to get a doctrine or an interpretation more or less "right." See Gale Heide, "The Nascent Noeticism of Narrative Theology: An Examination of the Relationship between Narrative and Metaphysics in Nicholas Lash," *Modern Theology* 12 (1996): 459–81.

vate good theological judgment so that it functions not so much as a script to be memorized and repeated verbatim but as a guide for learning one's role as a disciple of Jesus Christ. Rethinking doctrine as dramatic direction encourages us to think in terms of *doing* the truth.

The primary voice and actor to which doctrine attends is not the human subject but Jesus Christ. There is nevertheless a subjective aspect to doctrine, insofar as it lays claim to the subject's participation in the dramatic action of God.

Conclusion: A Plea for Amateur Theology

To sum up, I have commended the following three theses to evangelical theologians: (1) The Scripture principle—the way in which one identifies the Bible as the Word of God—should be formulated in terms of divine communicative action. (2) The canonical-linguistic approach conceives theology as the practice of indwelling the biblical texts, of looking along the texts so as to understand the judgments they embody, hence to learn canonical wisdom. (3) Doctrine is instruction or direction on how to participate fittingly in the ongoing drama of redemption. What might we hope to see in the church if such a model of theology were adopted?

Toward What Kind of Theatre?

It is the neglect of dogma that makes for dullness.[115]

Peter Brook's 1968 work *The Empty Space* is a profound essay on the theatre, its place in culture, and its contribution to an understanding and improvement of the human condition. Many of his descriptions apply equally well to another institution—the church—whose life is also played out before the watching world. "A man walks across [an] empty space whilst someone else is watching him, and this is all that is needed for an act of theatre to be engaged."[116] How should Christians today "walk" across the stage in such a way that it constitutes a good theological performance? Brook's discussion reveals an uncanny resemblance between different types of theatre and their theological counterparts.

The Deadly Theatre

The deadly theatre is deadly dull. This is the theatre of repetition, the theatre of set scenes, cliché, and stock effects. In deadly theatre there is no real connection between actor and audience, only a hollow spectacle. One approaches the classics from the viewpoint that "some-

---

115. Sayers, *Creed or Chaos?* 3.
116. Peter Brook, *The Empty Space* (New York: Atheneum, 1968), 9.

where, someone has found out and defined how the play should be done."[117] This is the theatrical equivalent of what we earlier called epic theology, in which the role of the theologian is simply to repeat the same formulaic confessions. The question that needs to be asked at this point, says Brook, is "Why theatre at all?" Indeed, why theology at all, if we already have the definitive interpretation for all times and places. Tradition is an important source for theology, but traditionalism—the excessive regard for tradition—is the enemy of vital theology.

The Holy Theatre

Brook's second type is the holy theatre, in which abstract ideas are made concrete, the invisible visible. Theatre originated in rituals "that made the invisible incarnate,"[118] but Brook believes these rituals have today largely lost their meaning and power. Theatre today becomes the means for liberating ourselves from the conventional forms in which we live our daily lives. This is why Brook considers the theatre holy— it is the place where secular society may discover a greater meaning. And yet, today "we do not know how to celebrate, because we do not know what to celebrate."[119]

The Vital Theatre

The immediate or vital theatre is assertive, "in your face," theatre— relevant, realistic, and revolutionary. It is live theatre that makes people feel alive. Vital theatre is that "in which there is only a practical difference between actor and audience, not a fundamental one."[120] What remains after a vital performance is the play's central image or idea, the essence of what it had to say, scorched into the memory.

Brook's description of actual theatre companies makes for an interesting analogy with church communities. One group, the Living Theatre, is a nomad company. The group of thirty live together and travel together. The community exists for the sake of performing, and its performances "contain the most intense and intimate moments of its collective life."[121] Because they lack a nurturing tradition, however, they have to look for the holy in unlikely places. Another company's members, based in Poland, are similarly committed, giving up everything except their own bodies: "The actor has himself as his field of work."[122] Brook likens performance to self-sacrifice, since the actor gives his all

117. Ibid., 14.
118. Ibid., 45.
119. Ibid., 47.
120. Ibid., 134.
121. Ibid., 62.
122. Ibid., 59.

to his role. The actor-audience relation thus resembles that between priest and worshiper: "The priest performs the ritual for himself and on behalf of others."[123] In Brook's view, vital theatre here plays a role that the church can no longer fill. The church has become the empty space.

An Evangelical Celebration: "Eucharisto, He Has Found Us!"

Evangelical theology serves the church by assisting it to become a holy and vital theatre once again. The church is not an empty space but the people of God filled with the Spirit of God. Moreover, we *do* know what to celebrate: the gospel. The voice and the action of the minister and the congregation should be such that the world sees the meaning of God's Word, the silhouette of Jesus Christ in his living body. Theatre is "a language of actions."[124] Calvin himself pictures the church as the theatre of the wisdom of God.[125] Do evangelical performances communicate the central image or idea of Scripture? Woe is me if I do not perform the gospel! For unlike their postmodern neighbors, Christians know what, and how, to celebrate.

Evangelicals typically are better at improvisation than ritual. Yet each has its place in creative fidelity. What matters most is expressing the main idea of the gospel. The main idea, of course, is celebrating the good news of salvation. In the present context, we need to put the Eucharist back into the Lord's Supper. *Eucharisto* means "I give thanks," and this should be the theme not only of our communion but of our entire individual and communal life. *Eucharisto* is the proper response to *euangelion*. The shared bread and wine recall the play's climax and rehearse the play's conclusion. It is a key scene, and it must affect our interpretation of all other scenes.

The Compleat Amateur

The church needs amateur theologians, persons who do theology for the love of it. Modernity encourages us to think in terms of professionalization, but let's not forget that the etymology of amateur is *amator*, "lover." Wayne Booth's *For the Love of It* is an autobiographical account of his passion for playing the cello, an instrument he began to study only late in life. Yet it is also a fascinating reflection on the meaning of being an amateur. What is an amateur? Not a professional, to be sure. Amateurs throw themselves into their work not with the hope of achieving perfection but for the love of the activity itself.[126] Being an

123. Ibid., 60.
124. Ibid., 49.
125. Calvin, *Institutes*, III.20.3. Calvin is reflecting on Ephesians 3:10. Elsewhere Calvin speaks of creation as the "theatre of God's glory" (I.6.2, II.6.1).
126. Wayne Booth, *For the Love of It: Amateuring and Its Rivals* (Chicago: University of Chicago Press, 1999), 10.

amateur is a matter of practicing one's art lovingly. Thus, I make my plea for amateur theologians.

The amateur theologian has a passion for performing the Scriptures, for practicing what he preaches. Theology aims at good practice, at training disciples to participate fittingly in the drama of redemption by making canonically competent judgments about what to say and do as disciples of Jesus Christ in new situations. Lesslie Newbigin urges the local congregation to be a "hermeneutic" of the gospel (and I would add, not of the gospel only, but of all the literary forms in Scripture). Our Christian witness consists in displaying the "lived meaning," and significance, of the text.

The voice and action of God call forth a corresponding obedient response on the part of the theologian—a response of voice and action, of witness and wisdom. Evangelical theology is a matter of cultivating Christian wisdom—a spiritual and intellectual *habitus*—through an apprenticeship to the diverse forms of biblical literature. Being biblical is not a matter of repeating biblical passages word for word, or even of summarizing the use of particular terms found throughout the Bible, but of making judgments that are informed, reformed, and transformed, as the case may be, by the wisdom embedded in biblical literature. Canonical-linguistic theology cultivates Christian wisdom: the ability to fit appropriately into the drama of redemption by saying and doing the right thing, by exemplifying right practical reason—in sum, by performing the wisdom of Christ.

Ecclesial Voice, Ecclesial Action: The Ministry of Theology and the Minstrelsy of the Word

What does the church have to say and do—to communicate through its action—that no other institution can say or do? What is the main idea of the play we call the Christian life? Theology yields doctrines—dramatic directions—learned from the canon and formulated to answer for our time just such questions.

Canonical-linguistic theology aims at cultivating minstrels of the Word—players who can interpret the text rightly in diverse situations; players who can stage the gospel anywhere, anytime. Like the medieval minstrel, theologians should think of themselves as part of a performing troupe. The etymology of *minstrel* (Provençal, Latin) is related to our term for minister. Yet the term *minstrel* specifies the way in which we minister the Word—through voice and action. The minstrelsy of the Word is its performance.

Theology serves the church; the church nurtures theologians. The theologian, as we have seen, is a performer, not an armchair critic. What exactly is the relation between the theologian, as an individual and critical thinker, and the theologian as a participating member of a particular ecclesial tradition? Whose judgments ultimately count, the individual's or the community's?[127] On the one hand, it would be absurd to require each individual theologian to "discover" every doctrine—say, the Trinity—afresh; on the other hand, the ultimate authority in theology is located not in church tradition but in the Triune God and in Scripture as God's communicative act.

We have already established that the understanding performance that constitutes good theology must be corporate in nature. The church is to be a "hermeneutic" of the gospel. The diversity of churches is therefore to be seen in terms of different interpretive traditions. The variety of ecclesial traditions represent so many "masterpiece theatres." And behind every theatrical tradition there is usually a "great performance"—the theology of an Augustine or a Luther or a Calvin. There is value in learning how to participate in the drama of redemption through participating in these venerable companies, so long as one remembers that the ultimate aim is creative fidelity not to an interpreter or to an interpretive tradition but to the divine drama and its script.

The task of the theologian in a particular community, I submit, is to instruct the community in what constitutes a fitting understanding of the faith and to monitor the integrity of its subsequent performance. In so doing, the theologian formulates the wisdom implicit in the community's practices and reforms the community's practice in light of the wisdom implicit in the canonical practices of its authoritative script. In brief, the theologian is to articulate and reflect back to the community what the community really is in Christ. If and when the reality of Jesus Christ contradicts the current beliefs and practice of the community, then the theologian must play the fool, the "fool for Christ."

There is a long tradition of the "wise fool" (e.g., the fool in Shakespeare's *King Lear*). According to Balthasar, the figure of the fool emerged as a distinctively Christian theme in Western literature (he comments that the figure of Don Quixote is "a piece of dogma that has been overlooked by Catholic theologians").[128] What Balthasar says about saints should be true, from an evangelical point of view, of all believers, namely, that they are "the great interpretation of the Gospel, more true and convincing than all exegesis."[129] There is biblical support for this notion, and for Lesslie Newbigin's idea that the church should be the

---

127. I am indebted to my teaching assistant, Dan Treier, for raising this objection, and for hinting at its solution!

128. Cited in Raymond Gawronski, *Word and Silence: von Balthasar and the Spiritual Encounter Between East and West* (Grand Rapids: Eerdmans, 1995), 195.

129. Cited in ibid., 204.

"hermeneutic" of the gospel. The church is the theatre of the wisdom of God, and the mission behind her performance of the gospel is to incorporate ever more players into the drama of redemption.

Paul in 1 Corinthians 4:9 says that he and the apostles have been "exhibited" by God as "a spectacle *[theatron]* to the world" (RSV). The apostles exhibit what God intends Jesus' followers to be: fools for Christ. "If any one among you thinks that he is wise in this age, let him become a fool that he may become wise" (1 Cor. 3:18 RSV). The actor's role here becomes the disciple's vocation: to speak and do one's part. Similarly, the author of Hebrews 10:32–33 asks his readers to remember their previous endurance of sufferings, which included "being publicly exposed *[theatrizo]* to abuse and affliction" (RSV). In this they are simply playing out Jesus' own scenes of humiliation—his trials before various publics—in another setting. In both cases, master and disciples, endurance makes for a show or spectacle of faith. What is shown in the theatre of faith is the truth that endures everything—critical testing, suffering, ridicule, death. This is the martyrdom of Christian life, a show of faith and rationality alike.

Evangelical theology is God-centered biblical interpretation that issues in performance knowledge on the world stage to the glory of God. It therefore prepares us for life in the real world, where reality is defined by the gospel of Jesus Christ. Herein is the sum of Christian wisdom: to know how to live "in Christ." Such is the aim of biblical-theological realism, in which the "real" is understood not as narrowly historical or empirical, but richly as historical, spiritual, and eschatological. Evangelical theology corresponds rightly and actively to evangelical reality, and evangelical reality is disclosed to us in plural form in the biblical witness to the life, death, and resurrection of Jesus Christ. The mission of theology is thus related to the mission of the church: creatively and faithfully—dramatically!—to interpret and perform the way, the truth, and the life.

4

Articulating the Christian Belief-Mosaic

Theological Method after the Demise of Foundationalism

STANLEY J. GRENZ

The closing two decades of the twentieth century have been marked by spirited theological engagement among evangelical thinkers.[1] Despite the great diversity this discussion represents, one reoccurring theme is emerging, at least among many voices. Evangelicals are increasingly concerned with the question as to what might be an appropriate response to the contemporary context, which for want of a better term is generally characterized as *postmodern*.[2]

1. A version of this chapter is also included in Stanley J. Grenz, *Renewing the Center: Evangelical Theology in a Post-Theological Era* (Grand Rapids: Baker, 2000). For a fuller explication of my theological method, see that book.
2. For an example of the current discussion of this theme, see David S. Dockery, ed., *The Challenge of Postmodernism: An Evangelical Engagement* (Wheaton, Ill.: Victor/ BridgePoint, 1994).

Postmodernism is a notoriously slippery word that defies definitive description.[3] Moreover, scholars are not of one mind as to what postmodernism is, what label ought to be used to describe the phenomenon, what its roots are, or even when it first developed. In addition, many critics of attempts by evangelical theologians to appropriate postmodern insights erroneously equate postmodernism with deconstruction. Despite these various hesitations and caveats, the term *postmodern* has gained widespread use as the designation for a highly complex phenomenon encompassing a variety of elements.

Whatever else it may mean, the situation is—as the designation itself suggests—*post-modern*. The postmodern ethos is on the one hand *modern;* it retains the modern. Rather than calling for a return to some premodern situation, the postmodern outlook accepts the Enlightenment, especially its elevation of skeptical rationality. On the other hand, the postmodern ethos is *post* modern; it sees the dangers inherent in the very skeptical rationality it accepts. For this reason, it seeks to live in a realm of chastened rationality.

One dimension of this chastened rationality is the transition from a realist to a constructionist view of truth and the world.[4] Postmodern philosophers assert that rather than viewing the world objectively from an Archimedean vantage point, humans structure their world through the concepts they bring to it. All human languages, these thinkers add, are human social conventions that map the world in a variety of ways depending on the context of the speaker. As a result, no simple, one-to-one relationship exists between language and the world. Nor can any single description provide an accurate "map" of the world.

The chastened rationality that typifies postmodernism is also evident in the "loss of the metanarrative" and the advent of "local" stories. Postmodern philosophers point out that not only have the grand narratives of scientific progress that legitimated modern society lost their credibility and power, but the idea of a grand narrative is itself no longer credible.[5] As Jean-François Lyotard stated tersely in his description of *The Postmodern Condition,* "Simplifying to the extreme, I define

3. For the author's fuller treatment of these topics, see Stanley J. Grenz, *A Primer on Postmodernism* (Grand Rapids: Eerdmans, 1996).

4. See, for example, Walter Truett Anderson, *Reality Isn't What It Used to Be: Theatrical Politics, Ready-to-Wear Religion, Global Myths, Primitive Chic, and Other Wonders of the Postmodern World* (San Francisco: Harper & Row, 1990), x–xi, 8; Hilary Lawson, introduction to "Stories about Truth," in *Dismantling Truth: Reality in the Post-Modern World,* ed. Hilary Lawson and Lisa Appignanesi (New York: St. Martin's Press, 1989), 4.

5. Jean-François Lyotard, *The Postmodern Condition: A Report on Knowledge,* trans. Geoff Bennington and Brian Massumi (Minneapolis: University of Minnesota Press, 1984), 37.

postmodern as incredulity toward metanarratives."[6] Nevertheless, narratives still function in the postmodern world. But these narratives are local rather than universal. That is, the narratives that postmoderns consider legitimate are the stories of particular peoples, the myths that lie at the genesis of human communities and provide the transcendent legitimization to particular societies.

The goal of this essay is to suggest the contours of a theological method that I believe holds promise for engaging theologically with the postmodern situation and for appropriating critically the central postmodern sensitivities so as to assist the church in being the community of Christ within, and in witness to, a postmodern context. To this end, the essay comes in two parts. In the first, I sketch the trajectory that led to the epistemological context in which contemporary evangelical theologians carry on their calling, a context characterized by the demise of Enlightenment foundationalist epistemology. In the second part, I offer an outline of a theological method that seeks to take seriously the postmodern situation. Such an evangelical theological method is a conversation involving Scripture, tradition, and culture, and results in a theology that is trinitarian, communitarian, and eschatological.

The Rise and Demise of Foundationalism

Connected to the demise of philosophical realism characteristic of the postmodern situation has been the undermining of the older foundationalist model of epistemology. This philosophical turn carries far-reaching implications for theology. Specifically, the discrediting of foundationalism in philosophy calls into question the reigning foundationalist theological method. As a result, theologians must now come to terms with, and even appropriate critically, the nonfoundationalist (or postfoundationalist[7]) philosophical turn.

Philosophical Foundationalism and Its Aftermath

In the modern era, Protestant theology was deeply influenced by the Enlightenment problematic, as well as the solutions proposed by thinkers in the Age of Reason. At the heart of the Enlightenment outlook was a specific understanding of the nature of human knowledge known as "foundationalism."

6. Ibid., xxiii–xxiv.
7. This is J. Wentzel van Huyssteen's preferred term. See his "Tradition and the Task of Theology," *Theology Today* 55, no. 2 (July 1998): 213.

Epistemological Foundationalism

In its broadest sense, foundationalism is merely the acknowledgment of the seemingly obvious observation that not all beliefs (or assertions) are on the same level; some beliefs (or assertions) anchor others. Stated in the opposite manner, certain beliefs (or assertions) receive their support from other beliefs (or assertions) that are more "basic" or "foundational."[8] Defined in this manner, nearly every thinker is in some sense a foundationalist.

In philosophical circles, however, foundationalism refers to a much more particular epistemological stance than is entailed in this observation about how beliefs relate to one another. At the heart of the foundationalist program is the desire to overcome the uncertainty generated by our human liability to error and the inevitable disagreements that follow. Foundationalists are convinced that the only way to solve this problem is to find some means of grounding the entire edifice of human knowledge on something that is unquestionably certain.[9] This quest for complete epistemological certitude is often termed "strong" or "classical" foundationalism.

Foundationalist epistemological proposals routinely draw from the metaphor of a building to conceive how human knowledge arises.[10] Like a physical edifice, knowledge must be built on a sure foundation. Proponents see this epistemological foundation as consisting of either a set of incontestable beliefs or a number of unassailable first principles, on the basis of which the pursuit of knowledge can proceed. These basic beliefs or first principles are supposedly universal, context-free, and available—at least theoretically—to any rational person. The foundationalist's initial task, then, becomes that of establishing an epistemological foundation for the construction of the human knowing project by determining, and perhaps even demonstrating, the foundational beliefs or principles on which knowledge rests. Viewed under the foundationalist rubric, therefore, reasoning moves in only one direction—from the bottom up, from basic beliefs or first principles to resultant conclusions.

Foundationalism, understood as the quest for epistemological certitude in the face of the problem of error, boasts a long pedigree dating to the ancient Greek philosophers. But in Western philosophical his-

8. For this definition, see, for example, W. Jay Wood, *Epistemology: Becoming Intellectually Virtuous* (Downers Grove, Ill.: InterVarsity Press, 1998), 78–79.

9. Ibid., 84.

10. For the use of this metaphor in René Descartes' writings, see his *Selected Philosophical Writings*, trans. John Cottingham, Robert Stoothoff, and Dugald Murdoch (New York: Cambridge University Press, 1988), 23, 24, 26–27, 76, 80.

tory, this epistemological difficulty became acute in the Enlightenment. Historians routinely look to the French philosopher René Descartes as the progenitor of modern foundationalism. In contrast to premodern Western philosophers who tended simply to assume the foundations for philosophical inquiry, Descartes began his philosophical work by attempting to establish that foundation.[11] To accomplish this task, Descartes brought all his beliefs under scrutiny, doubting everything until he arrived at a belief he could not doubt, namely, that he was doubting. In this manner, Descartes claimed to have established the foundation of knowledge by appeal to the mind's own experience of certainty. On this basis, he began to construct anew the human knowledge edifice, convinced that this epistemological program yields knowledge that is certain, culture- and tradition-free, universal, and reflective of a reality that exists outside the mind.

Although other philosophers took issue with specific aspects of Descartes' proposal, most readily adopted Descartes' concern to establish some type of firm foundation for the human knowing project. In keeping with this concern, the Enlightenment project assumed a realist metaphysic and evidenced a strong preference for the correspondence theory of truth, not only as an epistemological outlook focusing on the truth value of any individual proposition as reflecting some supposed "fact"[12] but more importantly as a program for "mapping" the supposedly objective world as it really is.

Foundationalist Theology

The concerns of Descartes and other Enlightenment thinkers spilled over the boundaries of the philosophical guild. Indeed, the foundationalist problematic challenged traditional viewpoints and reformulated thinking in every area of Western society, including theology. Soon theologians, swooning under the foundationalist spell, found themselves refashioning the theological edifice in accordance with the newly devised rationalist method.

Despite the efforts of Enlightenment theologians to construct a "religion within the bounds of reason alone," to cite the title of one of Immanuel Kant's books, as the Age of Reason came to an end, many intellectuals concluded that only two cogent alternatives were available: blind acceptance of classical Christian doctrine by appeal to the Bible (or the church) or the skeptical rationalism that seemed to be the final

---

11. See, for example, John E. Thiel, *Nonfoundationalism* (Minneapolis: Fortress Press, 1994), 4.

12. Bede Rundle, "Correspondence Theory of Truth," in *The Oxford Companion to Philosophy*, ed. Ted Honderich (New York: Oxford University Press, 1995), 166.

product of the enlightened mind.[13] In response, nineteenth-century theologians sought a new bedrock on which to construct the theological house, an impulse that eventually led to the division of theology in North America into the right-left dichotomy. Liberals constructed the house of theology on the supposedly universal human experience of the religious, together with what they saw as the religious (or moral) aspirations engraved, even if only in embryonic form, in (universal) human nature. Conservatives, meanwhile, devised a foundationalist theological method that appealed to an inerrant Bible, the veracity of which was thought to be unimpeachable by the canons of human reason.

Epistemology after Foundationalism

Foundationalism, allied as it was with metaphysical realism and the correspondence theory of truth, was undeniably the epistemological king of the Enlightenment era. Today, however, it no longer commands the broad, unquestioned acceptance it once enjoyed. In fact, among philosophers, foundationalism is in dramatic retreat.[14] As Merold Westphal observed about the reigning epistemological paradigm, "That it is philosophically indefensible is so widely agreed that its demise is the closest thing to a philosophical consensus in decades."[15] With this judgment Wentzel van Huyssteen concurs: "Whatever notion of postmodernity we eventually opt for, all postmodern thinkers see the modernist quest for certainty, and the accompanying program of laying foundations for our knowledge, as a dream for the impossible, a contemporary version of the quest for the Holy Grail."[16] And Nicholas Wolterstorff offers this sobering conclusion: "On all fronts foundationalism is in bad shape. It seems to me there is nothing to do but give it up for mortally ill and learn to live in its absence."[17]

The Quest for an Alternative Epistemology

Modern foundationalism has been the target of criticism since its genesis. Yet as the nineteenth century gave way to the twentieth, some philosophers, aware of the shortcomings of the Enlightenment epistemological program, sought a cogent alternative. These thinkers questioned the foundationalist assumption of the necessity of establishing

13. See, for example, Arthur Cushman McGiffert, *Protestant Thought before Kant* (London: Duckworth, 1911), 253.
14. See Thiel, *Nonfoundationalism*, 37.
15. Merold Westphal, "A Reader's Guide to 'Reformed Epistemology,'" *Perspectives* 7, no. 9 (November 1992): 11.
16. Van Huyssteen,"Tradition and the Task of Theology," 216.
17. Nicholas Wolterstorff, *Reason within the Bounds of Religion* (Grand Rapids: Eerdmans, 1976), 52.

the first principles of philosophy prior to engaging in the construction of knowledge, as well as the preoccupation with the quest for unassailable basic beliefs.[18] They also rejected the attendant understanding of truth as the correspondence of individual assertions with the world, each of which—in the words of one critic of foundationalism—is thought to be "true per se absolutely and unalterably."[19] Two alternatives emerged almost simultaneously: coherentism and pragmatism.

At the heart of coherentism is the suggestion that the justification for a belief lies in its "fit" with other held beliefs;[20] hence, justification entails "inclusion within a coherent system," to cite the words of philosopher Arthur Kenyon Rogers.[21] But what does it mean for a belief to cohere with other beliefs? Of course, noncontradiction must be an aspect of any coherence of beliefs. Coherentists, however, suggest that the "fitting together" of beliefs entails more than merely showing that the various assertions do not contradict each other. Rather, the corpus of beliefs must also be interconnected in some way. Rather than remaining an aggregate of disjointed, discrete members that have nothing whatsoever to do with one another, the set of beliefs must form an integrated whole, and this whole must carry "explanatory power."

Coherentists, therefore, reject the base/superstructure distinction so characteristic of foundationalism.[22] They argue that beliefs are interdependent, each belief being supported by its connection to its neighbors and ultimately to the whole.[23] Moreover, coherentists avoid picturing human knowledge as similar to constructing a building, choosing instead the image of a network, which sees beliefs as coming together to form an integrated whole. Hence, knowledge is a "web of belief,"[24] a

18. For a helpful summary of the arguments against foundationalism, see Wood, *Epistemology*, 88–98. For an early twentieth-century critique of the correspondence theory of truth by a sympathetic critic who does not reject the theory completely, see Charles A. Campbell, *Scepticism and Construction* (London: George Allen & Unwin, 1931), 82–96.

19. Harold H. Joachim, *The Nature of Truth* (1906; reprint, London: Oxford University Press, 1939), 72.

20. Wood, *Epistemology*, 114.

21. Arthur Kenyon Rogers, *What Is Truth?* (New Haven: Yale University Press, 1923), 12.

22. Jonathan Dancy, "Epistemology, Problems of," in *The Oxford Companion to Philosophy*, 246.

23. Nancey Murphy, *Beyond Liberalism and Fundamentalism: How Modern and Postmodern Philosophy Set the Theological Agenda* (Valley Forge, Pa.: Trinity Press International, 1996), 94.

24. See, for example, W. V. Quine and J. S. Ullian, *The Web of Belief* (New York: Random House, 1970).

"nest of beliefs,"[25] or, to cite the more generic designation, a "conceptual scheme."[26] In addition, whereas foundationalists tend to focus on
the task of determining the truth value of each assertion independently
of the others, coherentists find truth in the interconnectedness of beliefs. Truth is primarily a predicate of the belief system as a whole,
rather than of particular assertions in isolation. Hence, the turn-of-the-
century philosopher Harold H. Joachim criticizes the Cartesians for
their preoccupation with what he describes as "the smallest and most
abstracted fragment of knowledge, a mere mutilated shred torn from
the living whole in which alone it possessed its significance." For him,
the "ideal of knowledge . . . is a system, not of *truths*, but of *truth*."[27] Finally, for coherentists, the quest for knowledge entails a "research program"[28] in which advances occur through "paradigm shifts."[29]

Despite this shift in emphasis, many modern coherentists remain
committed to the quest for epistemological certainty. In fact, they embrace coherentism because they believe this approach provides a
greater possibility of justifying beliefs.[30] At the same time, some coherentists acknowledge that rather than a present reality, absolute justification of beliefs belongs to the realm of the ideal, although this does
not mean that the unattainable ideal is any less real.[31]

Turn-of-the-twentieth-century coherentists were joined in their critique of foundationalism by proponents of philosophical pragmatism.
Contrary to popular perception that defines pragmatism as the theory
that equates truth with "what works," modern pragmatist philosophers, especially Charles Peirce, proposed a far more sophisticated
epistemology. Peirce declared that the truth of any belief ought to be
measured according to the belief's success in advancing "factual in-

25. Wesley A. Kort, *Take, Read: Scripture, Textuality, and Cultural Practice* (University
Park, Pa.: Pennsylvania State University Press, 1996), 12.

26. Jack W. Meiland and Michael Krausz, eds., *Relativism: Cognitive and Moral* (Notre
Dame, Ind.: University of Notre Dame Press, 1982), 7. In his critique of the concept,
Donald Davidson offers the following summary of the typical definition: "Conceptual
schemes, we are told, are ways of organizing experience; they are systems of categories
that give form to the data of sensation; they are points of view from which individuals,
cultures, or periods survey the passing scene" (Donald Davidson, "On the Very Idea of a
Conceptual Scheme," in *Relativism*, 66).

27. Joachim, *Nature of Truth*, 73, 72.

28. Imre Lakatos, "Falsification and the Methodology of Scientific Research Pro-
grammes," in *Criticism and the Growth of Knowledge*, ed. Imre Lakatos and Alan Mus-
grave (Cambridge: Cambridge University Press, 1970), 132–33.

29. Thomas Kuhn, *The Structure of Scientific Revolutions*, 2d ed. (Chicago: University
of Chicago Press, 1970).

30. Rogers, *What Is Truth?* 12–13.

31. Joachim, *Nature of Truth*, 82.

quiry" (that is, "the activity aimed at the discovery of truth").[32] The pragmatists' innovation, according to Arthur E. Murphy's judgment, was "their insistence that the meaning and worth of ideas is rightly judged, not by their conformity to a 'reality' set up in advance as the final standard of truth and reasonableness, but by the way they function in the context of responsible inquiry."[33]

Peirce did not differ significantly with the foundationalists about the *goal* of inquiry. Nor did he reject the reigning metaphysical realism of the day. Rather, Peirce's pragmatism was largely an attempt to clarify the *method* of scientific advance. In his estimation, truth emerges as we engage in prediction followed by testing, observation, and experimental confirmation. And in contrast to the here-and-now individualism of the Cartesian method, this process requires both a long-term horizon and the cooperative contributions of a community of scientific investigators.[34] Although Peirce held to the objectivity of truth and the existence of reality independent of human subjectivity, he nevertheless posited an important connection between that reality and the pursuit of truth: "The reality of that which is real does depend on the real fact that investigation is destined to lead, at last, if continued long enough, to a belief in it."[35] Yet, he rejected the suggestion that this conclusion makes reality dependent on thought.[36]

William James explicitly advocated the connection between truth and the epistemological process implicit in Peirce: "Truth for us is simply a collective name for verification-processes, just as health, wealth, strength, etc. are names for other processes connected with life, and also pursued because it pays to pursue them. Truth is *made*, just as health, wealth and strength are made, in the course of experience."[37] For James, "the truth of an idea is not a stagnant property inherent in it. Truth *happens* to an idea. It *becomes* true, is *made* true by events."[38]

Coherentism and pragmatism provided ways to leave behind the foundationalist preference for the correspondence theory of truth. The means to overcome metaphysical realism, however, came from another source: the "turn to linguistics," especially as it is found in the

32. Arthur E. Murphy, *The Uses of Reason* (New York: Macmillan, 1943), 87.

33. Ibid., 85–86.

34. Charles Sanders Peirce, "How to Make Our Ideas Clear," in *Charles S. Peirce, Selected Writings (Values in a Universe of Chance)*, ed. Philip P. Wiener (New York: Dover, 1958), 133.

35. Ibid., 134.

36. Ibid., 133.

37. William James, *Pragmatism: A New Name for Some Old Ways of Thinking*, rep. ed. (New York: Longmans, Green and Co., 1928), 218.

38. Ibid., 200–201.

work of Ludwig Wittgenstein, who in a sense completed the shift toward belief systems and the communal dimension of truth pioneered by the coherentists and the pragmatists.

Midway in his career, Wittgenstein came to realize that rather than having only a single purpose—to make assertions or state facts—language has many functions (e.g., to offer prayer, make requests, and convey ceremonial greetings). This discovery led to Wittgenstein's important concept of "language games." According to Wittgenstein, each use of language occurs within a separate and seemingly self-contained system complete with its own rules. Similar to playing a game, we require an awareness of the operative rules and significance of the terms within the context of the purpose for which we are using language.[39] Rather than being directly or primarily related to an external world of "facts" waiting to be apprehended, meaning and truth are an internal function of language, and all utterances can only be deemed "true" within the context in which they are spoken.[40] Furthermore, language does not have its genesis in the individual mind grasping a truth or fact about the world and then expressing it in statements. Instead, for Wittgenstein, language is a social phenomenon, and any statement acquires its meaning within the process of social interaction.

Theology after Foundationalism

The Enlightenment quest for certitude served as a powerful molder of theology in the modern era. In recent years, however, several theologians have been looking to the insights of the nonfoundationalist philosophers in an effort to recast theology after the demise of philosophical foundationalism.

Perhaps no theologian has exemplified more clearly the application to theology of the non-correspondence epistemological theories of the modern coherentists and pragmatists than Wolfhart Pannenberg.[41] At the heart of Pannenberg's theological agenda is the task of demonstrating the internal coherence of the doctrines and the external coherence of Christian doctrine with all knowledge.[42] In so doing, Pannenberg

39. See, for example, the discussion in Ludwig Wittgenstein, *Philosophical Investigations*, 1.65, trans. G. E. M. Anscombe (Oxford: Basil Blackwell, 1953), 32. See also Robert C. Solomon, *Continental Philosophy Since 1750: The Rise and Fall of the Self* (Oxford: Oxford University Press, 1988), 150.

40. See Hilary Lawson, "Stories about Stories," in *Dismantling Truth*, xxiii–xxiv.

41. For my own lengthier treatment of Pannenberg's theological method, see Stanley J. Grenz, *Reason for Hope: The Systematic Theology of Wolfhart Pannenberg* (New York: Oxford University Press, 1990), 11–43.

42. Wolfhart Pannenberg, *Systematic Theology*, trans. Geoffrey W. Bromiley, 3 vols. (Grand Rapids: Eerdmans, 1991), 1:21–22.

seeks to devise a third way between Protestant scholasticism, which he accuses of unwittingly placing the Bible in contradiction to every new discovery of truth rather than integrating scientific discoveries into the truth claim of the Christian faith, and "neo-Protestantism" (e.g., pietism and liberalism), which in his estimation leads to a potentially irrational, subjectivist understanding of truth. According to Pannenberg, rather than being merely subjective, truth is universal, for any valid "personal truth" must be, at least in principle, true for all.

At the heart of Pannenberg's reformulation of a coherentist theological method is his understanding of truth. Reminiscent of modern coherentists and pragmatists, Pannenberg argues that truth is essentially historical. Truth is what shows itself throughout the movement of time climaxing in the end event.[43] Moreover, drawing from the classical Augustinian linking of truth with God, he asserts that the truth that emerges in the end is the truth of God,[44] who is "the reality that determines everything."[45] Consequently, all truth ultimately comes together in God, who is the ground of the unity of truth. This, in turn, leads to a coherentist theological method. For Pannenberg, the goal of theology is to demonstrate the unity of truth in God, that is, to bring all human knowledge together in our affirmation of God. Theology, therefore, seeks to show how the postulate of God illumines all human knowledge.[46] Because truth is historical, the focal point of certitude can only be the eschatological future. Until the eschaton, truth will by its own nature always remain provisional and truth claims contestable.[47] In the meantime, theological statements, like all human assertions, are hypotheses to be tested[48] according to the canons of internal and external coherence. Hence, resembling the modern pragmatists, Pannenberg maintains that the question of truth must be answered in the process of theological reflection and reconstruction.

Pannenberg draws from a coherentist/pragmatist approach in his attempt to carve out a theological method that is nonfoundational yet committed to a realist metaphysic. The widely debated program of

43. See the essays "On Historical and Theological Hermeneutic" and "What Is a Dogmatic Statement?" in Wolfhart Pannenberg, *Basic Questions in Theology,* trans. George H. Kehm, 2 vols. (Philadelphia: Fortress Press, 1971), 1:137–210.

44. Pannenberg, *Systematic Theology,* 1:53. See also, Pannenberg, "What Is Truth?" in *Basic Questions,* 2:1–27.

45. For a statement of this foundational definition of God, which Pannenberg articulates repeatedly, see Wolfhart Pannenberg, "The Nature of a Theological Statement," *Zygon* 7, no. 1 (March 1972): 11.

46. Pannenberg, *Systematic Theology,* 1:59–60.

47. Ibid., 1:54.

48. Ibid., 1:56–58.

George Lindbeck provides a clue as to what theology might look like if it not only rejected the correspondence theory of truth but sought to follow Wittgenstein and move beyond realism as well.

Lindbeck's primary goal is to call for an alternative to the "cognitive-propositionalist" and the "experiential-expressive" understandings of doctrine, both of which reflect the same discredited foundationalist epistemological assumptions. To provide a third view, which he calls the "cultural-linguistic" approach, Lindbeck not only follows the coherentist path but also gives it a Wittgensteinian twist. Lindbeck declares that doctrines are like rules of grammar, for they constitute what might be called the rules of discourse of the believing community. Doctrines act as norms that instruct adherents how to think about and live in the world. Hence, like rules of grammar, church doctrine has a "regulative" function, serving as "community authoritative rules of discourse, attitude, and action."[49] They are "teachings regarding beliefs and practices that are considered essential to the identity or welfare of the group." As such "they indicate what constitutes faithful adherence to a community."[50] In short, Christian doctrines establish the ground rules for the "game" of Christian thinking, speaking, and living.

Lindbeck's use of Wittgenstein has far-reaching implications for the concept of truth. He notes that rules of grammar are routinely stated in the form of propositions; nevertheless, asking whether any one of them is objectively "true" or "false" involves a fundamental misunderstanding of the type of proposition the rule in fact is. It entails ripping the assertion out of its context and treating it apart from its regulative role within the language itself. Because linguistic rules are not intended to say anything true about a reality external to the language they regulate, each rule is only "true" in the context of the body of rules that govern the language to which the rules belong. Lindbeck suggests that we might view doctrinal statements in a similar manner. Seen from this perspective, such statements do not make "first-order" truth claims; they do not assert something objective about reality. Instead, like rules of grammar, they are second-order assertions. This suggests that church doctrines are primarily rules for speech about God rather than actual assertions concerning the divine reality.[51] Hence, they make "intrasystematic" truth claims.[52] Doc-

49. George A. Lindbeck, *The Nature of Doctrine: Religion and Theology in a Postliberal Age* (Philadelphia: Westminster, 1984), 18.
    50. Ibid., 74.
    51. Ibid., 69.
    52. Ibid., 80.

trines are "true" primarily as "parts of a total pattern of speaking, thinking, feeling, and acting."[53]

With this in view, Lindbeck calls for an "intratextual theology" that "redescribes reality within the scriptural framework" and aims at "imaginatively incorporating all being into a Christ-centered world."[54] Such a theology draws from the text to explore what it means to articulate and live out the community's vision within a specific time and place.[55] Similar to Pannenberg, Lindbeck concludes that to this end, the theologian expounds the doctrinal core or framework of the Christian faith, determines that it coheres within itself, and indicates how doctrine illumines human existence.

Evangelical Theological Method after Foundationalism

In recent years, a growing number of evangelicals have become cognizant of the demise of foundationalism in philosophy and increasingly concerned to explore the implications of this philosophical development for theology. The new situation calls for an evangelical theological method that proceeds nonfoundationally and in so doing takes seriously the postmodern condition characterized by the move away from both realism and the metanarrative. In seeking to respond to this challenge, evangelical theologians can gain insight from thinkers such as Wolfhart Pannenberg and George Lindbeck, while not necessarily following either theologian's program in its entirety.[56] To this end, impulses from Pannenberg and Lindbeck can be combined profitably with reflections from philosophers and thinkers within the broader evangelical tradition.

Affirming a (Post)Foundation for Theology

During the Enlightenment, "strong" foundationalists sought to gain epistemological certitude by discovering an unassailable foundation of basic beliefs on which to construct the knowledge edifice. The post-

53. Ibid., 64.
54. Ibid., 118.
55. Ibid., 113.
56. For the author's summary of a critical engagement with Pannenberg's thought from an evangelical perspective, see Stanley J. Grenz, "Pannenberg and Evangelical Theology: Sympathy and Caution," *Christian Scholars' Review* 20, no. 3 (February 1991): 272–85. For representative evangelical engagements with Lindbeck's proposal, see Timothy R. Phillips and Dennis L. Ockholm, eds., *The Nature of Confession: Evangelicals and Postliberals in Conversation* (Downers Grove, Ill.: InterVarsity Press, 1996); Trevor Hart, *Faith Thinking: The Dynamics of Christian Theology* (Downers Grove, Ill.: InterVarsity Press, 1996), 81–89, 92–95; Alister E. McGrath, *The Genesis of Doctrine: A Study in the Foundations of Doctrinal Criticism* (Grand Rapids: Eerdmans, 1997), 14–34.

modern situation raises for evangelical theologians the question, Is there a way to avoid the error of foundationalism without following Lindbeck's proposal to the bitter end?

(Re)constructing a (Post)Foundationalist Epistemology

Perhaps the most helpful signpost pointing the way forward comes from a group of philosophers sometimes known as the Reformed epistemologists.[57] These thinkers, whose ranks include Alvin Plantinga and Nicholas Wolterstorff, question strong foundationalism while not rejecting the basic foundationalist insight. Plantinga and Wolterstorff join other nonfoundationalists in claiming, contrary to Enlightenment thought, that there is no universal human reason. That is, there is no single, universal set of criteria by means of which we can judge definitively the epistemic status of all beliefs.[58] Further, according to the Reformed epistemologists, reason is not the supposedly neutral medium in which human reflection takes place. Nor is it a purely formal and autonomous given that precedes and gives shape to intellectual reflection. Instead, reason is "person specific" and "situation specific."[59]

At the same time, the proponents of Reformed epistemology do not deny categorically the validity of the foundationalist search for a type of basic belief. In somewhat different yet complementary ways, Plantinga and Wolterstorff raise the question as to what—if anything—might be deemed "basic" for Christian theology. For the answer, these philosophers, like other nonfoundationalists, point to the believing community. In fact, this is in part what makes Reformed epistemology's seemingly weak brand of foundationalism at the same time nonfoundationalist and decidedly postmodern. Plantinga and Wolterstorff acknowledge the inevitability of our being situated in a particular community and the indispensable role our respective communities (or traditions) play in shaping our conceptions of rationality, as well as the religious beliefs we deem basic and thus by which we test new claims. They also readily admit the attendant loss of certitude involved with this acknowledgment, for they realize that these various communities may disagree on what should count as the relevant set of paradigm instances of basic beliefs.

57. For this designation, see, for example, Nicholas Wolterstorff, "Introduction," in *Faith and Rationality: Reason and Belief in God,* ed. Alvin Plantinga and Nicholas Wolterstorff (Notre Dame, Ind.: University of Notre Dame Press, 1983), 7. See also Alvin Plantinga, "Reason and Belief in God," in *Faith and Rationality,* 73–74.

58. Wood, *Epistemology,* 170.

59. Nicholas Wolterstorff, "Can Belief in God Be Rational If It Has No Foundations?" in *Faith and Rationality,* 155.

The difficulty this poses for any claim to universal truth ought not to be overlooked. Nevertheless, the communitarian turn returns theological reflection to its proper primary location within the believing community, in contrast to the Enlightenment ideal that effectively took theology out of the church and put it in the academy. More specifically, nonfoundationalist approaches see Christian theology as an activity of the community that gathers around Jesus the Christ. This has far-reaching implications for evangelical theology.[60]

The Communitarian "Turn" and the Casting of Evangelical Theology

Despite their differences, evangelicals share a common vision as to what it means to be the Christ-focused community. Most evangelicals would agree that at the heart of their vision of the faith is an emphasis on being encountered savingly in Jesus Christ by the God of the Bible and that this encounter is an identity-producing event. Through Christ, God constitutes us individually as believers and corporately as a community of believers. As a result, evangelicals are storytellers; we readily recite our "personal testimonies"—narratives that recount our historical and ongoing personal encounter with God. And these are cast in the categories drawn from the biblical narrative, as well as its explication in the didactic sections of Scripture. As evangelicals, therefore, we have come to see the story of God's action in Christ as the paradigm for our stories. We share an identity-constituting narrative.

This elevation of the role of an encounter—experience—ought not to be confused with the understanding that lay at the heart of the older Protestant liberalism. Two aspects separate the evangelical ethos as delineated here from the liberal project.

First, liberalism transformed religious experience into a new foundationalism. Liberal theologians assumed—and sought to discern—a single, universal, foundational religious experience that supposedly lay beneath the plethora of religious experiences found in the various religious traditions. What liberalism failed to see is that the various religions mediate religious experiences that are categorically different from each other. The encounter with the God of the Bible through Jesus, which is foundational to Christian identity, is shared only by those who participate in the Christian community (even though the experience is *potentially* universal, in that all persons might conceivably embrace the Christian faith). In fact, the commonality of this experience is the identifying feature of participation in this specific community, whereas a quite different experience would mark a person as a member of some other community.

60. Hart, *Faith Thinking*, 11.

Second, and providing the theoretical basis for the first, the proposal offered on these pages takes seriously the experience-forming dimension of interpretive frameworks. As Lindbeck has pointed out, the older liberal project tended to give primacy to experience and to view theological statements as expressions of religious experience. But this approach misunderstands the nature of experience. Experience does not precede interpretation. Rather, experiences are always filtered by an interpretive framework that facilitates their occurrence.[61] Hence, religious experience is dependent on a cognitive framework that sets forth a specifically religious interpretation of the world. In this sense, Lindbeck is correct in saying that religions produce religious experience rather than merely being the expression of it.

The move away from classical liberalism must proceed a step farther than Lindbeck seems to want to go, however. To Lindbeck's insight, I would add that there is no generic religious experience, only experiences endemic to specific religious traditions, that is, experiences that are facilitated by an interpretive framework specific to that religious tradition. And any such interpretive framework is theological in nature, for it involves an understanding that sees the world in connection with the divine reality around which that tradition focuses. More specifically, Christian experience is facilitated by the proclamation of the Christian gospel, and every such proclamation comes clothed in a specifically Christian theological interpretive framework that views the world in connection with the God of the Bible. In this sense, the specifically Christian experience-facilitating interpretive framework, arising as it does out of the biblical gospel narrative, is "basic" for Christian theology.

Christian theology, in turn, is an intellectual enterprise by and for the Christian community, in which the community of those whom the God of the Bible has encountered in Jesus Christ seeks to understand, clarify, and delineate the community's interpretive framework, connected as it is with the gospel, as informed by the narrative of the action of this God on behalf of all creation as disclosed in the Bible. Theology views this interpretive framework, however, not as something already residing as a given within the community as a particular visible, institutional reality. The task of theology is not purely *descriptive* (as is perhaps the case in Schleiermacher's view) but also very much *prescriptive*. The theologian seeks to articulate what *ought* to be the interpretive framework of the Christian community.

---

61. See, for example, Owen C. Thomas, "Theology and Experience," *Harvard Theological Review* 78, nos. 1–2 (1985): 192.

Re-forming the Mosaic

At first glance, the suggestion that the Christian interpretive framework is "basic" for theology might appear to be simply a return to Enlightenment foundationalism. In fact, however, it marks a radical departure from the Enlightenment while maintaining the central concerns of foundationalism. The cognitive framework that is "basic" for theology is not a given that precedes the theological enterprise; it does not provide the sure foundation on which the theological edifice can in turn be constructed. Rather, in a sense the interpretive framework and theology are inseparably intertwined. Just as every interpretive framework is essentially theological, so also every articulation of the Christian cognitive framework comes already clothed in a specific theological understanding. In fact, every such articulation is the embodiment of a specific understanding of the Christian theological vision; each embodies a specific understanding of the world as it is connected to the God of the Bible.

Consequently, the theologian's task is not to work from an interpretive framework to a theological construct. Instead, the theological enterprise consists in setting forth in a systematic manner a delineation of what ought to be the Christian interpretive framework for the sake of the mission of the church in the contemporary context. By its very nature, the systematic articulation of the Christian interpretive framework takes the form of an integrated and prescriptive statement of Christian doctrine.

This leads to the kind of coherentist theological method Pannenberg has pioneered. As I noted earlier, coherentist philosophers assert that knowledge is not a collection of isolated factual statements arising directly from first principles but a system in which each is supported by its neighbors and, ultimately, by its presence within the whole. If this is the case, theology can no longer model itself after the foundationalist metaphor of constructing an edifice. Nor need theologians any longer spin their wheels constructing elaborate prolegomena, thinking thereby they have laid a sure foundation for the compilation of seemingly separable units of biblical teaching they then elaborate as little more than "beads on a string."

The move to coherence suggests alternate images of the theological enterprise. Viewed from a perspective that takes the demise of foundationalism seriously, Christian doctrine comprises a "web of belief" or a "mosaic," and theology is the articulation of and the exploration of Christian doctrine viewed as an interrelated, unified whole. Hence, a helpful image for the nature of theological work is that of articulating the "belief-mosaic" of the Christian community, a mosaic consisting of interlocking pieces forming a single pattern (in which, of course, some pieces are more central to the "picture" and others are more peripheral). This mosaic consists of the set of interconnected doctrines that together comprise what ought to be the specifically Christian way of viewing the world. This worldview is truly theological and specifically Christian because it involves an understanding of the entire universe and of ourselves in connection with the God of the Bible and the biblical narrative of God at work bringing creation to its divinely destined goal.

Not only does the theological task entail explicating this doctrinal mosaic, however, but as Pannenberg has argued, it also includes demonstrating the explicative power of the Christian faith by indicating the value of the Christian worldview for illuminating human experience. In this way, theology becomes a second-order conversation that seeks to serve the mission of the church, understood as a people who proclaim and live out the biblical narrative of God's saving action in Christ through the Spirit.

Theology as Conversation

Not only is theology a conversation, it is a specific conversation. Viewed from the conversational perspective, theology is the ongoing process whereby participants in the faith community together seek to articulate what ought to be the Christian belief-mosaic by explicating the meaning of the shared cultural symbols—including sacred texts, language, rituals, and practices—through which Christians express their understanding of the world they inhabit. This is not a conversation in which "anything goes," however. Rather, constructive theological conversation emerges through the interplay, or perichoretic dance, of an ordered set of sources of insight.

The Primary Voice in the Theological Conversation

At the heart of evangelical theology is the Bible; evangelicals pride themselves on being a "people of the book." In the modern era, however, a misunderstanding of Luther's principle of *sola scriptura* led many theologians to trade the ongoing reading of the text for their own systematic delineation of the doctrinal deposit that was supposedly encoded in its pages centuries ago. Thereby, the Bible was all too readily transformed from a living text into the object of the scholar's exegetical and systematizing prowess. The postmodern situation has laid bare the foundationalist presuppositions lying behind this modernist program.

At the heart of the historical evangelical understanding of *sola scriptura* is the concern to bring Word and Spirit together in a living relationship. The paradigmatic statement of this viewpoint came in the description of the Protestant principle of authority found in the Westminster Confession. According to the Westminster divines, "The Supreme Judge, by which all controversies of religion are to be determined, and all decrees of counsels, opinions of ancient writers, doctrines of men, and private spirits, are to be examined, and in whose sentence we are to rest, can be no other than the Holy Spirit speaking in the Scripture."[62] This statement suggests the sense in which the Bible is the norming norm in theology. Scripture carries this lofty position because it is the instrumentality of the Spirit.

Insights from contemporary speech-act theory suggest how this principle can be effectively understood in the postmodern, postfoundationalist context. The Bible is the instrumentality of the Spirit in that the Spirit appropriates the biblical text so as to speak to us today. Through Scripture the Spirit performs the illocutionary act of addressing us. This address can take several forms, in keeping with the manifold diversity of writings that constitute the Bible.[63] For example, the Pauline statement to Timothy suggests that through Scripture the Spirit teaches, reproves, corrects, and instructs (2 Tim. 3:16). Also, through the text the Spirit informs us as to how we might voice our thoughts, feelings, and emotions to God, as, for example, in certain psalms. These dimensions, however, are parts of a larger whole, namely, the *goal* or *product* of the Spirit's speaking. By appropriating the text, the Spirit seeks to perform a particular *perlocutionary* act. And the specific perlocutionary act the Spirit performs is the creation of "world." As the life-giver, the divine power at work fashioning the universe, the Spirit creates through the Word a new world, a "centered" world, an eschatological world, a world that finds its cohesion in the Word, who is Jesus the Christ (2 Cor. 5:17). And this world consists of a new community comprised of renewed persons.

Through the Bible, the Spirit orients our present on the basis of the past and in accordance with a vision of the future. The Spirit leads the contemporary hearers to view themselves and their situation in the light of God's past and future and to open themselves and their present to the power of that future, which is already at work in the world. Thereby they are drawn to participate in God's eschatological world. The task of theology, in turn, is to assist the people of God in hearing the Spirit's voice speaking through the text so that we can live as God's people—as inhabitants of God's eschatological world—in the present.

62. The Westminster Confession of Faith, 1.10, *The Creeds of the Churches*, ed. John H. Leith, 3d ed. (Atlanta: John Knox, 1982), 196.

63. For a helpful delineation of the Bible as comprising four basic types of materials, see John Goldingay, *Models for Scripture* (Grand Rapids: Eerdmans, 1994).

The Hermeneutical Trajectory of the Theological Conversation

The Spirit's goal in appropriating the biblical text is to fashion a community that lives the paradigmatic biblical narrative in the contemporary context. The goal of reading the text, therefore, is to hear the Spirit's voice and to be formed into that community. Consequently, reading the text is a community event.

This idea is not foreign to the evangelical movement. As a people, evangelicals tend to elevate the reading and proclamation of Scripture within the local congregational setting. We come to Scripture aware that we are participants in a concrete, visible fellowship of disciples. Ultimately, therefore, our desire is to hear what the Spirit is saying to this particular congregation and to these particular believers who share together the mandate of being a fellowship of disciples in this specific setting. Hence, most evangelicals would readily agree with the words of the Mennonite theologian Walter Klaassen: "The text can be properly understood only when disciples are gathered together to discover what the Word has to say to their needs and concerns."[64]

Reading within community also means, however, that we approach the text conscious that we are participants in the one faith community that spans the ages. This consciousness involves recognizing the theological heritage—the tradition—within which we stand as contemporary readers of the text. The use of the word *tradition* here ought not to be viewed as reintroducing the medieval Roman Catholic idea of a twofold source of truth. Rather, the term stands as a reminder that Christians in every generation read the text through the lenses provided by a particular hermeneutical context. Understood properly, then, tradition plays an important (albeit secondary) role in theology. Like all Christians everywhere, we read the biblical text today conscious that we are part of an ongoing listening community and therefore are participants in a hermeneutical trajectory. We are not the first generation since the early church to seek to be formed into the community of Christ in the world. On the contrary, we are the contemporary embodiment of a historical people, the people of God throughout the ages.

Hence, the theological heritage provides a reference point for us today. This heritage offers examples of previous attempts to fulfill the theological mandate, from which we can learn. Looking at the past alerts us to some of the pitfalls we should avoid, some of the land mines

64. Walter Klaassen, "Anabaptist Hermeneutics: Presuppositions, Principles and Practice," in *Essays on Biblical Interpretation: Anabaptist-Mennonite Perspective*, ed. Willard M. Swartley (Elkhart, Ind.: Institute of Mennonite Studies, 1984), 10. For this idea, Klaassen cites John Howard Yoder, *Mennonite Quarterly Review* 41 (October 1967): 301.

that could trip us up, and some of the cul-de-sacs or blind alleys that are not worth our exploration. In addition to warning us of possible dangers, past theological statements can point us in directions that hold promise as we engage in the theological calling.

Theological heritage serves as a reference point in another way as well. Today we engage in theology conscious that we are members of a community of faith that spans the centuries. Because we come to the text as those who seek to understand the whole of Scripture as the instrumentality of the Spirit's speaking to us, we do well to keep in view what the church through the ages has considered this biblical "whole" to be. Further, consciousness of our participation in the one church of Jesus Christ also involves acknowledging that like others before us we desire to read the Bible "Christianly." This process is advanced as we take seriously the attempts of our forebears to engage in the hermeneutical task that now occupies us. Because we participate in the one church of Jesus Christ, we desire to be in hermeneutical fellowship with all the people of God. One aspect of this true evangelical "ecumenism" is our attempt to retain continuity of outlook with the church throughout the ages. In short, we desire to participate in a truly "catholic" reading of the text, even in those instances when such a reading leads us to differ with past luminaries on certain theological issues.

The Wider Context of the Theological Conversation

The ultimate authority in the church is the Spirit speaking through Scripture. This act of the Spirit, however, is always a contextual speaking; it always comes to its hearers within a specific historical-cultural context. The specificity of the Spirit's speaking means that the conversation with culture and cultural context is crucial to the hermeneutical task. We seek to listen to the voice of the Spirit through Scripture as the Spirit speaks to us in the particularity of the historical-cultural context in which we live.

This hermeneutical process occurs in part as contemporary "knowledge"—the discoveries and insights of the various disciplines of human learning—informs our theological construction. For example, theories about addictions and addictive behavior can provide insight into the biblical teaching about sin. Likewise, current discoveries about the process of human identity formation can lead to a deeper or wider awareness of the many dimensions entailed in the new identity the Spirit seeks to create in us through our union with Christ. Our theological reflections can draw from the so-called secular sciences, because ultimately no discipline is in fact purely secular. Above all, because God is the ground of truth, as Wolfhart Pannenberg so consistently argues, all truth ultimately comes together in God. Theology therefore looks to all human knowledge, for in so doing it demonstrates the unity of truth in God.[65]

These considerations, however, have not yet pierced to the core of the pneumatological basis for hearing the Spirit's voice in culture. Much of Western theology has focused on the church as the *sole* repository of all truth and the *only* location in which the Holy Spirit is operative. The biblical writers, however, display a much wider understanding of the Spirit's presence, a presence connected to the Spirit's role as the life-giver (Gen. 1:2; 2:7) and life-sustainer (Ps. 104:29–30; Isa. 32:15; cf. Job 27:3; 34:14–15). Because the life-giving Spirit is present wherever life flourishes, the Spirit's voice can conceivably resound through many media, including the media of human culture. Because Spirit-induced human flourishing evokes cultural expression, Christians can anticipate in such expressions traces of the Creator Spirit's presence. Consequently, in the conversation that constitutes theology, evangelical theologians should listen intently for the voice of the Spirit, who is present in all life and therefore precedes us into the world, bubbling to the surface through the artifacts and symbols humans construct.

A cautionary note is in order here, however. Whatever speaking that occurs through other media does not come as a speaking against the text. To pit the Spirit's voice in culture against the Spirit speaking through Scripture would be to fall prey to the foundationalist trap. It would require that we elevate some dimension of contemporary thought or experience as a human universal that forms the criterion for determining what in the Bible is or is not acceptable.[66] Hence, while being ready to acknowledge the Spirit's voice wherever it may be found, evangelical theology must always give primacy to the Spirit's speaking through the biblical text. Paradoxically, even though we cannot hear the Spirit speaking through Scripture except by listening within a particular historical-cultural context, hearing the Spirit in the biblical text provides the only sure canon for hearing the Spirit in culture, because the Spirit's speaking everywhere and anywhere is always in concert with this primary speaking through the Bible.

Furthermore, culture and biblical text do not comprise two different moments of communication (with tradition then forming a third); rather, they are ultimately one speaking. Consequently, even though the focus at any given moment might be Scripture, tradition, or culture, we do not engage in different "listenings," but one. Regardless of

---

65. Pannenberg, *Systematic Theology*, 1:59–60.
66. Darrell Jodock, "The Reciprocity between Scripture and Theology: The Role of Scripture in Contemporary Theological Reflection," *Interpretation* 44, no. 4 (October 1990): 377.

what may be the particular "text" being "read" in the moment, we always bring that specific "reading" into conversation with the other two partners in the perichoretic dance. In short, we listen for the voice of the Spirit, who speaks the Word through the word within the particularity of the hearers' context and who thereby can speak in all things, albeit always according to the Word, who is Christ.

Theology as Christian

The demise of foundationalism indicative of the postmodern situation opens the way for a nonfoundationalist theological method that views constructive theology as an ongoing conversation involving the interplay of Scripture, tradition, and culture for the purpose of articulating the church's mosaic of beliefs. This perspective, in turn, leads to the conclusion that ultimately all theology is—as the "postmodern condition" suggests—"local" or "specific." That is, it is the conversation involving, and the resultant articulation authored by, a particular group in a particular moment of their ongoing existence in the world. This observation raises the question as to what makes any particular local theology "Christian." In a word, a local theology can be designated Christian insofar as it reflects the specifically Christian pattern or "style,"[67] and this style entails a trinitarian structure, a communitarian focus, and an eschatological orientation.

The Triune God: Theology's Structural Motif

Early in the twentieth century, Emil Brunner noted, "The ecclesiastical doctrine of the Trinity, established by the dogma of the ancient Church, is not a Biblical *kerygma*, therefore it is not the *kerygma* of the Church, but it is a theological doctrine which defends the central faith of the Bible and of the Church."[68] Brunner's point is well taken. The doctrine of the Trinity as we know it came about as the result of a lengthy theological process during the patristic era. Once formulated, however, the understanding of God as triune became a nonnegotiable dimension of church teaching. Indeed, the concept of triunity lies at the heart of the unique biblical understanding of God, and therefore Christians through the years have seen it as crucial for maintaining the central message of the Bible.

While the confession of God as triune has become a standard component of the Christian faith, the question of its proper role in theology

67. According to Alfred Kroeber, culture provides "a far more natural and fit medium" for "style" to grow in than does "life" (Alfred L. Kroeber, *Style and Civilizations* [Ithaca, N.Y.: Cornell University Press, 1957], 76).

68. Emil Brunner, *The Christian Doctrine of God*, trans. Olive Wyon (Philadelphia: Westminster, 1950), 206.

is the subject of considerable debate. Many theologians give little place to the doctrine of the Trinity. Although this tendency has been represented in the Christian tradition in every age, it was exacerbated during the Enlightenment as thinkers under the banner of "reason" called into question not only its centrality for theology but also its veracity. Then, in the wake of Kant, skepticism about the very possibility of providing an ontology of God served to diminish, if not altogether eclipse, the doctrine of the Trinity in theology. As a result, the doctrine has become marginalized both by theologians who see it as little more than an abstract and indefensible example of the excesses of speculative theology and by Christians who view the doctrine as little more than an inherited dogma that is of no relevance to the modern world or to daily life.[69]

Yet, by its very definition, theology—the teaching about God—has as its central interest the divine reality as well as God's actions in creation. Rather than being mere speculation, therefore, unpacking the eternal trinitarian relations is endemic to the theological task. The trailblazer in the twentieth-century revival of trinitarianism was clearly Karl Barth. He "radically focused thought in a new way on the being and act of God as triune," to cite John Thompson's helpful description.[70] Since Barth's pioneering work, a host of theologians have taken up the task,[71] some even going so far as to suggest that the explication of this doctrine is a crucial safeguard against theological error.[72]

The chief inquiry for any theology, Christian or otherwise, is the question of the identity of God. The Christian answer to the question Who is God? ultimately surrounds the doctrine of the Trinity. The one God, Christians assert, is triune. God is—to cite the traditional theological designations—Father, Son, and Spirit. In keeping with this confession, both the Apostles' Creed and the Nicene Creed—these two ancient and ecumenical symbols of the church—are ordered and divided into three articles that correspond to the three persons of the Triune God: the Father and creation; the Son and reconciliation; and the Spirit, redemption, and consummation. For much of the history of the church,

69. Colin Gunton offers the following terse description of this position: "Overall, there is a suspicion that the whole thing is a bore, a matter of mathematical conundrums and illogical attempts to square the circle" (Colin Gunton, *The Promise of Trinitarian Theology*, 2d ed. [Edinburgh: T & T Clark, 1997], 2–3).

70. John Thompson, *Modern Trinitarian Perspectives* (New York: Oxford University Press, 1994), 3.

71. See the comment to this effect in David S. Cunningham, *These Three Are One: The Practice of Trinitarian Theology* (Malden, Mass.: Blackwell Publishers, 1998), 19.

72. See, for example, Jürgen Moltmann, *The Trinity and the Kingdom*, trans. Margaret Kohl (San Francisco: Harper & Row, 1981), 17, 64.

this creedal pattern gave rise to the classical trinitarian structure in theological construction.

The confessions of the church suggest that any truly Christian theology must be trinitarian theology. That is, because Christian theology is committed to finding its basis in the being and action of the Triune God, it should be ordered and structured in a manner that reflects the primacy of this fundamental Christian confession. At its core the content of Christian theology consists of a witness to, as well as participation in, the narrative of the being and act of the Triune God. As such, theology's structuring motif is rooted in the Christian confession of God as triune and hence must be trinitarian.

The centrality of God's triunity must go beyond the doctrine of God (or theology proper), however. Only as the fundamental Christian view of God as triune permeates the entire explication of the community's belief-mosaic, giving structure to the theological presentation in its entirety, does a local theology become truly trinitarian.

Community: Theology's Integrative Motif

Understood from the perspective of a theological ecclesiology that takes its cue from the Triune God, the church is a community. Indeed, community lies at the heart of the Christian concept of the church. But more importantly, all Christian theology is communitarian.

The Reformed epistemologists cited earlier maintain against Enlightenment foundationalism that there is no universal human reason[73] but that reason is "person specific" and "situation specific."[74] Nevertheless, Plantinga and Wolterstorff assert that certain beliefs are basic,[75] and to determine what might be deemed basic for Christian theology, these philosophers point to the believing community. Plantinga and Wolterstorff assert that to be human means to be situated in a particular community. As a result, our respective communities (or traditions) play an indispensable role in shaping our conceptions of rationality, as well as the religious beliefs we deem basic and thus use to test new claims.

Because following the lead of the Reformed epistemologists in declaring that the church is "basic" in theology can lead to a new "foundationalism of the church," this insight requires a nuanced understanding. Viewed from one perspective, what is "basic" for theology is not the church itself but the specifically Christian experience-facilitating interpretive framework, which in turn is connected to the biblical

73. Wood, *Epistemology,* 170.
74. Wolterstorff, "Can Belief in God Be Rational?" 155.
75. Westphal, "Reader's Guide," 11; Plantinga, "Reason and Belief in God," 73–78.

narrative. At the same time, there is a sense in which the church *is* basic for theology. In fact, only by viewing the church as basic can the foundationalism of modern theology, in both its liberal and conservative forms, be avoided.

The church is basic in that our participation in the faith community calls forth theological reflection. Theology is faith seeking understanding. Therefore, the very existence of the faith community—the community in which faith is present—leads naturally to the reflection on faith that we call *theology*. For this reason, theological construction needs no elaborate, foundation-setting, certainty-gaining prolegomenon. Instead, it arises out of the life of the discipleship community whose members are joined together by the Spirit and who join together in living out the mandate they share. Therefore, it is presence within the Christian community that leads to engagement in the theological task. And the existence of this community provides the only "foundation" necessary for launching into the process of delineating the mosaic of beliefs, or explicating the interpretive framework, Christians share.

The focus on the communal nature of theology as an activity of the faith community opens the way for introducing *community* as theology's integrative motif. That is, community is the central, organizing concept of theological construction, the theme around which a systematic theology is structured. Community provides the integrative thematic perspective in light of which the various theological foci can be understood and the significant theological issues ought to be explored.[76]

Christian theology must be communitarian because it is linked to a particular community, namely, the community of the disciples of Jesus. Theology has classically been understood as faith seeking understanding. At the heart of faith is personal response to the good news. Yet this does not mean that theology is solely the faith of the individual believer seeking understanding. Rather, as the Reformed philosophers declare, beliefs—and hence faith itself—are dependent on the community in which we are situated. More specifically, being a Christian entails membership in the fellowship of those who have come to know the God of the Bible through Jesus Christ by the Spirit. Theology, in turn, is the community seeking to understand the faith they share. Thus, James McClendon declares,"Theology is always theology of the community, not just of the individual Christian."[77] As the shared faith of the

76. For a discussion of the idea of the integrative motif in theology, see Gerhard Sauter and Alex Stock, *Arbeitswesen Systematischer Theologie: Eine Anleitung* (Munich: Kaiser, 1976), 18–19.

77. James William McClendon, *Ethics: Systematic Theology*, vol. 1 (Nashville: Abingdon, 1986), 36.

community seeking understanding, Christian theology is necessarily communitarian.

This same conclusion emerges as well from a parallel consideration. A central task of theology is to express communal beliefs and values, as well as the meaning of the symbols of the faith community. Theological construction has as its goal that of setting forth an understanding of the mosaic of beliefs that lies at the heart of a particular community. More specifically, the task of *Christian* theology includes the articulation of the belief-mosaic of the Christian faith, the interlocking doctrines that together comprise the specifically Christian way of viewing the world. As a result, Christian theology is by its very nature "church dogmatics," to cite Karl Barth's description. As church dogmatics—as the faith of the community seeking understanding—theology is inherently communitarian.

Further, theology is communitarian because it is the explication of the Christian conception of God. In addition to being faith seeking understanding, theology is by its very definition the study of God. This study, however, is never generic. Rather, it is always specific; it is always the explication of the understanding set forth within a particular community. Hence, *Christian* theology speaks about the God known in the Christian community. And the God to whom the Christian community bears witness is the Triune God. The only true God, Christians declare, is social or communal. Christian theology is inherently communitarian, therefore, because it is the explication of the Christian understanding of the God who is the Triune One.

This leads to a final reason why theology is inherently communitarian. Christian theology is the study of the narrative of this God fulfilling the divine purposes as disclosed in the Bible. The biblical narrative presents God's ultimate goal as the establishment of community. From the narratives of the primordial garden, with which the biblical drama begins, to the vision of white-robed multitudes inhabiting the new earth, which forms the drama's climax, the plot of Scripture is community. Taken as a whole the Bible asserts that God's program is directed toward the establishment of community in the highest sense of the word—a reconciled people living within a renewed creation, enjoying the presence of the Triune God.[78] Christian theology is the explication of this goal, and theologians engage in this constructive task for the purpose of facilitating the fellowship of Christ's disciples in fulfilling their calling to be the biblical community God destines them to become. For this reason, theology is by its very nature communitarian.

78. See, for example, Paul D. Hanson, *The People Called: The Growth of Community in the Bible* (San Francisco: Harper & Row, 1986), 510.

Eschatology: Theology's Orientating Motif

This understanding leads directly to the third in the triad of theological motifs: eschatology. Christian theology is inherently eschatological because it is the teaching about the promising God who is bringing creation to an eternal *telos*. Theology finds its orientation in eschatology, therefore, not so much as the compilation of what God has told us in Scripture "about the major events yet to come in the history of the universe"[79] but because of its connection to the narrative of God at work in creation as disclosed in Scripture. Taken as a whole, the biblical story is directed toward a *telos*. It speaks of the God who is bringing creation to its divinely intended goal.

The development of a *telos*-directed narrative is among the most significant theological contributions of the biblical communities. In contrast to other ancient Near Eastern peoples,[80] Israel came to understand time as a linear span[81] and developed a *historical* consciousness that arose out of their sense that Yahweh journeyed with them[82] and acts in time.[83] As a result, time—and history—became a narrative, the story of God at work. This story entailed as well a *future* consciousness,[84] the anticipation that the only true God would do a new thing that would include all peoples (Hab. 2:14; see also Ps. 102:15; Isa. 66:18–19) and even the entire creation.[85] This biblical narrative with its *telic* orientation, in turn, is formative for Christian theology. It provides the perspective from which theology proceeds.

The eschatological motif leads to a theology that is theocentric rather than anthropocentric. In contrast to "totalizing"[86] modernist metanarratives against which postmodernism rightly rebels, an eschatological theology views the God of the Bible, and not humankind, as the acting subject who unites the diverse moments of time into a single story. It rejects the modernist idea that history is *our* story (that is, the story of man or the tale of the progress of humankind), and it denies that the goal of history is a humanly devised utopia. Instead, Christian

79. Wayne Grudem, *Systematic Theology: An Introduction to Biblical Doctrine* (Grand Rapids: Zondervan, 1994), 1091.

80. Gerhard von Rad, *Old Testament Theology*, trans. D. M. G. Stalker, 2 vols. (New York: Harper & Row, 1965), 2:110.

81. Karl Löwith, *Meaning in History* (Chicago: University of Chicago Press, 1950), 19.

82. Werner H. Schmidt, *The Faith of the Old Testament: A History*, trans. John Sturdy (Philadelphia: Westminster, 1983), 52.

83. Von Rad, *Old Testament Theology*, 2:106.

84. Schmidt, *Faith of the Old Testament*, 22.

85. Ibid., 177.

86. Terry Eagleton, "Awakening from Modernity," *Times Literary Supplement* (20 February 1987): 194.

theology declares that history's goal is nothing less than the realization of God's purposes for creation, and this goal arrives only because the God who stands at the end of the human story is already in grace ordering the cosmic story toward its intended *telos*.

The eschatological motif leads likewise to a theology that takes its orientation from the perspective of our human *telos*, together with the *telos* of creation as a whole. It engages all theological questions from the perspective of the future consummation. It looks to the completion of God's creative work—that is, to the biblical narrative in its eschatological culmination—for the revelation not only of who God is but also of who we are and of what creation is, as well as for the revelation of God's purposes for all creation including humankind. In this manner, an eschatological theology anticipates the future within the present. It finds our human identity, as well as the identity of all creation, in the God who promises to make everything new (Rev. 21:5). And it speaks about the in-breaking of this new creation (2 Cor. 5:17) into our lives in the here and now.

The focus on the new creation indicative of an eschatological Christian theology brings the discussion full circle back to the postmodern rejection of realism with which this essay began. Social constructionists assert that the world we inhabit is not simply given but that ours is a world of our own construal,[87] a "socially constituted reality," to cite Peter Berger's phrase.[88] How can Christian theology continue to talk about an actual world, even if it is only future, in the face of the demise of realism and the advent of social constructionism?[89]

Similar to the so-called "critical realists,"[90] Christian theology maintains a certain undeniable givenness to the universe. But this givenness is not that of a static actuality existing outside of, and co-temporally with, our socially and linguistically constructed reality. It is not the objectivity of what some might call "the world as it is." Rather, the objectivity set forth in the biblical narrative is the objectivity of the world as

87. See, for example, Norwood Russell Hanson, *Patterns of Discovery: An Inquiry into the Conceptual Foundations of Science* (Cambridge: Cambridge University Press, 1958), 23–24.

88. Peter L. Berger and Thomas Luckmann, "Sociology of Religion and Sociology of Knowledge," *Sociology and Social Research* 47 (1963): 423.

89. See, for example, J. Wentzel van Huyssteen, "Postfoundationalism in Theology and Science: Beyond Conflict and Consonance," in *Rethinking Theology and Science: Six Models for the Current Dialogue*, ed. Niels Henrik Gregersen and J. Wentzel van Huyssteen (Grand Rapids: Eerdmans, 1998), 39.

90. See, for example, David Elton Trueblood, *General Philosophy* (New York: Harper & Row, 1963), 38–45. See also Arthur Peacocke, *Theology for a Scientific Age: Being and Becoming—Natural, Divine, and Human*, enlarged ed. (Minneapolis: Fortress Press, 1993), 21.

God wills it, as is reflected in the petition of the Lord's Prayer, "Your will be done on earth as it is in heaven" (Matt. 6:10 NIV). The universe as God wills it, however, is in its fullness not a present reality. Instead, the full measure of the divinely willed universe lies in the eschatological future (e.g., Isa. 65:17–19; Rev. 21:5), and this future, eschatological universe is nothing short of a *new* creation. Because the future reality is God's determined will for creation, as that which cannot be shaken (Heb. 12:26–28), it is far more real—and hence far more objective, far more actual—than the present world, which is even now passing away (1 Cor. 7:31). Therefore, the only ultimately valid "objectivity of the world" is that of a *future*, eschatological world, and the "actual" universe is the universe as it one day will be.

Rather than being antithetical to the social constructionist insight, the "eschatological realism" indicative of the Christian theological style actually takes it a crucial step forward. As the community of Christ, we have a divinely given mandate to be participants in God's work of constructing a world that reflects God's own will for creation, a world in which everything finds its connectedness in Jesus Christ (Col. 1:17), who is the *logos*—the Word—the ordering principle of the cosmos as God intends it to be. Because of the role of language in the world-constructing task, this mandate has a strongly linguistic dimension. We participate with God as through the constructive power of language we inhabit a present linguistic world that sees all reality from the perspective of the future, real world that God is bringing to pass.

Theology assists in this task. It explores the world-constructing, knowledge-producing, identity-forming "language" of the Christian community. The goal of this enterprise is to show how the Christian mosaic of beliefs offers a transcendent vision of the glorious eschatological community God wills for creation and how this vision provides a coherent foundation for life-in-relationship in this penultimate age as we anticipate the glorious fullness of the eschatological new creation. In short, the ultimate, highest, and final purpose of theology is to articulate the Christian belief-mosaic in accordance with the actual (that is, future) world God is fashioning and to do so for the sake of the church's mission as the sign in the present, anticipatory era of the glorious age to come.

Part 3
Engaging Tradition and Traditions

5

Engaging the Great Tradition

Evangelical Theology and the Role of Tradition

ALISTER E. MCGRATH

Evangelicalism has many ways of conceptualizing its identity.[1] I shall here suggest that one of the most fundamental distinctives of the evangelical approach to theology is its insistence that theology be nourished and governed at all points by Holy Scripture and that it seek to offer a faithful and coherent account of what it finds there.

At its best, evangelicalism recognizes there are limits to our knowledge—limits that are beyond our control and that must be discerned and acted on. Part of our task of being attentive and faithful to Scripture is to accept the discipline of recognizing our limitations and re-

1. For some reflections, see Alister McGrath, *Evangelicalism and the Future of Christianity* (Downers Grove, Ill.: InterVarsity Press, 1995); John Stott, *Evangelical Truth* (Leicester: Inter-Varsity Press, 1999); Kenneth S. Kantzer and Carl F. H. Henry, *Evangelical Affirmations* (Grand Rapids: Zondervan, 1990); George M. Marsden, *Reforming Fundamentalism: Fuller Seminary and the New Evangelicalism* (Grand Rapids: Eerdmans, 1987). In the Canadian context, see especially John G. Stackhouse, Jr., *Canadian Evangelicalism in the Twentieth Century: An Introduction to Its Character* (Toronto: University of Toronto Press, 1993).

spectfully declining to indulge in flights of speculative fancy where Scripture is silent or modest in its affirmations. I remain a firm supporter of what C. S. Lewis termed "mere Christianity" and have little personal interest in the boundary disputes that so frequently break out between different types of Christians.

As a historical theologian, however, I have a certain professional interest in this matter and feel obligated to note that many of these disputes result when evangelicals impose doctrines on their fellow evangelicals—doctrines that are actually somewhat speculative and far removed from the world of Scripture itself. While I am sure that discussions of these matters are appropriate and helpful, it is essential that they take place within what I have elsewhere termed "a culture of civility," in which we treat the views of our colleagues with the greatest of respect, views are clearly grounded in Scripture, and Scripture is honored and respected.

To understand the theological enterprise in such terms is to insist that theology is fundamentally an attentiveness to Scripture and encompasses a desire to express and communicate what is found there to the church and the world. Christian theology is under an obligation to pay respectful and obedient attention to the biblical testimony and allow itself to be shaped and *re*shaped by what it finds expressed there. Theology therefore has both catechetical and apologetic facets, just as it has immense relevance to spirituality and ethics.

We may well wish to use the best resources that human wit and wisdom can offer to help us articulate and proclaim what we find in Scripture. However, we must always realize that such canons of judgment are provisional and temporary; what one generation regards as wise, its successor may scorn as naïve. Yet there can be little doubt that we would be greatly assisted in the task of rendering a faithful and effective account of the biblical material if we were to draw on the rich witness of those who have reflected on Scripture before us. Whether we acknowledge it or not, we have a tradition of nearly two thousand years of engagement with Scripture at our disposal. The question I wish to discuss, therefore, is this: What use can we make of tradition in the evangelical theological enterprise?

Evangelicalism has, by and large, tended to neglect both the theological and spiritual role of tradition.[2] As I shall indicate, the reasons for this are entirely understandable. Yet, rightly understood, the idea of "tradition" has considerable importance to the evangelical movement

---

2. An exception that is as important as it is rare should be noted here: J. I. Packer, "The Comfort of Conservatism," in *Power Religion: The Selling Out of the Evangelical Church?* ed. Michael Horton (Chicago: Moody, 1992), 283–99.

as it seeks to foster and develop its sense of identity and purpose in the twenty-first century.

To begin with, let us consider why evangelicals have misgivings concerning the idea of tradition.

Evangelical Suspicions of Tradition

The word *tradition* comes from the Latin term *traditio,* which means "handing over," "handing down," or "handing on." At one level, it is a thoroughly biblical idea; after all, Paul reminded his readers that he was handing on to them core teachings of the Christian faith, which he had received from others (1 Cor. 15:1–4).[3] The term can refer to both the action of passing teachings on to others—something that Paul insists must be done within the church—and the body of teachings passed on in this manner. Tradition can thus be understood as a process as well as a body of teaching. The Pastoral Epistles in particular stress the importance of "guarding the good deposit which was entrusted to you" (2 Tim. 1:14). Yet the New Testament also uses the notion of tradition in a negative sense, meaning human ideas and practices that are not grounded in Scripture. Thus, we find our Lord openly critical of certain human traditions within Judaism that are in conflict with the Word of God (e.g., Matt. 15:1–6; Mark 7:13).

At first sight, then, evangelicals should not have any a priori difficulties with the notion of tradition, at least in the positive New Testament sense of the term. Yet anxieties do exist within the evangelical community over this matter, and it is important to identify and respect them. Two are of especial importance.

1. Tradition can be seen as a human fabrication, in opposition to the Word of God. The New Testament certainly notes this type of tradition and is vigorously critical of both the notion itself and its consequences. Developing this idea further, some evangelicals point out that the Council of Trent appears to give equal weight to Scripture and to what evangelicals view as merely human traditions. Such a view is irreconcilable with the Reformation emphasis on the priority of Scripture. This is a

3. For a full discussion of the relevant texts and issues, see G. E. Ladd, "Revelation and Tradition in Paul," in *Apostolic History and the Gospel,* ed. W. Ward Gasque and Ralph P. Martin (Grand Rapids: Eerdmans, 1970); James I. H. MacDonald, *Kerygma and Didache: The Articulation and Structure of the Earliest Christian Message* (Cambridge: Cambridge University Press, 1980); M. B. Thompson, "Tradition," in *Dictionary of Paul and His Letters,* ed. Gerald F. Hawthorne, Ralph P. Martin, and Daniel G. Reid (Downers Grove, Ill.: InterVarsity Press, 1993), 943–45.

major concern and needs to be taken seriously. For this reason, we shall give careful consideration later in this discussion to the relation of Scripture and tradition in the Reformation debates.

2. Tradition carries with it the sense of "traditionalism"—the dead hand of previous generations that demands we continue to think and act in precisely the same manner as earlier generations, thus locking evangelicalism into a sixteenth-, eighteenth-, or nineteenth-century worldview.[4] To give authority of any kind to tradition is to condemn evangelicalism to sleepwalking with the dead, as absurd as the wearing of eighteenth-century clothes in modern New York. In an age that is acutely aware of the importance of public perceptions of Christianity—witness the growth of "seeker-sensitive" worship services—a concern for tradition seems out of place. Tradition is directly opposed to contemporaneity.

These are real dangers that need to be taken seriously in our considerations. It is my contention, however, that the approach I shall present avoids these difficulties.

"Great Tradition" Christianity: The Critical Affirmation of Tradition

The approach to evangelical history, self-understanding, and theological method that I shall propose has its origins in the Reformation—that great period of Christian self-examination and self-criticism that led to spiritual renewal, theological reconsideration, and ecclesiastical reformation. Within that movement, two distinct tendencies can be discerned: what is generally termed the "mainline" or "magisterial" Reformation—exemplified by Martin Luther, Huldrych Zwingli, and John Calvin—and the smaller, and perhaps less coherent, movement that is often referred to as "the Radical Reformation."[5]

---

4. See the comments of Jaroslav Pelikan, *The Vindication of Tradition* (New Haven: Yale University Press, 1984), 65: "Tradition is the living faith of the dead, traditionalism is the dead faith of the living. And, I suppose I should add, it is traditionalism that gives tradition such a bad name."

5. For detailed studies of the history and terminology, see Hans Joachim Hillerbrand, *Radical Tendencies in the Reformation: Divergent Perspectives* (Kirksville, Mo.: Sixteenth Century Journal Publishers, 1988). See also James M. Stayer, Werner O. Packull, and Geoffrey Dipple, *Radical Reformation Studies: Essays Presented to James M. Stayer* (Aldershot, Hants, U.K.: Ashgate, 1999); George Huntston Williams, *The Radical Reformation*, 3d ed. (Kirksville, Mo.: Sixteenth Century Journal Publishers, 1992).

The mainline reformers argued that there was an urgent need for the reform of the church. A Christian church no doubt existed in Europe prior to the Reformation; it had, however, lost its way at the spiritual, theological, and ecclesiastical levels. The Reformation was a demand for the church to set itself in order and return to more authentic and biblical ways of living and thinking. The use of the word *reform* is of critical importance in that it points to the need for a reformation of an existing body. That is to say, a Christian church existed in the form of the medieval Catholic Church in Europe prior to the Reformation. Even though both Luther and Calvin were scathing in their criticisms of that church, their fundamental assumption was that it was a Christian church, even if it was severely distorted and confused.

Luther's initial agenda was to press for reform from within the church, along the lines of an evangelical *ecclesiola in ecclesia*. When this failed and he found himself excluded from that church, he began the process of renewal from outside by establishing a reforming evangelical group.[6] Calvin's doctrine of the church similarly worked on the assumption that the medieval church was Christian, even though he was severe in both his criticisms of that church and his demands for doctrinal and institutional reforms.[7] Calvin's program of "evangelization" of his native France, which began in earnest around 1555, was actually a program for the reform of the French Catholic Church.

Calvin is known to have had a particularly high regard for some medieval writers, such as Bernard of Clairvaux. Yet most interesting of all is the high esteem in which the mainline reformers held the patristic writers. Luther once styled his reforming program at Wittenberg as a return to "the Bible and Augustine,"[8] and he regarded Augustine as something of a theological lodestar.[9] Luther's colleague Philip Melanchthon developed similar ideas, arguing that reform should involve a return to the consensus of the early church, especially as found in the writings of Augustine and Ambrose.[10]

6. For details, see Scott H. Hendrix, *Luther and the Papacy: Stages in a Reformation Conflict* (Philadelphia: Fortress Press, 1981).

7. Alexandre Ganoczy, *Calvin: théologien de l'Église et du ministère* (Paris: Editions du Cerf, 1964).

8. Alister E. McGrath, *Luther's Theology of the Cross: Martin Luther's Theological Breakthrough* (Oxford: Blackwell, 1985), 47–53.

9. For detailed studies, see Adolf Hamel, *Der junge Luther und Augustin*, 2 vols. (Gütersloh: Mohn, 1934–35); Bernhard Lohse, "Die Bedeutung Augustins für den jungen Luther," *Kerygma und Dogma* 11 (1965): 116–35.

10. Peter Fraenkel, *Testimonia Patrum: The Function of the Patristic Argument in the Theology of Philip Melanchthon* (Geneva: Droz, 1961).

A similarly high evaluation of earlier Christian tradition can be found in the writings of Calvin.[11] Although especially concerned to maintain fidelity to Augustine,[12] Calvin also esteemed the thought of John Chrysostom.[13] This positive evaluation of the teachings and practices of the early church was of critical importance in the debate between Calvin and Jacopo Sadoleto over the nature of the true church,[14] and it was especially significant in relation to the Lausanne Disputation of October 1536.[15] At this important disputation, which took place shortly after Calvin's arrival in Geneva, a Catholic critic of the evangelical reformers suggested that the evangelicals despised the fathers (that is, the Christian writers of the first five centuries), regarding them as possessing no authority in matters of doctrine. Calvin declared this was simply not true. Not only did the evangelicals respect the fathers more than their Catholic opponents, they were also more familiar with the church fathers' views. Reeling off a remarkable chain of references to their writings—apparently from memory—Calvin clinched the evangelical case in the eyes of those present. The vote was taken, and Lausanne opted for the Reformation.

The magisterial Reformation thus offers an approach to engaging with the "great tradition" that has immense potential for their evangelical progeny today. Theology is not simply about giving priority to the Bible; it is about valuing and engaging with those in the past who gave priority to the Bible, and valuing and interacting with the ideas they derived from that engagement. Quite simply, the mainline reformers believed the Bible had been honored, interpreted, and applied faithfully in the past and that they were under an obligation to take past reflections into account as they developed their own.

This approach to theology may have been the dominant voice of the Reformation. We need to note, however, that it was not the only approach. Some representatives of the Radical Reformation had little time for what they regarded as the compromises and half measures of their mainline counterparts. Thus, Sebastian Franck argued that the true church had ceased to exist on earth and had been displaced by an

11. See the careful study of A. N. S. Lane, *John Calvin: Student of the Church Fathers* (Edinburgh: T & T Clark, 1999).

12. Luchesius Smits, *Saint Augustin dans l'oeuvre de Jean Calvin* (Assen: Van Gorcum, 1956).

13. Alexandre Ganoczy, *Calvins handschriftliche Annotationen zu Chrysostomus: Ein Beitrag zur Hermeneutik Calvins* (Wiesbaden: Steiner, 1981).

14. John Calvin and Jacopo Sadoleto, *A Reformation Debate: Sadoleto's Letter to the Genevans and Calvin's Reply,* ed. John C. Olin (New York: Harper & Row, 1966).

15. See Eric Junod, ed., *La Dispute de Lausanne 1536: La théologie réformée après Zwingli et avant Calvin* (Lausanne: Presses Centrales Lausanne, 1988).

apostate body. It was meaningless to speak of the "reformation" of the church, as there was no church to reform. What was required was a restoration of something that had ceased to exist after the time of the apostles.[16] Why bother engaging with people such as Augustine and other patristic writers, who were not even Christians (at least by Franck's criteria) and might even be apostles of the Antichrist? For Franck, true Christianity ended with the apostles and was born again in the sixteenth century. To engage with the "great tradition" was to become contaminated with the ideas of an apostate body that falsely claimed to be Christian. Christians, therefore, needed to engage directly with the Bible rather than pay attention to the views of those who went before them.

This distinction can be seen in the attitudes toward "tradition" adopted by the three major theological voices of the sixteenth century.[17]

1. The Council of Trent argued for a dual-source understanding of tradition in which unwritten tradition and Scripture were treated as equally valid and independent sources of revelation.
2. The mainline Reformation developed a single-source understanding of tradition in which tradition was understood as a "traditional method of interpreting Scripture," that is, an interpretation of Scripture mediated through documents such as the creeds, which were ultimately secondary to Scripture.
3. Some representatives of the Radical Reformation insisted that there was no place for any notion of tradition in Christian theology, for this notion presupposed the existence of an authentic Christian community of discourse and worship between the New Testament and the sixteenth century.[18]

The mainline reformers affirmed that theological debate and correction could take place within the "great tradition" without the need to

16. Sebastian Franck, Letter to John Campanus, 1531, in B. Becker, "Fragment van Francks latijnse brief aan Campanus," *Nederlands Archief voor Kerkgeschiedenis* 46 (1964–65), 197–205. Only part of this letter exists in its original Latin; for the complete letter in German and Dutch translation, see Manfred Krebs and Hans-Georg Rott, eds., *Quellen zur Geschichte der Täufer*, vol. 7 (Gütersloh: Mohn, 1959), 301–25.

17. For what follows, see the detailed discussion in Alister E. McGrath, *The Intellectual Origins of the European Reformation* (New York: Blackwell, 1987), 140–51; Paul de Vooght, *Les sources de la doctrine chrétienne d'après les théologiens du XIVe siècle et au début du XVe* (Desclée: De Brouwer, 1954); Hermann Schüssler, *Der Primät der heiligen Schrift als theologisches und kanonistisches Problem im Spätmittelalter* (Wiesbaden: Steiner, 1977).

18. See further Alister E. McGrath, *Reformation Thought: An Introduction,* 2d ed. (Oxford: Blackwell, 1993), 135–36, 144–47.

break from it. We should stress that, while the historical outcome of this process in the sixteenth century was indeed the breaking away of the evangelical churches from the medieval church, this outcome was not inevitable. Nor was it the only theologically justifiable outcome. Nor—and this point must be stressed—was it the outcome Luther desired or expected, based on his early approach to reforming the church.

So what is the relevance of this excursus into the theology of the Reformation for our purposes today? It draws our attention to two points that are of significance in understanding both the options that are available today to evangelical theological method and the tension that can arise within the evangelical theological community.

1. The mainline Reformation makes it clear that a legitimate and persuasive option for evangelical theological method is that of engagement with the "great tradition," while recognizing at all times that interpretations of Scripture are secondary to Scripture itself.

2. Evangelicalism is a complex movement and contains within itself elements that are either directly influenced by or sympathetic to both the mainline and Radical Reformations. A person should expect, therefore, to encounter in contemporary evangelicalism the tensions whose origins lie within the Reformation—such as the tension concerning the role of tradition. This tension may be lesser than in the past, and it may well be modulated by a spirit of graciousness and longing to understand one another that is characteristic of evangelicalism at its best. Yet such tension is present and affects reflection on the proper role of tradition in evangelical theological method.

My concern, therefore, is to explore the strengths and weaknesses of an approach to theology that aims to take seriously the long history of Christian engagement with Scripture.

The Importance of History

Yet why bother with history? It seems to many that we have quite enough ideas and positions to consider in the present without complicating things by turning to the past. On the other side of the coin, history is often the refuge of people who cannot cope with the present and find consolation in turning over the pages of the past in a wistful manner. Some are disconcerted with the directness of the question, What should we believe about God? and find it much easier to offer a historical answer: "Let me tell you what Augustine (or Luther, or Pascal) said about God." Those who find theological self-disclosure embarrassing, or who have no concern with the issue of truth, can thus retreat into the relative safety of reporting what others have said. A concern for history thus ultimately degenerates into a contempt for truth. But it need not; indeed, it should not.

Part of our theological method must include an examination of the past to understand how we came to be where we are. Studying the past allows us to gain insights into how the thinking of our forebears was shaped by the biblical text and by factors outside that text, such as cultural assumptions, understandings of rationality, and notions of logic. Much more of the furniture of our intellectual world than we care to admit is culturally conditioned and socially constructed. For example, the notion of common sense varies enormously from one culture to another, as do understandings of what constitutes "rationality."

We all read Scripture through spectacles that shape, to a greater or lesser extent, what we find as we read. This is a fact of theological life, and it is one we can learn to live with without much difficulty. Some are, of course, reluctant to concede this point and suggest that they are able to read and interpret the Bible objectively. They feel liberated from the awkward intrusion of the subtle influences of culture, personal history, notions of truth, and the lengthening shadows of great individuals who have shaped our evangelical culture. But this is not the case. Many recent American evangelicals read Scripture with spectacles that reflect the strongly individualist assumptions of late-twentieth-century American culture[19] and are consequently prone to overlook the corporate themes of both Old and New Testaments, such as sin as a corporate entity that affects generations to come, or the church as the body of Christ. Equally, many British evangelicals read Scripture with spectacles that have been subtly configured, like a distorting mirror, with the moral assumptions of middle-class England of the postwar period, quite unaware that they are doing so. Thus, the New English Bible is widely regarded as locating the world of Jesus in the polite society of English high teas.[20]

I could cite additional examples without difficulty. For example, do Western Christians tend to overlook the many biblical texts that speak of poverty and its potential remedies, perhaps believing this is not an important topic in comparison with that of eschatology? Do male readers of the Old Testament, as many feminist writers suggest, approach

19. See the rich documentation in Robert N. Bellah, *Habits of the Heart: Individualism and Commitment in American Life*, 2d ed. (Berkeley: University of California Press, 1996).

20. See the witty comments in David Norton, *A History of the Bible as Literature*, 2 vols. (Cambridge: Cambridge University Press, 1993), vol. 2, 408–32.

it with unconscious patriarchal assumptions that color their rendering of that text? Or are those feminists themselves simply projecting onto the biblical text the assumptions of their worldview? These are no idle questions; they probe at the heart of our biblical interpretation and invite us to examine ourselves and the rich and complex bundle of assumptions we bring—often unwittingly—to our task.

The consequences of ignoring such questions are painfully evident. Well-meaning Western missionaries to China and India in the nineteenth century seemed to work under the assumption that the Christianization and Westernization of those nations went hand in hand, in some theologically legitimated covenantal relationship. In reality, they had allowed their perception and presentation of the gospel to be shaped by their Western context and had failed to extricate Western assumptions from their evangelism. The result in China was the Boxer Rebellion, which sought to exterminate Christianity from Chinese soil on the grounds that it was a Western import. Similarly, in Japan Christianity was stigmatized as a Western phenomenon. The nineteenth-century Japanese colloquial term for Christianity was *bata kusai*, "it tastes of butter," referring to the fact that both butter and Christianity were seen as Western imports to the region!

Precisely the same issue can be seen as underlying the surprising failure of Marxism to gain a foothold in North America. In the course of an important debate over this matter between Karl Kautsky and Edward Bernstein,[21] Bernstein argued that Marxism failed to win a following in the United States because its outlook was too deeply embedded in the social situation of 1830s Germany. It did not relate to the social realities of twentieth-century America, and Marxist theoreticians were making no effort to alter this situation by interpreting Marxism in a North American context. In short, it had become so conditioned by its original context that it lost any ability it originally possessed to relate to dissimilar contexts.

We all read the Bible through a filter of assumptions, many of which we have failed to identify. One of the relatively few insights of postmodernism with which I find myself in full agreement is that there is no privileged vantage point independent of tradition that allows us to read any text—biblical or otherwise—devoid of prior assumptions and precommitments.[22] For example, many evangelicals find that they are unable to approach Paul's statements on justification by faith, and James's on justification by faith *and*

---

21. See Peter Gay, *The Dilemma of Democratic Socialism: Edward Bernstein's Challenge to Marx* (New York: Octagon, 1979).

22. For justification of this point, see Alister E. McGrath, *The Genesis of Doctrine: A Study in the Foundations of Doctrinal Criticism* (Oxford: Blackwell, 1990), 81–102.

works, without reading them in the light of Luther's views on justification by faith alone. Here the text is being read and interpreted within a specific framework reflecting the debates of the sixteenth century.

Now, this is not a fatal difficulty—unless, of course, we pretend there is no problem and insist that our unconsciously assumption-laden and theory-driven interpretation of the Bible is neutral, detached, objective, and permanently valid for all peoples and all times. The study of historical theology encourages us to operate a "hermeneutic of suspicion," which demands that we *justify* our interpretations of Scripture. For example, why do many evangelicals affirm "justification by faith alone" when no biblical text explicitly affirms this and at least one explicitly denies it (James 2:24)? We are encouraged to be on our guard and understand why we believe certain things rather than just accepting them passively from those we recognize as masters and teachers. Tradition is something that is to be actively and selectively appropriated, not passively and unthinkingly received.

Engaging with church history and historical theology serves three critically important functions, which evangelical theology cannot afford to ignore.

First, it demonstrates how the interpretation of the Bible was governed, often to an uncomfortable extent, by cultural and philosophical assumptions. Such assumptions often intruded into the hermeneutical process without any awareness on the part of those engaged in this matter that they were allowing extra-biblical considerations to influence their reading of Scripture. Thus, Platonic notions had a significant impact on Origen as he read and interpreted both the Old and New Testaments, as did Aristotelianism on Aquinas, as did the Scottish Common Sense philosophy on Charles Hodge, and as did Enlightenment rationalism more generally on the Old Princeton School. This is not, it must be stressed, a criticism of these individuals or schools. It is simply a recognition that this subtle influence *does* take place and that it needs to be acknowledged. Otherwise, we will be left with the naïve and potentially damaging view that evangelicals can read Scripture and reflect on it in a detached, objective, and culture-free manner.

Second, engaging with church history and historical theology indicates that the use succeeding generations are able to make of the work of earlier generations is limited by shifts in cultural and philosophical assumptions. For example, because Luther vigorously rejected the intrusion of Aristotelianism into Christian theology, he rejected a substantial tract of medieval theology, precisely because he considered it dependent on extra-biblical norms and assumptions at this point. Likewise, the widespread rejection of Enlightenment rationalism within modern Western culture, popular and academic, is widely shared within evangelical circles. It is quite difficult, therefore, to make use of some of the foundational theological assumptions that have undergirded the work of some earlier evangelical writers such as Carl Henry—including the notion that revelation must be *purely* propositional, which rests on an Enlightenment rather than a biblical understanding of truth.[23] This observation forces us to note that evangelicals are not immune from being shaped, whether consciously or not, by their culture, and that the use to which future generations will be able to put their ideas will be determined, at least to some extent, by the manner in which they are able to minimize the critical role played by extra-biblical foundational assumptions.

Third, the study of history discloses that evangelicals regard their tradition as determined by Scripture, not by what evangelicals have historically thought. Thus, contemporary evangelicals have not felt obligated to mechanically repeat the theologies and ethics of, for example, their eighteenth-century forebears. Rather, they have felt free to appropriate the ideas that resonate with Scripture and discreetly pass over those that are obviously incorrect or shaped by outdated cultural norms. Evangelicalism is thus able to undertake a critical appropriation of its own heritage. This attitude avoids the dangerous position of what comes close to idolatry, as it sets up certain evangelical figures as infallible guides to the truth. We recognize instead that we are all engaged in the search for biblical truth and all prone to error. To give one very obvious consequence of this, an evangelical theologian should not be challenged concerning his evangelical credentials merely because he fails to agree completely with Jonathan Edwards, or B. B. Warfield, or John Stott—to offer a generous spectrum of possibilities. We must acknowledge the provisionality of our interpretations of Scripture—which is, of course, what all good theology ultimately is—and be prepared to have them challenged and corrected by others as part of the corporate evangelical quest for biblical authenticity.

These thoughts are perhaps unsettling for some. It is natural, as Max Weber pointed out in a seminal essay, to long for certainty and to look for charismatic figures to sort things out and tell us what is right.[24] And

23. See the criticisms of evangelical rationalism offered in Alister McGrath, *A Passion for Truth: The Intellectual Coherence of Evangelicalism* (Downers Grove, Ill.: InterVarsity Press, 1997). For a useful comparison of the notions of "truth" in some recent evangelical writers, see James Emery White, *What Is Truth? A Comparative Study of the Positions of Cornelius Van Til, Francis Schaeffer, Carl F. H. Henry, Donald Bloesch, Millard Erickson* (Nashville: Broadman & Holman, 1994).

24. Max Weber, "The Sociology of Charismatic Authority," in *From Max Weber: Essays in Sociology*, ed. Hans H. Gert and C. Wright Mills (London: Oxford University Press, 1946), 246–52.

there will always be a scattering of evangelicals who seek to make absolute conformity to the ideas of some favored individual the litmus test of evangelical identity and orthodoxy. Yet this must be rejected as unbiblical, for it places the authority of an interpreter of Scripture over that of Scripture itself. The priority of Scripture over all other sources and norms, including its interpreters, must be vigorously maintained as a matter of principle by evangelicals. Otherwise, it is not the ultimate authority of Scripture that is defended but a penultimate authority. Further, according to this approach, it is not Scripture that is infallible but a specific interpretation of Scripture. Evangelicalism simply cannot allow itself to be trapped in this kind of theological personality cult, and it must vigorously resist all who seek to place themselves or others in such a privileged position.

Evangelicalism must see tradition as its servant, not its master. To affirm the supreme authority of Scripture in matters of doctrine should not prevent us from paying attention to what others who have gone before us have found in their engagement with Scripture. Indeed, the fundamental evangelical theme of obedient attentiveness to Scripture makes it all the more important to listen respectfully to the views of our forebears who paid respectful attention to the biblical materials. A willingness to listen—not to agree uncritically, I stress, but to *listen*—is of considerable importance in securing the stability of evangelical theological reflection. Such an approach can be found in the writings of many evangelical writers, such as James Orr and J. I. Packer, who see themselves as standing within the "great tradition."[25] While engagement with these approaches has much to commend it, I propose to revert to what is, in many respects, the *fons et origo* of such approaches: the theology of John Calvin.

Tradition and Theology: The Contribution of John Calvin

As I pointed out earlier, the magisterial Reformation witnessed the development of an approach to theology that gave priority to Scripture

25. The most significant studies of Orr have been Alan P. F. Sell, *Defending and Declaring the Faith: Some Scottish Examples, 1860–1920* (Exeter, U.K.: Paternoster Press; Colorado Springs: Helmers and Howard, 1987), 137–71; and Glen G. Scorgie, *A Call for Continuity: The Theological Contribution of James Orr* (Macon, Ga.: Mercer University Press, 1988). See also Packer, "The Comfort of Conservatism," 283–99; "On from Orr: The Cultural Crisis, Rational Realism, and Incarnational Ontology," *Crux* 32, no. 3 (September 1996): 12–26. On Packer, see Alister McGrath, "The Importance of Tradition for Modern Evangelicalism," in *Doing Theology for the People of God*, ed. Donald Lewis and Alister McGrath (Downers Grove, Ill.: InterVarsity Press, 1996), 159–73.

while fully acknowledging the sapiential and critical role of tradition. To allocate supreme authority to Scripture does not, as the writings of the magisterial Reformation make clear, involve rejecting the role of tradition. Tradition is allocated a positive and critical role as a servant in the interpretation and application of Scripture. In what follows I propose to examine the approach of Calvin as a means of encouraging others to engage with tradition.[26]

To begin with, let us reflect on the role played by tradition in Calvin's defense of the Reformation. An excellent example lies in the Lausanne Disputation of 1536—the first major public debate to involve Calvin as an authorized representative of the Reformation.[27] In the course of this dispute, the evangelical contingent was accused by the Catholic theologian Jean Mimard of despising Christian tradition, especially the theological witness of antiquity. Calvin's response was immediate and decisive: Far from "despising" this witness, the reformers took it with the greatest seriousness. It was a matter of considerable importance to Calvin to be able to demonstrate that the Reformation belonged within the "grand tradition" of critical theological reflection, which embraced such luminaries as Augustine.

Calvin carefully navigated his theological flagship between two unacceptable positions. First, he explicitly rejected the idea that tradition has authority precisely on account of its antiquity. This view—which he associated with his Roman Catholic opponents—was untenable. The Christian tradition contains errors, and it is important to identify and eliminate them. An uncritical repetition of the teachings of the past dishonors Scripture, in that it raises human interpreters and interpretations of Scripture above Scripture itself. In the end, it is not what Augustine or any other Christian writer believes that matters; the final court of appeal must be what Scripture itself has to say.

Yet Calvin was also critical of those who rejected tradition as a matter of principle. This is clear from the Lausanne Disputation and Calvin's dispute with Sadoleto, in which the extent of the continuity between the Reformation and the apostolic church was a matter of considerable importance. It must be conceded that tradition includes mis-

---

26. For a full study of this important question, see Lane, *John Calvin*, and references therein. Older studies that merit attention here include J. Boisset, "La réforme et les pères de l'église," in *Migne et le renouveau des études patristiques*, ed. A. Mandouze and J. Fouilheron (Paris: Beauchesne, 1988), 39–51; D. Fischer, "L'histoire de l'église dans la pensée de Calvin," *Archiv für Reformationsgeschichte* 7 (1986): 79–125; David C. Steinmetz, "Luther and Calvin on Church and Tradition," in *Luther in Context* (Bloomington, Ind.: Indiana University Press, 1986), 85–97.

27. See E. M. Braekman, "Les interventions de Calvin," in *La Dispute de Lausanne*, 170–77.

takes. Well, what else can you expect? Theologians are human beings and hence prone to error. The important thing is to identify and correct these errors in the light of Scripture itself.

While he was not prepared to endorse the theological opinions of the fathers uncritically, Calvin stressed their stabilizing and ministerial role for evangelical theology: "We do not exalt their authority in such a way as to debase the dignity of the word of our Lord, to which alone total obedience is due within the church of Christ." Having made it clear that the patristic testimony is subordinate to Scripture, Calvin proceeded to establish the ministerial role of tradition for evangelical theology:

> Although we hold that the Word of God alone lies beyond the sphere of our judgement, and that the fathers and councils are of authority only to the extent that they concur with the rule of the Word, we still give to those fathers and councils such rank and authority as it is proper for them to hold under Christ.[28]

The area in which this became of critical importance was the issue of the relation of private and public beliefs. Calvin, in common with all reformers, believed strongly in the right of all believers to interpret Scripture. Yet how was this private interpretation of Scripture, and the doctrinal affirmations made on its basis, to be related to the public teaching of the church? Having explicitly rejected the notion of the infallible *magisterium* of the church, Calvin initially seemed vulnerable at this point. Is not the recognition of the private judgment of the individual tantamount to giving every believer the right to believe what he pleases, providing he can offer some kind of biblical sanction for the view in question?

In dealing with this question, Calvin set out some ideas that can be of immense benefit to modern evangelicalism. Calvin explained the perceived difficulty and his proposed solution in a discussion of 1 John 4:1 as follows:

> If everyone has the right and liberty to make judgements, nothing will ever be settled as certain, and the whole of religion will falter. Yet I reply

---

28. I have used the same citations brought forward by Lane, *John Calvin,* 15–47, apart from some minor alterations made in the light of the original. Other references may be found in Lane's excellent discussion, as well as other words noted above. In that the account offered of Calvin's approach represents a general consensus among Calvin scholars, it seemed unnecessary to provide detailed documentation of the various points being made. If any aspect of what follows is contestable, I daresay it is the application of Calvin's approach to modern evangelicalism, not what Calvin himself has to say on the issue.

that there is a twofold test of doctrine—private and public. The private test is that by which each individual settles his own faith, and rests securely in that teaching which he knows comes from God. . . . The public test relates to the common consent and *politeia* of the church. For since there is a serious danger of fanatics rising up and presumptuously declaring that they are endowed with the Spirit of God, it is a necessary remedy that believers should meet together and seek a way of godly and pure agreement.

The issue then became ascertaining what the corporate judgment of the church might be, in response to these highly individualist and charismatic declarations. Calvin argued that, while tradition could not be regarded as an infallible guide to theological orthodoxy, it was helpful in meeting this challenge of radical individualism. The teachings of the councils, for example, were not infallible, but they were immensely valuable in establishing some theological landmarks against fanatics.

The general position Calvin developed can be summed up in the following phrase: Tradition has a *critical ministerial role* to play for evangelical theology. It alerts us to highly suspicious teachings and biblical interpretations. It forces us to develop a hermeneutic of suspicion with regard to some of the more puzzling and problematical biblical interpretations and theological formulations of American evangelicalism, all too painfully evident in some recent controversies. Rediscovering the corporate and historic nature of the Christian faith reduces the danger of entire communities of faith being misled by charismatic individuals. Doing so also affirms the ongoing importance of the Christian past as a stabilizing influence as we prepare to theologize in the twenty-first century. This is surely something we need to reappropriate.

Yet Calvin also offered us a vision of the place of evangelicalism within the grand tradition of Christian theologizing that can help modern evangelicalism gain a sense of historical perspective and location. There can be no doubt the church had fallen into times of corruption and decline, yet it remained the Christian church despite these distortions. God raised up champions of truth and orthodoxy during those dark periods—people such as Gregory the Great and Bernard of Clairvaux. Such people struggled for truth against the odds. Did Paul not teach that the Antichrist would have his seat in the midst of God's temple (2 Thess. 2:4)? And does this not point to corruption at the very heart of the church? For Calvin, the reformation was about the purging and reforming of a corrupt church—yet a church Christ had never abandoned. The important thing was to struggle for truth, knowing that one stood in a long line of faithful witnesses down through the ages.

This great vision of the "grand tradition" of Christian theology holds the key to the evangelical quest for biblical integrity and for liberation from what is perhaps the deadliest virus to infect modern evangelicalism—the demands of our modern "fanatics" (to use Calvin's term) to obey them unthinkingly because they have direct access to the Word and Spirit of God. Perhaps they do. Yet Calvin demands that we treat them critically and judge them publicly by Scripture and the great weight of the Christian tradition.

Modern evangelicalism should see itself as continuing in this "grand tradition," represented by Calvin, Luther, and Melanchthon. Do we see Augustine, Gregory the Great, and Bernard of Clairvaux as our forebears in our struggle for authenticity of Christian life and thought? Calvin certainly did, and he regarded an engagement with such luminaries as both polemically advantageous and theologically constructive. Might not we learn from this? Calvin challenges us to develop a more comprehensive vision of the nature and scope of evangelical theology, inviting us to enrich our theological vision by engaging with dialogue partners from the past—dialogue partners he himself found helpful in illuminating the meaning of Scripture and combating heresy.

Theology as a Corporate Activity

To take tradition seriously is to recognize the importance of the historical community of faith, whether past or present. One of the greatest threats to evangelical theology is that it becomes the arena of individuals who have no sense of belonging to, or having responsibilities toward, the body of Christ. To theologize is to take responsibility for one's views in relation to the people of God as a whole, for those who claim to speak on behalf of that people will one day have to give an account of their views, not simply to God, but also to the community of faith, whose views they presume to voice and guide. Theology is a matter for the people of God, not just certain individuals, and those individuals who seek to set out a theological vision do so as representatives of their communities of faith.

The Reformation set out a vision of the "priesthood of all believers." That fundamental doctrine has theological aspects in that—at least in theory—the views of individual believers had to be taken into account by theologians. Evangelicalism has little time for the elitism characteristic of so much academic theology. It is primarily concerned with addressing the issues faced by ordinary people. Yet evangelicalism can and should aim to encourage the emergence of sustained serious theological reflection from a committed standpoint within the Christian community. It should also see theologians as believers who think for themselves and for others within the community of faith. There is no shame in being an "amateur" theologian. After all, amateurs may be defined precisely by the fact that they are not professionals—and the professionalization of theology may be one of the most serious causes of the dysfunctionalism of the modern church.

The Italian writer Antonio Gramsci took the sixteenth-century Reformation idea of the theologian as the basis for his influential notion of the "organic intellectual."[29] Gramsci argued that two distinct types of intellectuals can be discerned. In the first place, there are those who arc imposed upon a community by an external authority. These "traditional intellectuals" are not chosen by that community and have influence only insofar as their authority is forced on the community. They have power by virtue of an external agency.

In contrast to this, Gramsci notes and commends the idea of "organic intellectuals"—that is, thinkers who arise within a community within which they operate and are respected. They gain respect, not on account of an externally imposed authority, but on account of being seen to represent and respect the outlook of that community. Their authority is thus not imposed but emerges naturally, reflecting the esteem in which the community holds them and its willingness to regard them as its representatives and thinkers.

This model of the theologian resonates with the experience of many evangelicals who have come to regard "professional theologians" with intense skepticism. This attitude is the result of the gross theological irresponsibility of much modern academic theology, which showed itself to be the willing prisoner of the latest cultural whim and treated the pastoral and spiritual needs and concerns of the church with a scarcely disguised contempt. The British evangelical writer John R. W. Stott is an excellent example of an "organic intellectual" in this respect. He possesses no overwhelming academic or institutional authority but rightly enjoys enormous status within the evangelical community (and beyond) on account of having *earned* that respect. There has been an organic and natural relationship between Stott and the community for whom he has spoken and to whom he so clearly has held himself responsible.

A careful reading of Gramsci's work, echoing the outlook of the Reformation, will encourage evangelicals to look toward the community

29. See Antonio Gramsci, *Gli intellettuali e l'organizzazione della cultura*, 6th ed. (Rome: Giulio Einaudi Editore, 1955).

of faith and to seek and find authority in individuals with a proven record of fidelity to the Christian tradition, a concern for the *consensus fidelium,* a love for the gospel, and a responsible and informed concern to relate it to the world—whether this is recognized by the academy or not. The best intellectuals indeed may well exist and operate outside the academy.

Evangelical theologians are conscious of a dual responsibility in that they are writing for other theologians yet also on behalf of the evangelical community. This dual responsibility entails a willingness to listen to others. And it is here that engaging with the great tradition becomes important—for those whose views we must seek and value include both those who are now alive and those who have gone before us. We must realize that faithful and obedient men and women were wrestling with the meaning and application of the gospel before we were born and that their views have a right to be heard. To take tradition seriously is to acknowledge both the existence and theological importance of the rich treasury of past Christian faithfulness and obedience.

This insight offers us two immediate benefits.

1. We are safeguarded from the shallow individualism of theologians for whom innovation and "creativity"—to use a word that has often come to mean little more than a determination to abandon traditional viewpoints—are of prime importance. If an evangelical theologian confronts us with a demand to "believe me!" when offering us a radical new teaching, we can respond with an obvious challenge: Why has no one believed this before? Why, throughout two thousand years of faithful Christian reflection, has this doctrine never been taken seriously? Such a critical approach is liberating, as it frees us from the authoritarianism of maverick preachers and writers.

2. We are offered stability in both our faith and our theological reflections in that we have access to traditions of interpretation that have been tried and tested and whose strengths and weaknesses are well-known. A modest acquaintance with historical theology makes it clear that radical new teachings, which are allegedly the only viable option for biblically serious people, emerge throughout Christian history. They need to be seen in perspective. The arguments offered against them in the past can speak to us today. The positions that theologians adopted, as a consequence of wrestling with Scripture and dialoguing with the past, can be our positions. This is no demand to woodenly repeat the past or become trapped in its idiosyncrasies; it

is a recognition of the continuing role of dialogue with the past in maintaining stability, integrity, and authenticity in Christian life and thought.

Conclusion

The approach I have been commending in this essay encourages evangelicals to value history and engage with the "great tradition" in its totality. It invites evangelicals to enter into dialogue with the past—with Athanasius, Augustine, Anselm, Aquinas, Luther, Calvin, and Edwards, to mention but a few. To do so is to learn from the past without in any way being bound by that past. It is to be nourished, encouraged, challenged, and excited by the witness of those who have wrestled with Scripture before us, without allowing these servants of the gospel to become our masters. Certainly, we will wrestle with those with whom we disagree—often profoundly. But such engagement is a superb means of sharpening our own understanding of the nature of the gospel and seeing the fresh vistas that good theology affords us.

But it also encourages us to see ourselves as standing within that great tradition of Christian faithfulness, which has been there before us and will still be there after us. It reminds us that we are standing on the shoulders of giants. If we can see farther than they did, it is because they raise us up—as we trust and pray that we may encourage, enlighten, and strengthen the faith of those to whom we minister now, and who will follow us in the future.

6

The Theological Task and Theological Method

Penitence, Parasitism, and Prophecy

STEPHEN WILLIAMS

It is fair to admit that, to some extent, this essay is perched on the boundary of the issue of theological method, rather than being centered on it. The matter of theological method inevitably raises the question of presuppositions about the theological task, and I believe that, within evangelicalism, attending to the task means raising some broader questions than we often do and raising them urgently. So the question of task has been allowed to govern the overall structure of this present contribution. The methodological implications, however, are spelled out, for that is our focus in this book, and in any case, it will be clear in our discussion how they inseparably accompany the issue of task.

Indeed, it is as well that theologians root their consciousness of the task in some perspectives that are beyond the boundaries of this particular discussion. At the risk of courting the disease of thinking in triads (the material in this paper is presented under three headings), this perspective can be set out by means of three quotations. The first is from a figure who will loom large later—Dietrich Bonhoeffer: "The time when people could be told everything by means of words, whether theological or pious, is over."[1] The second is from the black liberation theologian James Cone: "Because white theologians are well fed and speak for a people who control the means of production . . . they spend more time debating the relation between the Jesus of history and the Christ of faith than probing the depths of Jesus' command to feed the poor."[2] The third is from Martin Luther: "What makes the theologian is living—better, dying and being condemned—certainly not understanding, reading and speculating."[3] We may find fault with aspects of these quotations, but let us extract from them the good and the true. Bonhoeffer teaches that theologians must live with a shot of word-weariness, something that descends naturally on people seriously committed to action. Cone implies that theologians should live with a burden of wealth-wariness and that attending to the material base from which one speaks is a precondition of the authenticity of that speech. Luther reminds us that the theologian is first a species of disciple. Theology is not just generally a form or expression of discipleship, but in particular can only grasp in thought Christ crucified and risen if the self is united to him in death and resurrection.

It would be more than enough if we were to order our reflections on evangelical theology to the matters that arise in these statements, but our present purposes are not best served by doing so. Then why the quotations? Because our purposes are ill-served if we do not carry their weight with us wherever we go, and even a modest attempt at theological statesmanship surely does well to be haunted by them. Taken together, they direct us to renewed selfless worldly action.[4] And although the intention in this paper is to highlight those things that seem noteworthy in relation to task and method, the unifying principle is the worldly concern of theology. I hope it is with sincerity that the appropriate first note is struck—the note of penitence.

Confession of a Penitent

About thirteen years ago, Robert Banks produced a short but challenging book titled *All the Business of Life: Bringing Theology Down-To-*

---

1. Dietrich Bonhoeffer, *Letters and Papers from Prison* (London: SCM, 1971), 279.
2. Quoted in J. Andrew Kirk, *Theology Encounters Revolution* (Leicester: Inter-Varsity Press, 1980), 99.
3. Taken from Luther's *Operationes in Psalmos* (1519–21) WA 5, 163.
4. Luther, in his classic 1520 treatise on "The Freedom of the Christian," insists that the renewed self, through justification, dwells in the neighbor by love just as we dwell in Christ by faith.

Earth.[5] The argument was simple: The things that most occupy us receive the least theological attention. The back cover selectively listed "work, commuting, chores, shopping, sport, family, health, security, hobbies, bills, sleep, waiting, friendship." Some will wonder how theological thinking on at least some themes in everyday life can actually go on. Still, there are enough uncontroversial concrete examples here for us to agree with Banks that giving theological attention to the mundane is a less familiar and less welcome operation in the guild of theologians than is concerning ourselves with what we regard as the great theological themes. Why is this so?

I have come to see that the kind of theological reflection to which we are summoned by Banks can take place properly only if it is done cooperatively, in the context of congregational church life where we think together in fellowship. Theological expertise in such a context is optimally deployed to enable the faithful to think theologically, by which one basically means thinking Christianly. From this it is but a small step to conclude that we might need to make a move parallel to the one people have made over the years in relation to the concept of ministry. The one we traditionally call "minister," we know, ought to be releasing people into their ministries. So shouldn't the one we presently call "theologian" help enable people to become theologians? That is surely a necessary task. We shall not venture here to suggest that it is a task for all whom we customarily call theologians. But the day may come when we shall democratize the word *theologian* as many of us have long done with *minister.* As theologians we need to consider whether it is a task at least for a good number of us. The point is not to get away from traditional theological responsibilities. It is to correct an imbalance: to supplement, to diversify, and to expand the theologian's vocation.

"A necessary task," but difficult, for reasons that overlap with the reasons why ordained leaders find it difficult to be committed enablers of others' ministries. For the fact is that we find ourselves a little more detached from the body of Christ than we should be according to the theology we profess. An extreme form of detachment is solitude. René Descartes regularly gets singled out for criticism for something or other, so let us also pick on him here. In a famous passage, William Temple said, "If I were asked what was the most disastrous moment in the history of Europe I should be strongly tempted to answer that it was that period of leisure when René Descartes, having no claims to meet, remained for a whole day 'shut up alone in a stove.'"[6] He was al-

5. Sutherland, Australia: Albatross; Tring, England: Lion, 1987.
6. William Temple, *Nature, Man, and God* (London: Macmillan, 1934), 57.

luding to that passage in which Descartes described his discovery of the elements of a philosophical approach that would center thought on the existing, thinking self. That momentous afternoon was a continental fatality, Temple held, because Descartes thought subject and object apart. Actually, Descartes' philosophy is not our quarry here. But his personal style is: Descartes, *spectateur* and *voyeur* of, rather than *acteur* in, human existence, wandering the streets of Amsterdam and seeing people as trees in the woods or as the animals that inhabited them, he himself being as free and peaceful in the crowd as in a quiet street.[7] Despite the fact that Descartes is credited with a method and a philosophy designed to be universally prescriptive, he trumpeted his discoveries as his own and for himself.[8]

There is an attractive kind of solitude here whose nature, power, and prevalence we must not forget, however remote from us its temptation may seem.[9] Temperamentally, we may be gregarious rather than solitary, but we rather like the self-image of producing the theological goods from our solitude. Theologically, we may be convinced of the importance of interpersonal relationships, but unless we can choose our company, we find humans more interesting and less demanding when viewed from within the abstracted sphere of speculation. Of course, theologians need solitude and space for what we might call speculation, as all thinking people do and as most conscientious Christians do who are aware that they are personally accountable to their Maker and Redeemer. Obviously so.[10] But wheeling ourselves into the position in which our theological thought has, for its backdrop, mundane concerns and theological sharing, has, for its locus, ordinary Christians

7. See Helmut Thielicke, *Modern Faith and Thought*, trans. Geoffrey W. Bromiley (Grand Rapids: Eerdmans, 1990), 58–62.

8. René Descartes, "Discourse on Method" in *Philosophical Writings*, vol. 1, ed. J. Cottingham, R. Stoothoff, and D. Murdoch (Cambridge: Cambridge University Press, 1985), 112; René Descartes, "The Search for Truth" in *Philosophical Writings*, vol. 2 (Cambridge: Cambridge University Press, 1985), 419.

9. This is not to collapse our temptations into the Cartesian one or to collapse different kinds of solitude. But I suspect that more theologians than will readily admit it can sympathize rather strongly with strains in either Thomas Wolfe in "God's Lonely Man," *The Hills Beyond* (New York: Harper, 1941); or Friedrich Nietzsche in *Daybreak* (Cambridge: Cambridge University Press, 1982). In the latter, solitude is advertised from the first sparkling section of the preface, later emerging, along with science, as a new law that must govern our reflective life. Of course, Nietzsche's celebration of it is extreme in the self-commendatory jubilation that marks his intellectual autobiography, *Ecce Homo* (London: Penguin, 1979).

10. In his preface to *The Grammar of Faith* (San Francisco: Harper & Row, 1978), Paul Holmer says that "the reflections in these pages have mostly come about when attempts were being made to make sense for and by myself." This may be legitimate, and it would be preposterous to pass judgment otherwise, but peril lurks none too far away.

thinking about all the business of life—that is a different matter. The visceral resistance in some of us to such a reorientation signals an element of detachment from the ecclesia. This is to put it mildly. Those happily engaged in theological teaching and stimulated by theological exchange may feel they are not tempted to be as Descartes. When, however, we are confronted with the possibility of being summoned to the theological responsibilities I have outlined, a flash of envy for Descartes lights the heart.

Surely the cost of a failure to propel ourselves in the direction of the theological enterprise in question is high. We forfeit hearing the Word of God across all the business of life. As evangelicals, whether theologians or not, we are often most comfortable handling the issues that lie on the surface of the Bible. We are less comfortable with those matters on which Scripture is silent. On the question of justification, for instance, we think that God has spoken. On the other hand, on a host of issues in medical ethics, for example, which can press on ordinary people for swift resolution, he has not. The place where the doctrine of justification is resolved, we may suppose, is in the study with concordance and commentaries. Perhaps we are not quite right in that supposition, but for sure our works of reference will not resolve issues in medical ethics. So at the very least we have to get interdisciplinary. And still less is the study the place, and the concordance the tool, that will enable us to think through those things that constitute all the business of life. Here we need the fellowship. Here we engage in theology together, just as we worship and pray together.

Of course, appropriate theological expertise and leadership are to be retained, not jettisoned. Apparently, Jürgen Moltmann used to tell students in his Christian ethics courses that when a doctrinal dispute emerges in the church, theologians are the experts, but when ethical dilemmas in secular life emerge, the expertise is in the hands of those relevantly involved.[11] In order for that expertise to be theologically informed, theologians can aptly guide. But this may be less a direct theological guidance in the issues than a matter of guiding people to be theologians. At root, we are enquiring into the implications of a sound pneumatological ecclesiology, for the Spirit who leads is given to the body joined to its risen head, not to the professional theologian. Indeed, the concordance or common sense in interpretation is no substitute for the Spirit working in the body, whatever issue we are thinking about. However, it sometimes takes confrontation with those issues to which the concordance and common sense give no instant answers for us to truly appreciate the fact. Sometimes the Word of God is scarce,

11. Banks, *All the Business of Life*, 130.

and God himself shrouded in silence, in lands or ecclesial groupings where guidance is urgently needed. Surely it will remain so all too often unless the *whole* church immerses itself in the Word, pursuing a theology of everyday life collectively and deliberately in intra-congregational and trans-denominational groups.

It is worth following this through with a supplementary point, though one that can be made in a different connection and on a separate basis. Attending to all the business of life in the context of Christian community also encourages the theologian to redirect theological energy professionally in an interdisciplinary direction, something already entailed by one reference to medical ethics. Banks proposes that if we take up the responsibility of thinking effectively about a wide range of issues in a functional environment that enables sharing, commitment, and cooperation, we cannot do so consistently without prescribing to theology an interdisciplinary task.[12] Evangelical theologians probably spend proportionately too much time talking to each other or to non-evangelical theologians and too little talking to Christian artists, scientists, political thinkers, and activists. Here a concrete suggestion may be in order: It would be no idle ambition if a squad of theologians sought to team up with a number of Christian thinkers in different subject areas to work out a contemporary theological anthropology that adumbrates the Christian understanding of the human person right across the spectrum of academic disciplines.

We are not trading in theological novelties here. "If any group of Christians took seriously the importance of relating their systematic beliefs to all the business of life, it was the Puritans."[13] Nor are the remarks necessarily bound to an evangelical perspective, though offered from within it. They are truly confessions of a penitent. The principal entailment that arises from them for the matter of theological method is not novel either; but if novelty is the goal of a proposal, that itself should be a cause for penitence! That theology should be done *by* the people and *for* the people has been argued most influentially in modern theology by liberation theologians. They have allied their appeal to a specific conception of the theological task, derived from the perceived imperatives of liberation. Here we are not entering into that aspect of things, though the opening quotation from Cone indicates sympathy

---

12. Those whose ecclesiology makes them unhappy with home churches should not be put off by Banks's argument. Its essentials can be preserved if one thinks alternatively of structures such as house fellowships that function within the more traditionally established denominations. I am deliberately drawing a great deal of attention to his work, since its simple but trenchant claim, unheeded by too many of us, impels us to give an account of ourselves.

13. Banks, *All the Business of Life,* 127.

with features of the liberation theologians' program, passé as that program now seems to many. Several factors, including the democratizing
of education, have forced us to rethink the relation of "minister" to congregation and world. We must be forced also to rethink the question of
the theological method by which we pursue the theological task. If believers are priests and kings, there is every reason why they should be
theologians. Theology proceeds by community; that is its true method.

Of course, we speak of what many have known and practiced over
the years. My suggestion is that to evangelical theologians and theology
is committed the task for the future of developing and extending this
practice. The aim is to get the theological most out of each in the body
of Christ according to his or her ability and situation.[14]

From Penitent to Parasite: Bonhoeffer and Evangelicals

It is not only that no one knows where Bonhoeffer's thought would
have come to its theological term had he lived to think things through.
The fact is that one cannot be entirely confident of knowing its direction. Or, if some think this is too skeptical, we may think we know its
direction—but had he come to a fork in the road he was traveling,
which way would he have gone? All this is to express a familiar caution
in the interpretation of Bonhoeffer. The radicalism of his "religionless
Christianity" has frightened off some who have concluded that he
began to lose the church, to lose the distinctives of Christianity with it,
and certainly to lose all possibility of affirming a robust orthodoxy for
his day and ours. To such, and not to such alone, the words of Georg
Huntemann are startling.

> [Bonhoeffer] is a theologian of an era that has not yet begun in theology
> or the church . . . very close in spirit to the evangelicals. . . . He will be
> their church father in the future—or else evangelicals will have no future.
> Bonhoeffer is in fact so similar to the evangelicals that it will become un-
> comfortable for them. For Bonhoeffer's theology could bring the neces-
> sary catharsis for the "evangelicals of all lands."[15]

There is more to Huntemann's claim than we can unpack here, and
in any case, I shall be taking a line that is independent of his. I am going
to be parasitic just on this strong formulation, and on Bonhoeffer's
own thought. Lest this sound like a ringing endorsement of Bonhoeffer

14. For some further thoughts, see Stephen N. Williams, "Theology: A Task for Non-
Theologians," *Frontiers* (spring 1997): 39–44.
15. Georg Huntemann, *Dietrich Bonhoeffer: An Evangelical Reassessment* (Grand Rapids: Baker, 1996), 12.

and of Huntemann's judgment of him, let me qualify, lapsing once more into triadic mode. First, what follows does not imply comprehensive agreement with the key points in Bonhoeffer's theological thought. Second, much that is crucial in Bonhoeffer's theology is patient of insertion into a rather traditional evangelical framework, and many of us feel more comfortable in doing that than in substituting a Bonhoefferian mode for that rather traditional framework. Finally, let me say that Huntemann's claim is an overstatement. Having said all that in order to prove that parasites too can take pride in their orthodoxy and their independence, the question is now, What gives Bonhoeffer such a high claim on our attention?

The integrity of Bonhoeffer's thought and life of discipleship is perhaps the most striking thing about him, and as often as one queries or disagrees with his thought, one keeps coming back to this. Although the body of his book does not always identify with precision what it is that evoked his claims, Huntemann himself had in mind both Bonhoeffer's realization that a new era had dawned and his response to it. Huntemann is right to locate where he does much of the significance of his subject's thought, and, although this has been said by a number for some decades now, Huntemann thinks that evangelicals are yet to catch on. Toward the end of his days, Bonhoeffer explored the notion of a "religionless Christianity."[16] All things considered, Bonhoeffer seems to have had in mind a form of Christian thought and life that inwardly retains the basic apparatus of traditional belief and spirituality but emphasizes the external task of living humanly, this being *the* form of witness and communication. Interpretation of Bonhoeffer at this point is bound to be controversial, of course, and it is not a controversy that can profitably be joined here. The background to his famous inchoate and controverted remarks in the *Letters and Papers from Prison* is found in the more thought-out reflection that goes on in the unfinished *Ethics*. To this we turn.

Writing in Germany in the early 1940s, Bonhoeffer spoke of a

> western world brought to the brink of the void. . . . This is not a crisis among other crises. It is a decisive struggle of the last days. . . . It is a rebellious and outrageous void, and one which is the enemy of both God and man. . . . It is the void made god. No one knows its goal or measure.

16. In the earlier stages of the Bonhoeffer industry, the English-speaking world concentrated on this phrase, but the German-speaking world attended more to the proximate matter of what Bonhoeffer said about the nonreligious interpretation of biblico-theological concepts. See Eberhard Bethge, "Bonhoeffer's Christology and His 'Religionless Christianity,'" *Union Seminary Theological Quarterly* 23, no. 1 (fall 1967): 61–77.

Its dominion is absolute. . . . The void engulfs life, history, family, nation, language, faith. The list can be prolonged indefinitely.[17]

There is a case for believing that sadly the study of inter-war Germany helps us understand what is now happening elsewhere in the West and beyond, again something that cannot be pursued here.[18] What worried Bonhoeffer was the concomitant collapse of Christianity and the collapse of "natural" structures, such as family and government. This phenomenon, and our observation of it, has become more familiar in the decades since Bonhoeffer wrote. His response to it, however, merits our serious interest.

Rightly or wrongly, Bonhoeffer was implicated in a plot to assassinate Hitler and found that whereas church members were cravenly capitulating to the Führer, a number of unchurched people, concerned in all integrity for justice, truth, and freedom, were upholding principles and values that Christians ought to hold dear. These folk, he found, could be drawn some way toward, and were not distant from, Jesus Christ. Bonhoeffer remarked that in a time of such crisis and peril, it is found not that Christianity must prove that it measures up to certain standards of justice, truth, and freedom. These standards have publicly collapsed. It is "not Christ who must justify himself before the world by the acknowledgement of the values of justice, truth and freedom, but it is these values which have come to need justification, and their justification can only be by Jesus Christ" (59). Things have somewhat changed since Bonhoeffer wrote, and committed Christians and atheists alike often balk at talk of canons of justice, for instance, in anything like a universal or normative sense, as they do at talk of "the reasonable," of which Bonhoeffer also speaks, or of the "natural."[19] He appears to belong to another era when he avers, "There seems to be a general unconscious knowledge which, in the hour of ultimate peril, leads everything which desires not to fall victim to the Antichrist to take refuge with Christ" (56). Yet what Bonhoeffer says about those who pursue justice,

17. Dietrich Bonhoeffer, *Ethics* (New York: Macmillan, 1965), 105ff. Page references to this work are placed in the body of the text from now on.

18. See, e.g., Allan Bloom, "The German Connection," in *The Closing of the American Mind* (New York: Simon & Schuster, 1987), 141ff.; or Nigel M. de S. Cameron, *The New Medicine* (London: Hodder & Stoughton, 1991). Elton Trueblood's *The Predicament of Modern Man* (New York: Harper & Row, 1944) still merits careful reading in this connection. Huntemann himself is eloquent on this point though we suspend judgment here on the merits of his contentions.

19. Even if we are justified in balking at the language, it would be a pity if we missed the depth and force that inform a sentiment like this, expressed in *Ethics:* "One is distressed by the failure of reasonable people to perceive either the depths of evil or the depths of the holy" (65).

truth, and freedom, and about the nature of that pursuit, is abidingly important.

In his *Ethics,* he makes a distinction between the ultimate and the penultimate. The ultimate is the justification of the sinner *sola gratia,* received *sola fide.* But Christ is Lord of, present in, and returning to a world spoiled by poverty, injustice, and hunger. The attempted rectification of such an order is our mandatory task, and the zealous quest for its establishment is no deviation from the business of proclaiming grace. On the contrary:

> There are conditions of the heart, of life and of the world which impede the reception of grace in a special way, namely by rendering faith infinitely difficult. . . . For him who is cast into utter shame, desolation, poverty and helplessness, it is difficult to have faith in the justice and goodness of God. For him whose life has become prey to disorder and indiscipline, it will be difficult to hear the commandments of God in faith. . . . The hungry man needs bread and the homeless man needs a roof; the dispossessed need justice and the lonely need fellowship; the undisciplined need order and the slave needs freedom. (136)

So, far from denying the need for faith, Bonhoeffer expresses things in a way that would infuriate many people if it came from the lips of evangelicals: They care for bodies only in order to get at souls. But the words do not demonstrate all the angles of Bonhoeffer's approach.[20] Broadly speaking, we are being presented with the task of the preservation, restoration, and renewal of the natural order, the task of a proper Christian humanism. By the time the letters from prison had been written, it seemed to be not only *a* task but *the* vital task. And its dimensions were large. Bonhoeffer's ruminations on the form of Christ's lordship over a world in which people are no longer religious, taken along with the overall thrust of his work, show that Bonhoeffer is not regarding the accomplishment of such a task as merely instrumental to having faith, as though faith alone were all that really mattered. Bonhoeffer speaks as strongly as any in the tradition of Luther of the paramount place of faith. Yet in concentrating his thought relentlessly on Jesus Christ, Lord of all, who must return to a world over which he has claims and for whose advent we must prepare, his thought takes a distinctive turn. Truth, justice, and freedom matter intrinsically to Jesus Christ. Those who love and practice them must be claimed for him, for they are

---

20. Anglo-Saxons will often identify a typically Germanic dialectical cast of mind and form of expression in Bonhoeffer's writing that can render quotation invidious and summary difficult.

claimed by him.[21] Put this together with the description of our task of preservation, restoration, and renewal, and we find that Bonhoeffer's program of Christian humanism aims, let us dare to say, at a kind of moralization of humankind.

Now, clearly Bonhoeffer had to tread with the most delicate of steps here, and we need to hasten slowly lest the word *moralization* settle too quickly in the reader's mind. It appears to announce a breach with the gospel, which surely disestablishes all human righteousness in order to enable the receipt of divine righteousness. It is a gospel that summons us out of vaunted morality into faith. How can a son of Luther commission us with the task of moral edification?[22] There were risks here, but he stood in the tradition of that greater verbal virtuoso who was never prone to hide reality under a bushel for the sake of the safe form of words. So Bonhoeffer would have aligned himself with the words that he read on a postcard sent by a friend in February 1943, quoting none other than the man himself, Martin Luther. "A Christian is a strange bird, would to God that most of us were good pagans who keep the natural law—to say nothing of the Christian law."[23] In his *Letters and Papers,* Bonhoeffer says, "Kierkegaard said that today Luther would say the opposite of what he said then. I think he was right—with some reservations."[24] Bonhoeffer believed that we misunderstand justification *sola fide* if we think it entails divine displeasure toward the pursuit of justice, truth, and freedom outside the church and toward its practitioners irrespective, or in the midst of, their engagement in this pursuit. The Reformation talked of Christ and the sinner; what of Christ and the good man? Bonhoeffer is objecting to the belief that one must tear down human striving for justice, the virtues of human courage, and so on in a bid to identify all people as sinners who are to be saved *sola gratia.*

This needs to be appropriated with sober care. I take as nonnegotiable the beliefs that "all have sinned and fall short of the glory of God" (Rom. 3:23 NIV) and that the gospel summons all people indiscriminately to repentance, faith, and salvation in Christ alone. At the same time, we must insist that justice, truth, and freedom, as Christians understand them, are precious to a God of holiness and of goodness; that

21. See the way in which Bonhoeffer tried to formulate this with the aid of the Synoptic texts: "He that is not against us is for us" and "He that is not with me is against me" (*Ethics,* 57).

22. "Concretely, two things are called penultimate in relation to the justification of the sinner by grace, namely being man and being good" (*Ethics,* 134).

23. Quoted in Eberhard Bethge, *Dietrich Bonhoeffer* (New York: Harper & Row, 1970), 619.

24. Bonhoeffer, *Letters and Papers,* 123.

he cannot, without inconsistency, condemn their pursuit and preservation; that the natural order is under severest threat in and beyond the West today; and that those who contend for it are to be welcomed as such contenders. Resistance to the destruction of the natural is precisely what God is calling us to in his world when his own divine and holy order, which sustains humanity, is engulfed by dire threat. It is in this light we should interpret the ruminations that gave birth to the notion of religionless Christianity, although there is admittedly more going on there than that. The humanizing of men and women and the edification of natural goodness are appropriate Christian responsibilities; in a world come of age, Bonhoeffer seems to make them our central responsibilities.[25] Far from displacing the gospel, this project is supposed to establish it in terms of a message and mandate that humanity needs.

The dangerous waters that swirl about the text of the *Letters and Papers* need to be charted in relation to their tributary sources in the *Ethics* (and, indeed, previous work). The deeper thrust of Bonhoeffer's thinking in the *Ethics* is toward an enrichment, not denigration, of Christ and of justification. We need a theology of justification that maintains the essential Reformation discovery but fearlessly grants a profound biblical realism to Bonhoeffer's insights. Indeed, if we are in the habit of reading thinkers according to their better part (scriptural part, as evangelicals have it), what Bonhoeffer has to say is absolutely vital. For the benefit of hardened theologians, one could advocate a dialogue between the theology of Abraham Kuyper and Dietrich Bonhoeffer as one way in to the discussion of all this.[26] For the benefit of the saner, one simply advocates that we ponder sympathetically and urgently the insights and proposals of Bonhoeffer at a time of civilizational collapse.

For the collapse coming in the train of the current destruction of the "natural" is terrifying. One example among many: Discussions on the sexual needs of children and intimacies between humans and animals occasionally break the public surface in ways that are ominous for the future. These things have a period of subterranean incubation first, but undercurrents seem to be flowing rapidly. In our situation, any person concerned for the natural—for justice, truth, and goodness—is more the ally of the church than its foe. The gospel of saving grace need not be compromised one whit; rather, we should be clear on what we are

25. One must interpret carefully, as ever, but it is disquieting to read Bonhoeffer's negative comments about "evangelizing intention" in this context. See the letter of 30 April 1944.

26. Huntemann takes steps toward it but exaggerates the proximity of Kuyper's view of common grace to Bonhoeffer's thinking (*Dietrich Bonhoeffer*, 80ff., 97ff.).

saving people to and for. It is not heaven alone, for God is Lord of the earth and its fulness. We should not fear that the cultivation of moral consciousness and the celebration of extra-Christian goodness weaken the claims of Christ's gospel. The higher in our estimation the glory of Christ, the greater our celebration of fidelity and compassion, justice and truth without, as well as within, the Christian community. Many Pharisees apparently failed to recognize extra-Pharisaical goodness because it was adrift from orthodoxy. We are altogether encouraged by the biblical narratives to maintain that encounter with Christ can mean submission of human goodness to his service; its transformation, not destruction, by acknowledgment of its origin and Lord; and its glad relocation in the sphere in which you are saved by grace alone, appropriated by faith alone, so that the recipient knows that all things good and true whatsoever are to be wrought only in God and by God. And we should gladly fling aside all reference to human goodness if it for one moment negates the *sola gratia* and *sola fide*.

But what precisely are the implications of all this for theological method? Superficially, they are quite mundane, immediately amounting just to the reminder that experience and discernment of life and of our times, when rooted in the habit of faithfulness to Christ and to Scripture, must be allowed to shape our interpretation of the biblical kerygma. More specifically, we should say two things. First, there is a neglected text in the Book of Hebrews: "But solid food is for the mature, who by constant use have trained themselves to distinguish good from evil" (5:14 NIV). We might instantly think the text pregnant with possibilities for our thinking about Christian ethics, but it is more useful than that. It tells us that insight comes from life and conflict, and it suggests that discernment of Christ's work, spirit, and lordship is acquired in the context of sensitivity to the good and the evil. Methodologically, this is important, and Bonhoeffer's thought shows just how and why. Second, it is particularly apt for us self-styled evangelicals to take this to heart. For many evangelicals, exegesis suffices for understanding. The life of Christian obedience is commanded, but it has little or no hermeneutical significance. Involvement in God's world is not a condition for understanding what Scripture says about that world. In such a context, Bonhoeffer's integration of thought and life constitutes a momentous proposal that we have got this badly wrong. If as penitents we need to move from the individual to the church, so as parasites (on Bonhoeffer) we need to move from ecclesial ghettos to the world.

It was intimated earlier that it is an open question whether or not Bonhoeffer should have been politically complicit in the way he was. We can conscientiously opine that by the time his authorship ended he had come closer to losing the church than to finding it. But only in the world could Bonhoeffer learn of Christ and the world, and there he is our teacher. His particular enterprise does not only constitute a challenge to deepen our understanding of justification. It not only constitutes an imperative to keep hammering away at the question of church and world. It also constitutes a claim about theological method whose force is only felt when we see what immersion in the world does to the character and fabric of theological thinking. Plenty of others may teach us what Bonhoeffer does, but the course of Western history since the collapse of the Weimar Republic bids us listen to him with some care and heightens our sense of urgency in relation to Christ and the natural. Discussion of the task and method of theology is futile unless informed by such a sense of urgency.

For the Future: Small-Time Prophecy

Those who have read up to this point may well have already couched their thoughts in prophetic terms. So far, we have been reconceiving the theological task and appropriating Bonhoeffer's thought. Actually, it will be said, success in such tasks will lead to the attenuation of evangelical theology as such. For there has been nothing evangelical about the proposals and evangelical identity being merged into a wider scheme of things. That is a grim prospect. Worse than placing questions of theological method rather too close to the boundaries of discussion is the crime of expelling evangelical theology over the borders altogether.

A combative response to this objection comes to mind in the form of the words of Samuel Taylor Coleridge. "He who begins by loving Christianity better than Truth, will proceed by loving his own Sect or Church better than Christianity and end in loving himself better than all."[27] Fraught as these words are with multiple possibilities of interpretation, Coleridge was nevertheless more right than reckless. Jesus commended himself to his disciples as the Truth and invoked the witness of the Father and the Spirit. Coleridge's words do not entail the denial that Truth and Christianity are one. The conceptual distinction is stated in order to get at the psychology of people's religious adherence. Nor do they entail the a priori impossibility that a sect or church should appropriate that truth and that faith aright, as far as is humanly possible and as far as we can humanly tell. Again, the words are putting the spotlight on the psychology of adherence to particular traditions. Evangelical-

27. Samuel Taylor Coleridge, *Aids to Reflection* (London: Pickering, 1836), Aphorism XXV.

ism, like any worthy religious tradition, is interested in the truth, the whole truth, and nothing but the truth. Suppose that evangelicals had got all their theology right except on the matter of Sabbath observance. Then a theology of the Sabbath would be *the* subject for theological development and reflection. This principle holds even for wild hypothetical cases; if evangelicals had got everything right except that they failed to appreciate the religious value of Gothic architecture, then let us concentrate on architecture. However, we seem to be leaping out of the frying pan of the combative into the fire of the trivial, so another approach is in order.

The term *evangelical* commonly signifies a distinction, particularly a doctrinal one. This misleads us all too often into equating the distinctive with the essential. For example, we believe that all life and thought must be grounded in the twin injunctions to love God and neighbor. Yet if one were asked, "What do evangelicals believe?" and answered, "Essentially in the love of God and neighbor," it would be puzzling. Why should we not so answer? Because, we think, these do not constitute distinctives. Non-evangelical liberals, non-Christian theists, non-theistic adherents of other faiths, and nonreligious humanists may affirm one or both of these commandments. Of course, we will say that a description in terms of love of God and neighbor is inadequate rather than false. If one were allowed to spell out their meaning, one would come up with what is distinctively evangelical. That is true enough. But it remains that the word *evangelical* in practice, if not in principle, has a polemical definition whether we think in terms of the Protestant Reformation or modern evangelical-liberal differences. This means that we have often concentrated our thought on what makes us distinctive. And this has frequently, though not always, resulted in attending more to dogmatic than to moral theology or, if you prefer, doctrine rather than ethics. There are great resources for moral theology in the traditions stemming from the Protestant Reformation, and certainly there is contemporary literature on Christian ethics from the evangelical stable. Yet, however dangerous it is to generalize, it seems that our ethical thought is proportionately underdeveloped in relation to our doctrinal thought.

In light of this, it is interesting to read a prophecy uttered at the end of the nineteenth century by one whose feet were as firmly on the ground as any. In lectures he delivered in 1897, the great Scottish theologian James Orr granted that work still needed to be done in the area of doctrinal theology. But he concluded:

> If, however, I were asked in what I think the distinctive peculiarity of twentieth-century Christianity will lie, I should answer that it is not in

any new or overwhelmingly brilliant discovery in theology that I look for it. The lines of doctrine are by this time well and surely established. But the Church has another and yet more difficult task before it, if it is to retain its ascendancy over the minds of men. That task is to bring Christianity to bear as an applied power on the life and conditions of society; to set itself as it has never yet done to master the meaning of the "mind of Christ," and to achieve the translation of that mind into the whole practical life of the age—into laws, institutions, commerce, literature, art; into domestic, civic, social and political relations; into national and international doings—in this sense to bring in the Kingdom of God among men. I look to the twentieth century to be an era of Christian Ethic even more than of Christian Theology.[28]

As a matter of fact, Orr's work portends more theological development than this quotation indicates. And it is not difficult in the present climate to prophesy the continued importance of theological debate over the key doctrines of God and Scripture, the discipline of hermeneutics forging a vital connection between the discussions. Whatever else one is doing, one is not decrying the significance of ongoing consideration of classical doctrinal themes. Nevertheless, and without asking whether Orr's prophecy came true in the last century, there is much to be said for the claim that we need to concentrate our energies on the production of a social ethic in this one.

This is contestable on more fronts than one, particularly if we attend to those who emphasize that it is the responsibility of the church to be church, to concentrate on the dynamics of its community life, and thus to *be* a social ethic rather than *have* one for the world.[29] The issues involved here need more sifting than we have space available. What we need to say is that while love extends beyond the bounds of the Christian community, we must attend to worldly structures just as an expression of that love. Certainly the ecclesia is our concern. Certainly it may be that the best way to attend to the world is by attending to the ecclesia. But neither of those things should obscure the fact that the neighbor, and therefore the world, is one of the two points of religious orientation specified by Jesus.[30] This is, indeed, to

28. James Orr, *The Progress of Dogma* (London: Hodder & Stoughton, 1901), 383.

29. Stanley Hauerwas is particularly influential here. Samuel Wells has recently tried to capture his thought in *Transforming Fate into Destiny: The Theological Ethics of Stanley Hauerwas* (Carlisle: Paternoster, 1998), and note the significantly different sort of treatment given in Arne Rasmusson's work, *The Church as Polis* (Lund, Swed.: Lund University Press, 1994).

30. In another place, we should examine whether love of neighbor is not the logical basis for love of the brethren. Further, we should point out that there are important obligations toward the nonhuman creation.

fail to put things theocentrically and Christocentrically enough: Our friends Kuyper and Bonhoeffer would swiftly tell us that. In these questions, it is important to recover a sense of the dimensions of reformation that shaped the thoroughgoing endeavors of Zwingli, Calvin, Bucer, and Knox. The changed situation in relation to Church and State, and the decline of Christianity in Europe, makes it easy to overlook the way in which concern for the whole city or nation, not ecclesia alone, drove their work. Their situation is not ours, and perhaps they were significantly mistaken, as Anabaptists and others will maintain. But the scope of both our heart's concern and our action cannot be less than theirs.

The need for a social ethic in whatever form is connected to the reasons for the rejection of Christianity. These are many and complex, of course, but perhaps the most widely voiced criticism is that Christianity has deleterious social effects, oppressive and intolerant as it is. Because its truth claims are held to have had this impact historically, our direct discussion of its truth claims often yields less than we tend to hope, as its perceived social performance militates against my claim for its truth. The ability of Christianity to formulate a fresh social ethic in contemporary society will surely play a large part in its self-commendation. We are bound to be far less sanguine than Orr was about the social prospects, one hundred years on, yet we can and should own his prophecy, or at least his hope.

From a point of view in (generally) Western experience, we know how widespread is practical atheism and that its modern, post-Christian nature makes it a novelty and not just a return to the paganism of the ancient world. In the nineteenth century, Friedrich Nietzsche trumpeted forth the death of God, an accomplished fact whose implications only he could really see. But there are divine aftereffects. "After Buddha was dead, his shadow was still shown for centuries in a cave—a tremendous, gruesome shadow. God is dead; but given the way of men, there may still be caves for thousands of years in which his shadow will be shown. And we—we still have to vanquish his shadow too."[31] The darkest part of the shadow is Christian morality. So Nietzsche set about a revaluation of all values that made the individual the creator of values.

The extent of Nietzsche's influence is enormous, and one must always pay heed to what he says.[32] Shortly after the words quoted, he

31. Friedrich Nietzsche, *The Gay Science* (New York: Random House, 1974), III.108.

32. At random, see the various statements noted by Robert B. Pippin, *Modernism as a Philosophical Problem: On the Dissatisfactions of European High Culture* (Cambridge, Mass.: Blackwell, 1991), 84. Alasdair MacIntyre has described Nietzsche as "the moral philosopher of the present age" (*After Virtue* [London: Duckworth, 1981], 107).

makes a lapidary remark of great import. "What is now decisive against Christianity is our taste, no longer our reasons."[33] The force of this should not be lost on those who wonder whether he is reading, and is right in reading, the story of Western anti-Christianity as a move from rational to aesthetic objections. For in directing us here and now to the question of taste, Nietzsche hits the modern nail on the head. The taste of our day is a taste for autonomy or autarchy with a corresponding distaste for the principle and content of imposed authority unless, perhaps, it is a practical social necessity. What happens in the world between today and tomorrow is unknown to us, and so few of us dare strictly prophesy. But it looks as though our present situation calls for both a social ethic and a restoration of taste   a restoration of taste, we may hope, in the train of the formulation of a coherent and fruitful ethic. Let us hope that the church is not overwhelmed by opposition before it can undertake much of the task.

Of course, we are being one-sided here. The aspiration to social reconstruction must be set in the context of our responsibilities in worship, evangelism, and the edification of the church. Systematic theology grounded in sound theological method is still important. But those who have an eye on the Christian contribution to worldly life know that a theological method is called for that is different from the one we customarily use in the construction of conceptual schemes. After expending all our energy and rigorous thought on social questions, we shall yet cry out to heaven for a word from God in guidance. What some will call intuition, what all will hope is the leading of the Spirit, is necessary. So it is the task of theology to bring the church to the place where the voice of God may be heard. It will position people in relation to God even more than it will coordinate statements in relation to each other. Its principle will be service more than system. It would rather change the world without quite understanding it than understand the world without changing it. Methodologically, it will have as its first principle the use of Scripture in order to make sure that the Spirit can communicate to the church what the Scriptures do not directly contain.

So we are back with things raised in the first two sections. We are back, too, with our first three quotations. Theological accomplishment will in the future happen largely in the valley of growing persecution, a phenomenon that in its way forced Bonhoeffer, who endured suffering, to reflect on the place of words today. It will happen only in the flight from materialism as Cone, like many others, has said. It will happen,

33. Nietzsche, *Gay Science,* III.132.

as Luther knew as well as anyone, only in the communion of Christ. In-scribed on the banner of its enterprise will be something like the words of Abraham Kuyper: "There is not a square inch in the whole domain of our human existence over which Christ, who is Sovereign over *all*, does not say: 'Mine.'"[34]

34. From the inaugural address at the Free University in Amsterdam, 20 October 1880, in James Bratt, ed., *Abraham Kuyper: A Centennial Reader* (Grand Rapids: Eerd-mans; Carlisle: Paternoster, 1998), 461.

Part 4
Responses

7

Maintaining Evangelical Theology

J. I. Packer

Christian theology is an art, as it is also a craft, and a science, and a mode of wisdom. As an art, it is both fine and useful, and when well-done, it has a doxological elegance that is all its own. As a craft, it calls for strategy, tactics, and technique, plus a workmanlike discipline within recognized parameters. As a science, it requires scrupulous attention to all relevant facts and an understanding of theory formation that lets those facts confirm or correct its proposals. As a mode of wisdom (that is, of insight into the right way to live with God in his world), it necessitates spiritual and pastoral discernment—qualities, alas, that are not always in evidence in theological discussions. Theology is thus an exacting study, in which it is easy to fall short.

To explore, then, the state and task of evangelical theology today from the standpoint of method, as the essays in this book do in their different ways, is an instructive exercise, provocative, corrective, and directive by turns. Conference papers, which the essays originally were, cannot cover all the ground in treatise fashion, but if they start us thinking in ways that to some of us, at any rate, are new, they will serve us well. My remarks here are meant only to establish the wavelength we must tune in on if we are to benefit from these soundings.

Our starting point has to be a recognition that because Christianity is unlike any other religion in this world, Christian theology is correspondingly different from any other intellectual enterprise, not only in its content but also, indeed primarily, in its aims and method. To explain this, let me pose and sketchily answer three basic questions.

The Marks of Christianity

First, What is distinctive about Christianity?

Christianity is the world religion that grew two millennia ago out of the life, death, resurrection, and ascension of Jesus of Nazareth and the Pentecostal outpouring of the Holy Spirit. The identity of the individual Christian, and of the Christian church (which is one but takes form here on earth in the multitude of Christian churches that are its outcrops), lies in a relationship to Jesus, the incarnate Son of God, that has in it faith, repentance, love, hope, joy, obedience, gratitude, self-denial, crossbearing, and worship—in other words, a relationship with the divine one who is at once teacher, rescuer, master, and friend. This relationship has been verbalized in different ways at different times against different cultural backgrounds, and a certain internal pluriformity has developed in the world church—Roman Catholicism, Eastern Orthodoxy, and Reformational Protestantism being the main types, with various subtypes, ethnic, theological, and ideological, within each. But the constant core has been a cluster of convictions—Christological, soteriological, trinitarian, ecclesiological, and eschatological—that are based on, exhibited in, and vindicated by the canonical New Testament. This convictional continuity warrants the claim that under God Christianity is both transcultural and (if a word from the kitchen may be used here) self-cleaning, for when Christianity goes out of shape, resources in due course appear from within itself to overcome error and reform (re-form!) what has become disordered.

Nothing in other world religions is anything like the Christian belief in a tri-personal God in whose saving work the Father, the Son, and the Holy Spirit act as a team. Wholly without parallel are the Christian contentions that, in John Betjeman's phrase, God was man in Palestine, where he died and rose, and that he lives as man to all eternity; and that he imparts a salvation that first to last is a gift of grace—God's Riches At Christ's Expense, as the Sunday school acronym puts it— freely bestowed on those who deserve from God only rejection. Where non-Christian religions say, work for life, Christianity says, admit that you cannot secure life by working and learn to receive it as a free gift. Nor, again, do non-Christian faiths contain anything matching the claim that the church is God's new humanity, an international society of sinners re-created in Christ. All these beliefs are unique to Christianity, springing from faith in Jesus Christ as God and Savior.

Evangelical Christians sometimes speak of the evangelical church and evangelical people as if evangelicalism were something entirely distinct from the rest of the professing Christian world. Some who call themselves fundamentalists (as distinct from the near half billion worldwide who are labeled fundamentalists by their critics) actually seem to believe this. Most evangelicals, however, see such talk as misleading. To be sure, evangelicalism is an identifiable form of Protestant Christianity. Rooted in Reformational theology, Puritan-type pietism, and eighteenth- and nineteenth-century ideals of evangelistic outreach, evangelicalism appears in all mainline denominations and is the accepted norm in quite a number. John Stackhouse's essay notes the chief emphases that distinguish it: the centrality of Christ as mediator and of his cross as the basis of forgiveness and justification; the authority of a trusted Bible; the need for regeneration and conversion, that complex work of inner renewal that Paul denominates *calling;* and the priority of evangelistic and church-planting mission. But these emphases mark mainstream Christianity across the board, more or less. All evangelicals could claim is that they maintain them more insistently and consistently than do others.

And that is what evangelicals do in fact claim. They hold that, far from being marginal in relation to the larger Christian world, they are in fact at its center, upholding mainstream Christian faith in a way that is demonstrably more biblical than any alternative. It is true that during the first half of the last century, when the rules of cross-traditional dialogue were being worked out under ecumenical auspices, evangelicals were for the most part left out of the conversation. That is understandable in light of the hammering evangelicals took in the mainline churches as liberals gained leadership, and of the liberals' certainty that classic evangelicalism had nothing to give to the Christian future, being intellectually untenable, backward-looking, censorious, and divisive. (I remember hearing exactly that said when I became a Christian—an evangelical, in fact—in 1944.)

Today, however, evangelicals regularly converse with Christians of other stripes. Evangelical theological scholars flock to the meetings of the professional guilds in their various fields, and evangelical spokespeople at all levels seek to share what, as they see it, they hold in trust for the rest of God's people, recognizing that because values are scattered in our fragmented Christian world, they may have something to learn as well as something to give in these exchanges. Undeniably, the worldwide multichurch charismatic renewal has made some of these

exchanges easier by prioritizing Christ-centered life over all forms of
ecclesiasticism—and it should be remembered that the origin and essence of that renewal itself is a mutation of historic evangelical pietism.
Generally, then, involvement in the wider theological community, without loss of identity or compromise of conviction, is a mark of evangelicalism today, and who would deny the healthiness of this trend?

The conclusion is that evangelical distinctives, both of emphasis and
of variant conviction, do not set evangelicals apart from the rest of the
Christian world in the way that Christian convictions as such set that
world apart from all the worlds formed by other faiths.

The Marks of Christian Theology

On, then, to our second question: What are the characteristic marks
of Christian theology?

Theology (the *logos*, meaning account, of *theos*, meaning God) exists
wherever people speak of God. Thus, there is Jewish theology, Muslim
theology, Sikh theology, and so on. Christian theology focuses on the
Triune Creator-Redeemer of Christian faith. In this Christian context,
theology has become an umbrella term for a wide spectrum of intellectual endeavors, all aimed on the one hand at establishing churches and
guiding Christians in ways of belief and behavior, life and work, mission and ministry, thought and speech that truly reflect and express
God's redemptive revelation, and on the other hand at straightening
out sin-twisted lives and life patterns through applying that same truth
in evangelism, nurture, education, and culture criticism. The noun
theologian is usually reserved for those who as teachers, writers, and resource specialists pursue these concerns at a technically competent
professional level, though every Christian is perforce a theologian of
sorts, and as Stephen Williams indicates, it is most desirable that as
many Christians as possible share in the theological life of the church.

In theology, as in every intellectual pursuit in this world, the mere
advancement of learning, pushing out the walls of human knowledge,
exerts a constant fascination in and of itself, and there are always some
in the theological guilds whose interest goes no farther. But it is vital
to realize that truth is for people, and therefore, the pastoral function
of theology is ultimately primary. Professional theologians should be
winning their spurs as pastors no less than as scholars. Augustine,
bishop of Hippo and theologian extraordinaire, would remind us that
the goal of theology as science *(scientia)* is to lead us to wisdom for living *(sapientia),* and when the sixteenth-century Puritan William Per-
kins defined theology as the science of living blessedly forever—a practical science, therefore, as he and his fellow Puritans never tired of

insisting—he was right on Augustine's wavelength. The supreme skill in the art and craft of theology is to link the theoretical and cognitive aspects of God's revealed truth with its practical and transformative aspects in an unbreakable bond. For God shows himself to us and tells us about himself so that we may not just know of him but know him relationally in a life-changing way and taste the full joy of that knowledge in our fellowship with the Father and with his Son, Jesus Christ.

Throughout Christendom up to the eighteenth century, theology was seen as a single many-sided activity; those called theologians were exegetes and Bible teachers, expositors and vindicators of dogma, pastors and physicians of the soul, all in one. Today, however, the theological disciplines have been separated out in the universities and seminaries where theology is taught, and in the publishing programs that feed and are fed by the technicians in each department. With this, the disciplines themselves have become more complex so that it is hardly possible for individuals to have an expert acquaintance with all that goes on in their own fields, let alone with all the disciplines together in the manner of Augustine, Aquinas, Luther, Calvin, or the seventeenth-century polymaths. The disciplines in question include exegesis, which now involves hermeneutics (principles of interpretation, semantics, semiotics, and the study of communication and rhetoric); biblical theology; church history framed by the historical theology that it yields; dogmatic, symbolic, and systematic theology; ethics, which takes a student into many fields of secular learning; apologetics and philosophical theology, both requiring that one should have logical theory at one's fingertips; liturgics; missiology and ecumenics; spiritual, ascetic, moral, or devotional theology (the study of communion with God); and poimenics or practical theology (the study of all forms of pastoral care). Daunting as it sounds, we who feel swamped by this proliferation of complexities must face the fact that competence in our craft requires some thoughtful acquaintance, however sketchy, with each of them. The old tag, that pastors must keep reading, seems truer than ever today.

The first authentic mark of Christian theology, then, is its embrace of Paul's twin goals: The church should ever be "the pillar and bulwark of the truth" (1 Tim. 3:15 RSV), and it should ever be laboring to "present [everyone] mature in Christ" (Col. 1:28 RSV). The second mark involves taking responsible ownership of the wide range of studies described above and aiming at full competence in them all, for the furthering of the stated goals. The third mark is its direct engagement with its own heritage, which it sees as embodying divine discernment and wisdom as well as human blindness and folly; with the secular and pagan crosscurrents of thought that swirl around the church, eroding its faith and offering alternative ideals for life; and supremely with the Bible, in which resources for tackling all these tasks are found. Theology in which these features fail in any measure to appear is to that extent less than authentically Christian.

How well does evangelical theology measure up to these criteria? It has long been thought that, as an activist movement with a pietist value system, evangelicalism characteristically undervalues theology, and as Alister McGrath notes, a jeremiad on the decay of evangelical theology in North America has recently emerged from the ranks and made considerable waves. But the truth appears to be that in intensity of engagement with Scripture, with modern and postmodern aberrations, with the evangelistic and pastoral task, and with the implications of historic Christian orthodoxy for today, evangelicalism as a whole is strong, certainly in North America, seemingly in other places too, and if anything is getting stronger. Could it be that God is grooming evangelicalism for leadership in the new millennium? It appears that way.

The Marks of Christian Theological Method

Our third question picks up from the second: In light of what has been said, how should we describe the authentic Christian theological method, or methods, for today? Since, as must by now be plain, I see evangelicalism as true mainstream Christianity, in relation to which all forms of non-evangelicalism are sub-evangelical and eccentric, I shall direct my answer specifically to evangelicals, with the hope that others too might find it relevant.

What I have written so far, along with the other essays in this book, suggests five principles that should guide our practice of theology in the twenty-first century.

First, maintain the trajectories, or, putting the point in golf slang, keep your eye on the ball. In theology, as we saw, the focus of the questions asked and the thrust of the answers given must ever, on the one hand, further the faith, penitence, holiness, righteousness, and Christlikeness of sinners (the aretegenic task, as Ellen Charry calls it) and, on the other hand, maintain, explore, and vindicate historic supernaturalist Christian orthodoxy (the apologetic task, as classically conceived), which skeptical critics both outside and inside the church are constantly chipping away at. The liberation theologies (socioeconomic, feminist, and black), the process theology with its growing God, and the range of syncretistic theologies that confront us today have lost these trajectories to a significant degree, for they have in effect displaced the Christ of Scripture from his central and determinative place in both. We must not let that happen in our own theology.

Second, maintain the organism—that is, keep theology intact. Centrifugal fragmentation, the fruit of specialization whereby, as we saw, one comes to know more and more about less and less, is the way of the modern academic world and is likely to continue to be so. It is crucially important that tomorrow's theology buck this trend. Systematicians must exegete Scripture, keep up with biblical theology, and weigh the implications of their views for ethics, spiritual life, and pastoral care. Exegetes must build bridges linking the Bible world with our own, making possible a surefooted application of Bible teaching to the life of today's church. Pastors and spiritual guides must know enough about the aretegenic theology of the church's past to discern the values and correct the lopsidednesses of yesterday's devotional models, and so work toward genuinely nourishing patterns of praise and prayer for our time. And so on. As was said above, the only safe and sound way of pursuing particular interests in theology is within the frame of at least a general working knowledge of the other theological disciplines. Only when the entire organism of theology is recognized and kept in view will wisdom result from specialist work.

Third, maintain constant dialogue with the Bible, "God's Word written" as the Anglican Articles call it. The Bible is, in Calvin's phrase, the scepter of God, the instrument of divine rule, whereby the Father and the Son personally and authoritatively communicate with us through the Spirit, instructing, enlightening, feeding, warning, forming, assuring, encouraging, and equipping us for every form of service to God and our fellow human beings. Evangelicals know this and have proved it to be so in experience. To them the variegated literary sprawl that is Holy Scripture is, as the moderator of the Church of Scotland declares in Britain's coronation service, "the most valuable thing that this world affords." To evangelicals, therefore, the to-and-fro of searching Scripture and finding in it answers to their questions is the heart of theological life and work. The witness of the Holy Spirit to the divine authority of Scripture, which Calvin affirmed so categorically, is sometimes spoken of as if it were prior to, and distinct from, the illumination of the Spirit whereby the theological contents of Scripture are understood. But it is not. The witness of the Spirit and the spiritual understanding go together and come to us together. Those who want to be credible when affirming the former must have a convincing way of affirming the latter. In this connection Kevin Vanhoozer's hermeneutically driven, dynamically structured proposal of a dramatic model for this ongoing dialogue, in which God performs his communicative action through the text and his devotees perform what they hear and see as canonical wisdom, merits serious attention. Losing the ability to listen to the Bible, whether through strength of preoccupation, as typically with liberals, or through lack of imagination, as (so says Vanhoozer) sometimes with evangelicals, is the ruin of theology. It would be a supreme tragedy should we lapse at that point.

Fourth, maintain constant dialogue with the culture, with a view to fulfilling Paul's agenda to "destroy arguments and every proud obstacle to the knowledge of God, and take every thought captive to obey Christ" (2 Cor. 10:5 RSV). Christian theology is not just for in-house consumption; it must ever be used to persuade the world. But for this aspect of our theological task, we need to be clear on our own faith, and with that on two things more. We must know the ideas that are being spread and institutionalized around us today at all levels, from highest culture to lowest pop. We must also see that community thinking always moves forward to some next thing that is supposedly better (truer, wiser, more useful, more helpful) than the last thing. As a result, we must present the gospel, not as a way back to yesterday, but as a way that points forward from today's world, the world of postmodernism, postfoundationalism, post-Christianity, and potent paganism, to a richer and more rational future for all who turn to Christ. Stanley Grenz urges that we shall be better placed to do this if as trinitarian, communitarian (meaning, churchly), and eschaton-oriented believers we reposition ourselves clearheadedly in a Pannenbergian type of coherentism. This suggestion differs from Vanhoozer's, though there is some overlap, but like Vanhoozer's it deserves to be thoroughly discussed. And in any case, theology must always be watchful lest anything in the church's way of stating the gospel reduce rather than enhance its credibility in our benighted modern world.

Fifth, maintain constant dialogue with non-evangelical theology, both Roman Catholic and Orthodox (where mutual dissent on the church and salvation is framed by substantial agreement on most else) and liberal Protestant (where on most matters of faith there is disagreement, while on the ramifications of the second great commandment evangelicals are often outshone). The fact that all who know and trust the Christ of Scripture are brothers and sisters in one family, and that the trinitarian model of personal identity is one of total openness, makes separatist isolation from other sorts of Christians indefensible for the individual, whatever may be necessary at the denominational level. In the divided visible church, values are scattered, and we gain as well as give by fraternizing with persons and exploring books for public discussion that convictionally are not entirely where we are.

So to conclude, these essays should be seen as a sample—no more, no less—of what is coming nowadays from evangelical centers of theological learning. Contrary to what some have imagined, the collection surely shows that evangelical theology enters the new millennium alive and well and raring to go on a number of fronts. The essays themselves are more stocktaking than they are anything else, but stocktaking is preparation for future trading, and these particular stocktakings hint at many good things to come. Take note, and stay tuned.

8

Imagining Evangelical Theology

TREVOR HART

It may be helpful to begin by setting my response in a context, and thereby account for those particular themes in the book that grabbed my attention and provoked the flow of my own thoughts. As several of the essays in this volume make clear, the task of responsible reading (whether of Scripture, tradition, or a collection of essays) is one that involves the reader in an active (and therefore responsible) rather than a purely passive role. We need not capitulate to the wilder excesses of some reader-response models of interpretation in order to admit that reading is an activity in which what we bring with us has a part to play in shaping the event of "meaning" that occurs. In this sense, as Stanley Grenz urges, *sola scriptura* must not be understood in any way that either constrains the Spirit's activity in bringing the text to life in relevant patterns of response within the particularity of our ever changing circumstances, or robs us of our moral obligation in the face of the text. What we bring to and do with texts matter, in other words, as much as what texts (and in this case God through texts) bring to and do with and to us. Meaning is had in a dynamic dialogue in which, as Grenz rightly insists, Scripture furnishes the "primary voice," but we are equally drawn in and called to participate and faithfully correspond with what we hear. Kevin Vanhoozer's essay offers us a series of vital images for appropriating this perlocutionary aspect of the text of Scripture: the-atre, drama, performance, plot, voice, actors, play, improvisation, and so on. As well as furthering consideration of the relevant methodolog-ical point, Vanhoozer's own practice thereby also raises a significant and discrete methodological question: What role ought to be afforded to the image, and the imagination, within Christian theology, whether at the level of first-order engagements with the primary realities known to faith, or second-order discussions such as those carried on in this volume ("talking about talking about God" as it has been put)?

Other essays in this volume also raise this issue indirectly—notably, Grenz's central appeal to the image of tradition as a mosaic, and his passing reminder of just how many prior images have variously en-abled and held our thinking captive in this field of discourse: founda-tions and building; cartography and horizons; frameworks; networks; the "fitting together" of pieces; and so on. How should we view such imaginative takes on vitally important issues? Should we eschew them altogether in preference for the sort of "plain speech" that (according to John Locke, for example) simply says what it means and means ex-actly what it says? Should we permit them a useful illustrative or lubri-cative function but be sure to resort to more hard-edged and precise analysis at the vital moment at which truth comes into view? Or might we actually suppose imagination itself to be a vital tool and resource for our grasp and elucidation of the substance of theology, enabling us, in certain circumstances at least, to go farther and to see more than other more discursive modes of theological reflection? These are im-portant questions and ones around which my own recent research has recently centered. This, I hope, explains what it is that I, as reader and respondent, bring to the text, do with it, and take away from it. Whether it is a responsible reading is for others to judge. I hope that the result will at least contribute helpfully to the wider discussion this book initiates.

No Place for Imagination?

The status of the image within Christian theology has usually been at best a precarious one. The vulgar fact that the gospel proclaims the ap-pearance among us of one described by Scripture as "the image of the invisible God" and God's Word rendered (would "performed" be stretch-ing things too far?) in the flesh, has not dissuaded Christian theology from a widespread eschewal of imagination as a theological tool and re-source. Our theology has, as John Baillie observed long ago, too often been preoccupied with the intellectual and neglectful or downright sus-picious of the imaginative. If this observation needs any qualification, it is perhaps only by way of a challenge laid to the neat distinction that it seems to permit: The intellect is not an imagination-free zone. From first to last the exercise of reason, like the functioning of moral consciousness and our capacity for empirical engagement with the world around us, is contingent upon the varied benefits bestowed by this arcane benefactor. Yet theologians, in step with wider currents in Western culture, have preferred to pretend otherwise, claiming to have disentangled the imaginative from the rational, the empirical, the moral, and then subjected it to their allegedly superior and more trustworthy judgments.

This odd form of epistemic apartheid can be observed in attitudes regarding the ways in which the Bible functions as Scripture. It is ironic, if not perverse, that this most imaginative of texts, this literary production line of power-packed images, has so often been approached with an imaginative sympathy worthy of Dickens's Thomas Gradgrind, "a man of facts and calculations. A man who proceeds upon the principle that two and two are four and nothing over, and who is not to be talked into allowing for anything over. . . . With a rule and a pair of scales, and the multiplication table always ready in his pocket, sir, ready to weigh and measure any parcel of human nature, and tell you exactly what it comes to."[1] Gradgrind's cadaverous positivism, for which all that matters is hard facts and a grasp of the intellectual principles that link them together, has its exegetical counterparts. Whether it is the conservative evangelical's concern that a certain sort of inerrancy be ascribed to the text, or the liberal's passion to identify and pare away the trimmings of myth and theological elaboration, very often the same basic set of assumptions is operative; namely, that what is of permanent value for faith must be reducible in the final analysis either to fact (history) or to eternal truths that can be shown to be rationally and morally satisfying.

In this respect, that very impact of foundationalism on theological method to which Grenz alludes has produced a pair of oddly related Siamese twins, joined at a methodological hip and almost impossible to separate. The "biblicist" insistence on the "historicity" of such books as Job and Jonah, or on reading the apocalyptic visions of Daniel and Revelation as straightforwardly predictive (the "facts" of the future), and the liberal passion for demythologizing the gospels and Old Testament patriarchal narratives actually (and ironically) amount in practice to much the same thing: a stripping of the textual altars in a bid to purge all hint of imaginative influence. The tacit (and shared) assumption is that imagination as such can have no serious or positive contribution to make or role to play in the mainstream of Christian faith and theology.

1. Charles Dickens, *Hard Times* (London: Penguin, 1969), 48.

Similar attitudes may be traced more widely within our churches, in "tradition" in its widest senses. As Stephen Williams's essay suggests, in our reflections on theological method, this category of *traditio* must be deliberately broadened out beyond the steady effluence of words in creed, confession, liturgy, proclamation, and the rest to embrace all the ways in which we are called to "interpret" or "perform" the gospel in the most diverse and the most mundane aspects of life lived Christianly. For what is handed on from one person, group, culture, and generation to the next is not just words and ideas, important though these will always be, but a set of vital practices and roles that must constantly be improvised upon in order to meet the demands of particular environments. Whatever the activity, though, the truth is that we do not generally expect imagination to be the locus of any significant encounter with God (and are immediately suspicious of any claim to this effect), nor to furnish the tools and other resources for a genuinely theological engagement with reality, divine or mundane. A paucity of imagination is something with which we have become all too familiar. Like Plato we have banished the artists from the city-states of our traditions, and for some essentially similar reasons. We are inherently suspicious of them as weavers of fictions and conjurors of illusions that we suppose can serve only to detract from the truth rather than to illuminate it.

When imagination is welcomed into our worship, for example, it is frequently heavily sedated and placed on a thick leash. If we allow something so radical as dramatic sketches, we nonetheless want the point that they are making to be clearly explained later in a sermon of a mostly conceptual nature. The function of the poetic or the dramatic, therefore, is purely illustrative of something else, a matter of communicative lubrication rather than substance. But imaginative forms cannot be translated into purely rational/conceptual versions without significant loss. The following words from Flannery O'Connor point toward the difficulties inherent in this unthinking subjugation of the imaginative by the intellectual: "When you can state the theme of a story, when you can separate it from the story itself, then you can be sure the story is not a very good one. The meaning of a story has to be embodied in it, has to be made concrete in it. A story is a way to say something that can't be said any other way, and it takes every word in the story to say what the meaning is. You tell a story because a statement would be inadequate. When anybody asks what a story is about, the only proper thing to do is to tell him to read the story."[2] Something similar could be said, I believe, about most of the forms of creative

2. Flannery O'Connor, *Mystery and Manners* (New York: Farrar, Straus & Giroux, 1969), 96.

imagination. Yes, of course they *can* be used in a purely illustrative fashion, to make intellectual truths or moral precepts more palatable, but at their best these forms resist any such merely subservient role and stand alone as the vehicles of a truth that all the resources of rational and empirical method can neither reach nor explain.

And yet theology (and evangelical theology as much as any other and perhaps more than most) has so often prized itself on being a Gradgrind discipline, concerned, if not exactly or always with "facts" in the usual sense, nonetheless with "facts" of a sort, with the exploration of concepts, ideas, and truth claims, and with the sort of rigorous argumentation in which we could easily imagine (were we permitted to do so) Gradgrind finding some deep sense of satisfaction. That we have not been entirely successful in the attempt is testimony perhaps both to the ineradicability and all-pervasiveness of the imaginative itself as a force in human life, and to the preserving providence of the God the activity of whose Spirit is characterized by the dreaming of dreams and the seeing of visions. Where there is no vision, as the proverb reminds us, the people perish. And if theology has not exactly perished, it may be precisely because it has not entirely lost sight of vision and surrendered its imaginative instincts; but it has often deliberately sought to do so, and there have doubtless been costs to pay.

Evangelical Suspicion of Imagination

Ironically, the roots of evangelical suspicion of imagination where it persists are likely to lie in some well-motivated but less well-conceived attempts to resuscitate its theological fortunes (always uncomfortable and awkward when something isn't really dead in the first place). Some, for example, especially in the modern period, have supposed all talk about "God" to be, in essence, imaginary, a construction or projection of the human quest for a transcendent Other whose reality (if he/she/it actually transcends our imagining at all) must not be supposed to be correlated closely with the images that we deploy in theology and spirituality.

This approach has its roots and its most extreme expression in the nineteenth century with Ludwig Feuerbach's *The Essence of Christianity* (New York, 1957), but it appears in more moderate contemporary versions among writers such as Gordon Kaufman (*The Theological Imagination*, Philadelphia, 1981) and Sallie McFague (*Metaphorical Theology*, London, 1983). It is an approach that understands imagination as an essentially free and creative manifestation of the human spirit and traces strong connections between theology and the sort of activity we naturally associate with the arts. So McFague, for example, in her writings likens the theologian to a "philosopher-poet" whose role is to fashion and test on her contemporaries ever new metaphors for God, seeking those images that will best facilitate the expression of the God-world relation as it is currently experienced. Such a creative task, she admits, involves daring and imaginative leaps across distance (i.e., the distance that separates us from God) and is fraught with danger: Being open initially to all possibilities, there is always the risk "that the leap across the abyss will be unsuccessful."[3] Kaufman, meanwhile, also appeals to the ancient recognition of imagination's capacity for sheer creativity and sets it deliberately over against the category of "revelation" as a source for God-talk. We must choose—either imaginative construction or the "positivism" of revelation.

Faced with such a choice, it is not surprising that theologians in the evangelical mainstream have shied away from any embrace of imagination. For many, such language inevitably suggests the substitution of the creations of an untrammelled human imagination ("figments" as the popular phrase has it) for the reality of God, with spiritually and theologically damaging consequences. Unfortunately, the bid to be rid of the imaginative is a futile one. It is no more possible to purge imagination from our theology than it is to dispense with the poetic in our language. To succeed would be to reduce ourselves finally to silence. "Metaphor, simile, analogy, synecdoche, and so on are common in the simplest attempts to understand and explain, and are not restricted to poetry. Take the common expressions 'I see what you mean,' 'I follow your argument,' or 'I get your point.' These are all metaphors, but if we were to try and purge them from argument and explanation, what could we put in their place?"[4]

The poetic undergirds even our most straightforward engagements with the real and furnishes the grid that enables us, bit by bit, to chart its mysterious contours. George MacDonald makes this point very clearly when he directs us to the etymology of the word *attention* (from *attentio*, meaning a "stretching to"). "Take any word expressive of emotion," MacDonald writes (and we may broaden this to include the inner and outer "spiritual" or "psychic" realm), "and you will find that its primary meaning is of the outer world."[5] Such a quarrying of the physical-created realm is inevitable when we wish to speak of the invisible, since if we are to picture something to ourselves it must be in terms of other

3. Sallie McFague, *Models of God: Theology for an Ecological, Nuclear Age* (London: SCM Press, 1987), 35.

4. Gordon Graham, *Philosophy of the Arts* (London: Routledge, 1997), 115.

5. George MacDonald, *A Dish of Orts* (London: Sampson Low, Marston & Co., 1891), 8–9.

things that we can see or otherwise perceive via our senses. The invisible cannot be pictured in terms of the invisible. And if this is true more widely in the field of the human, it is all the more true in relation to matters of faith and theology. To the extent that Christian faith is rooted in realities that transcend the flesh and blood realities of nature and history, it is inevitable that it should be "a faith that subsists in the symbolic realm and is appropriated through imaginative indwelling,"[6] hence, the predominance of metaphor, symbol, myth, and story in its scriptural source text, its doctrine, and its liturgy. We cannot avoid "imaging" the realities in which our faith is finally invested, including the God who lies at the heart of it all.

The Importance of Imagination

To recognize this, though, is far from being driven onto some slippery slope leading to the jaws of idolatry. The golden calf can safely be put back in the cupboard. Nor is it even to cut ourselves loose from the firm moorings of revelation and tradition, free to drift endlessly on a sea of postmodern open-mindedness, velcroing our colors to the mast and allowing ourselves to be cast hither and thither toward new shores by the tides of *difference*. Imagination is not opposed to revelation and tradition, nor to the sort of identifiable horizons for faith, discipleship, and theological reflection that these furnish. As some of the essays in this collection make clear, revelation and tradition are themselves imaginative in provenance and in practice, and demand from us imaginative modes of engagement with the realities that they mediate. Both Scripture and the tradition, in which in the most diverse forms of life its story is taken up and "performed" again and again on ever new stages with ever new casts and to an ever changing audience, are storehouses of images in terms of which the gospel may and must be proclaimed and imagined and acted out.

Amos Wilder's plea, made some twenty-five years ago now, that the church wake up to its imaginative resources and develop a "theopoetic" to match its theology and theopraxis (again these ought not to be set alongside one another as if they were not meshed together in reality) still needs to be heard and taken to heart, and not least in evangelical circles. We must insist, to be sure, that God's self-revealing initiative (in Scripture, in his own self-imaging in his Son, and in his personal indwelling of the church in his Spirit) be taken absolutely seriously and accounted for adequately in Christian discipleship and theological con-

---

6. Paul Avis, *God and the Creative Imagination: Metaphor, Symbol, and Myth in Religion and Theology* (London: Routledge, 1999), 7.

struction. Yet we must also acknowledge the vital roles played by imagination in laying hold of the reality of this same God and in enabling our response to God's engagement with us. For faith, as evangelicals above all know very well, is a relationship with God that transforms and transfigures. It is a relationship in which the Father's approach in Word and Spirit calls forth from us ever and again imaginative responses as we seek to interpret, to "make sense" of, and to correspond appropriately with what we hear God saying to us. It is not a matter of having a divine image impressed on us like tablets of wax but of having our imagination taken captive and being drawn into a divine drama, playing out the role that the Father grants us in the power of the Spirit, whom he pours out on the entire group of players.

The series of images that Vanhoozer offers us in his essay are thus supremely healthy and "enabling" images, helping us to picture a form of responsible (response-able) participation in the tasks of theology (defined, as he urges, in its broadest sense to embrace all those who would "image" the gospel in word or gesture or way of being) that secures the proper order of godly initiative and "direction," and human performance and interpretation. Its health is all the more apparent when set alongside a related but altogether different imagining offered recently by the Anglican Bishop of Edinburgh, for whom God may helpfully be pictured as "one who accompanies creation in its evolving story like a pianist in a silent movie."[7] Such a suggestion issues, I think, not from taking imagination too seriously but from failing to take it seriously enough. This is precisely the sort of Promethean usurping of the divine copyright that Plato so chastised and that led him duly to undervalue the roles of imagination in bringing us into a proper relationship with truth, a deeper and more resonant relationship than unaided reason can aspire to.

But take imagination seriously we must. For, we might say, while the stuff of Christian faith and theology is certainly not *imaginary*, it is highly *imaginative* and cannot avoid being so. Therefore, one recent consideration of this matter insists "that Christianity lives supremely from the imagination," and "unless we attempt to do full justice to the part played by imagination, we cannot understand the Christian faith and we cannot ourselves truly believe."[8] Evangelicals, I believe, have no reason to demur from this judgment and every reason to embrace and own its force and implications. Yet imagination is not just at the core of what it means to be Christian but more significantly at the core of

    7. Richard Holloway, *Godless Morality: Keeping Religion Out of Ethics* (Edinburgh: Canongate Publishers, 1999), 33.
    8. Avis, *God and the Creative Imagination*, 3.

what it means to be human. There are few if any activities or experiences known to us that do not involve the imagination in one way or
another. Might it be the case that recognition and exploration of its
roles within faith and theology could offer one important way into a
"theological anthropology that adumbrates the Christian understanding of the human person right across the spectrum of academic disciplines" (see Stephen Williams's essay)? This is not to suggest some new
natural theological project rooted in the claim that humans are *capax
imaginatio* and therefore in some sense *capax Dei;* it is simply to note
that imagination seems to run through every sphere, layer, dimension,
nook, and cranny of our humanity, and since as Christians we believe
God to be present and known in the midst of all this, the category of
imagination may provide a convenient focus for an accounting of what
it means to be human in God's world.

We need do nothing whatever to detract from either the importance
or the benefits of that proper use of "reason," which generally gets
listed alongside Scripture, tradition, and experience in accountings of
the various "tools" or "resources" of theology. This familiar image cluster itself surely needs supplementing by others that emphasize the way
these realities are tangled up together and that picture them not as set
over against us as discrete objects to be picked up and "used," but
rather as the elements that furnish the very milieu of our existence, on
which we depend from moment to moment for the survival of our
Christian identity in the world. Whatever set of images we use, though,
it is high time that we granted imagination its proper place on the list
(or in the mix), for it is there whether or not we recognize or like it, and
it will have its impact on our theology whether or not we take account
of and responsibility for it. Evangelical theology must take seriously
the poetic as a mode of theological exploration and engagement, alongside and interwoven with the conceptual and the empirical in ways that
it has not often been hitherto. The deliberate, sustained appeal to imagination in this collection is thus welcome both in itself and as an indi-
cation of a wider growing awareness of the importance and promise
that this dimension of our humanity offers to all "theologians," that is,
to all those who think, and act, and bear witness together in fellowship.

There is, I think, an important sense in which those many "theologians" (in Stephen Williams's democratized sense) who daily indwell
and "perform" the imaginative story of a Father who sends his Son em-
powered by the Spirit into the world for its salvation have a more secure grasp on the mysterious reality of just who this God is than some
of "those whom we customarily call theologians," who feel more at
home amid the bloodless ballet of concepts: *ousia, hypostasis, peri-*

choresis, filioque, communicatio idiomatum, and the rest. Of course the two belong together, and both, finally, matter; but if forced to choose, I think I would opt for the drama over the algebra every day of the week. Imagination, the poetic, can help us to bring to expression, for ourselves and for others, reality in its most mysterious and complex dimensions and yet, having brought it to an appropriate level and form of expression, to remain tantalizingly aware of the symbolic shortfall of our utterance. For reality, in all its mysterious depths, is the great iconoclast; and God is the greatest iconoclast of them all.

9

Reforming Evangelical Theology

Roger E. Olson

In a *Christian Century* essay, I coined the label "postconservative" to describe a new mood arising within North American evangelical theological circles. Some critics and commentators have identified this new mood (not movement!) as "the evangelical left." The essays on evangelical theological identity and methodology in this volume demonstrate that theological reflection can be both postconservative and neither "left" nor "right" but solidly evangelical. Not every author would identify himself as "postconservative." In fact, only one uses that modifier for his proposal (Vanhoozer). In the sense I had in mind, however, the term well describes the overall tenor of the essays included here. These essays show how a truly evangelical theology can move along a trajectory away from fundamentalism and even conservatism (i.e., traditionalism, rigid preservation of the "received evangelical tradition") and toward a more biblically faithful, more culturally relevant, and therefore more evangelical theology. These essays and their publication by Baker Book House represent a most hopeful sign that evangelical theology may yet escape the tendency toward "hardening of the categories" that set in sometime during the Reagan era.

What do these essays have in common that qualifies them (taken together) as postconservative? Overall and in general they display a certain set of characteristics that is quite different from the controlling motifs of earlier, more conservative evangelical theological proposals and programs (to say nothing of fundamentalist ones!). While acknowledging differences among them, I will risk making certain generalizations about the group. These general characteristics are not true to the same extent of each and every essay, but I see them as markers of the group as a whole that indicate progress in reforming evangelical theology in a non-fundamentalist, non-liberal, postconservative direction.

A Lack of Fear

First, notably lacking in these essays is obsessive fear of liberal theology. Understandably, much conservative theology throughout the twentieth century was governed by reaction against the liberal reconstruction of Protestant theology in the previous century and against its reverberations and echoes in the twentieth century (e.g., in neo-liberal theological paradigms). To a large extent, even postfundamentalist evangelical theology was and is held captive to the liberal-fundamentalist crisis of the 1920s through the 1950s. This captivity inevitably gave to conservative theology a certain reactionary cast. Conservative theologians felt they had to draw firm boundaries around authentic Protestant Christianity (i.e., evangelical theology) without becoming separatistic or sectarian à la fundamentalism. A major task of evangelical theology, then, became that of fending off all forms of liberal theology. For conservatives this included some that were decidedly anti-liberal, such as Karl Barth's dialectical theology. In spite of itself, conservative evangelical theology often came (and still comes) close to that which it perceived as the enemy: accommodation of the biblical witness and of the gospel of Jesus Christ to a secular spirit. This danger appeared in the tendency of many of its most noted leaders to wed theology to a highly rationalistic epistemology that focused on demonstrable correspondence between revealed propositions (or propositions deduced directly from revelation) and empirical reality and/or between revealed propositions themselves. Aggressive critique of liberal (experiential-expressivist) theology, rationalistic prolegomena and methodology, and rigid traditionalism marked the scholastic spirit (mood) of much conservative evangelical theology in the latter half of the twentieth century. This manifested itself in the harsh polemics over not only the concept of inerrancy but also over its hermeneutical functions.

In recent years (1990s) certain leading spokespersons for conservative evangelicalism have extended the "battle for the Bible" (i.e., the battle for biblical inerrancy) into an aggressive battle for epistemological realism and rationalism (as necessary for healthy evangelical theology) and against all innovations in or adjustments to what they regard as "the received evangelical tradition." In an article in *Christianity Today*, I identified a crisis in evangelical theological circles in North America between "reformists" and "traditionalists." By "reformists" I meant those evangelicals with a postconservative spirit—in other words, those committed evangelical theologians who are determined to break free with bold confidence from captivity to categories of "right" and "left" and develop a liberated evangelical theology that is more and not less biblical because it is open to radical challenges from the word of God in Scripture. The essays contained in this volume breathe that liberated and liberating spirit that I call postconservative while strictly avoiding a "liberal trajectory." Such is the case because the authors have broken free from being governed by modernity (or postmodernity for that matter!). This is not to endorse each and every proposal. Nor do I intend by this admittedly general characterization to blend them all together. There are notable differences among them, and each author speaks with his own voice. Yet, the chorus has a new and exciting harmony that is recognizably evangelical without parodying past arrangements. The first general characteristic of these essays (as a group), therefore, is that they are postconservative without being theologically "left." There is nothing either fundamentalist or modernist about them.

A Concern with Evangelical Identity

The second general characteristic I find in these essays as a group is a concern with evangelical identity apart from rigid boundaries and "gatekeeping." John Stackhouse's essay, "Evangelical Theology Should Be Evangelical," is a model of broad but never shallow evangelical description. It helpfully and quite accurately identifies the core commitments of evangelical theology, and I find insightful the addition of a fifth to the oft-used "Bebbington four": transdenominationalism. This fifth characteristic commitment is fleshed out by Stackhouse in a charge to would-be self-appointed conservative gatekeepers of "authentic evangelicalism": "We simply can't afford the luxury of continual heresy hunting and the division that it produces. . . . Such intra-evangelical wars are actually anti-evangelical." Stackhouse's call for intra-evangelical dialogue as a practical aspect of evangelical theological methodology is welcome.

Other essays in this collection also speak to the issue of evangelical identity in a manner that does not seek so much to exclude persons (or institutions) as to include all those whose basic commitments are to the supreme authority of God in Jesus Christ as revealed in the inspired canon of Holy Scripture and impressed upon the hearts of women and men through the transforming work of the Holy Spirit. I do detect a certain favoritism toward the Reformed theological heritage in Alister McGrath's otherwise fine essays, but even this is ameliorated by inclusive references to the Radical Reformation and John Wesley. My own hermeneutic of suspicion—faulty as it probably is—leads me to suspect that McGrath's version of evangelical identity would include among the core commitments a Reformed accent that stands in some tension with Stackhouse's transdenominationalism (which really seems to mean "transconfessionalism"). Nevertheless, even McGrath's contributions to this collection breathe a fresh spirit of critical appropriation of the "great tradition" within evangelical theological methodology.

A Search for Truth

A third unifying characteristic of these essays that makes them (as a whole) postconservatively evangelical is liberation from Enlightenment realism and rationalism combined with a preservation of objective truth and coherence. For many conservative evangelicals, of course, this move is impossible. Epistemological realism and rationalism are inextricably tied to ontological realism and belief in objective truth. For many conservative critics of postmodern and postliberal moves in theology, the only real alternatives in this basic area of foundational theology are commonsense realism and Richard Rorty's relativism. (Of course, this is unfair to any individual conservative evangelical theologian and possibly to Rorty as well, but it is a relatively accurate representation of the impression given by some conservative critics of the postmodern approaches of evangelical theologians such as Stanley J. Grenz, James McClendon, Nancey Murphy, Brian Walsh, and Richard Middleton.)

Especially Stanley Grenz and Kevin Vanhoozer raise fresh and fascinating possibilities (however inchoate they may be) for truly evangelical approaches to theological methodology that avoid both the Scylla of Protestant scholasticism and the Charybdis of postmodern relativism. This is not to imply that their proposals are completely commensurate with one another; they are quite distinct. Yet they do have a common concern: to provide a postfoundationalist vision for a truly Christ- and Bible-centered evangelical approach to theological reflection and doctrinal construction. Each uses George Lindbeck's postliberal approach to theology (cultural-linguistic) as a foil, and each transcends Lindbeck's three categories of defining doctrine to one that seeks to preserve what is of value in each while leaving behind their be-

setting weaknesses. For Grenz, the tools of coherentism and eschatological realism help construct such a new approach. For Vanhoozer,
the tools are canonical-linguistic approach (to understanding doctrine)
and the dramatic analogy (for conceiving and communicating theology
as performance). Both emphasize the importance of community for
positive and constructive evangelical theology, and both also emphasize the constitutional-regulative authority of Scripture. At the same
time, they (and perhaps other essays in this collection, though less notably) transcend the old correspondence theory of truth to visions of
truth that are not tied to the Enlightenment project. For Grenz, objective truth is the future world of God (eschatological realism); for Vanhoozer, it is the divine drama of redemption played out in the biblical
witness and our Spirit-inspired inclusion in the play. Truth is in the
performance as much as or more than in the proposition.

A Respect for Doctrinal Heritage

Fourth, as a group these essays reflect respect for doctrinal heritage
without rigid traditionalism. This characteristic of postconservative
theology comes through especially in McGrath's two essays. The others
say less about the roles of doctrinal heritage and tradition while reflecting respect for the great tradition. Some readers (and perhaps even
McGrath himself!) may question my identification of McGrath's essays
as "postconservative." Without doubt such identification is more problematic in this case. Nevertheless, McGrath goes out of his way to underline the secondary status of doctrinal heritage and tradition compared with the authority of the biblical witness itself. He chides those
who regard a form of absolute confessionalism or traditionalism as a
warranty against doctrinal downgrade. He correctly affirms and asserts that any part of the great tradition of Christian teaching could be
in need of correction by better understanding of Scripture. This is a
postconservative move. So is McGrath's hearty acceptance and endorsement of evangelical diversity.

I cannot help but wonder, however, why McGrath makes two moves
within his recommendation of the great tradition as a source (and possibly a norm?) for evangelical theological methodology. First, he seems
to baptize as mainline a theological tradition running from Augustine
through Gregory the Great through Bernard of Clairvaux through
Luther, Zwingli, Calvin (the "mainline reformers") and up to J. I.
Packer. Almost everything McGrath says about the roles of non-Augus-
tinian-Reformed theologians is seriously qualified as if even the best
representatives of non-Reformed theological traditions were at best
flawed guides and models. Was Wesley's approach to Scripture and tra-

dition really all that different from Calvin's? I don't think so. Wesley's
"Quadrilateral" is widely misunderstood as an "Equilateral" of authoritative sources and norms. Rather, Wesley placed Scripture on a higher
plane than tradition, reason, and experience while respecting the great
tradition of doctrinal teaching. There is a subtle but discernible bias in
McGrath's account of the valuable heritage of the past in favor of mon-
ergistic theologians. (Gregory the Great and Bernard of Clairvaux may
be anomalies, but why are they mentioned at all? That remains unclear.) My point is simply that if McGrath really wishes to recognize
evangelical diversity, he should include in a more positive light the he-
roes of non-Reformed evangelicals, such as Menno Simons and Balthasar Hubmaier, Jacob Arminius and John Wesley, Philipp Spener
and August Hermann Francke. And Clark Pinnock.

A Role for Experience

Finally, a fifth general postconservative characteristic of these essays is fusion of the practical-spiritual with the theoretical-intellectual
in evangelical theological methodology. That is to say, theology cannot
be divorced from concrete experience. While most of the essays in this
collection in some manner tip the hat to experience as having an inevitable and positive role to play in theological methodology (contrary to
much conservative evangelical methodology that tends to play exegesis
against experience), Stephen Williams especially emphasizes the inex-
tricable connection between lived experience and theological reflection
in a positive way. For Williams, "experience and discernment of life
and our times, when rooted in the habit of faithfulness to Christ and to
Scripture, must be allowed to shape our interpretation of the biblical
kerygma." He especially recommends a retrieval of Dietrich Bonhoeffer's Christian ethics of the penultimate as a powerful tool for evangelical theological method. Exactly how this will contribute to doctrinal
development and construction is left unclear, but the vote for a vigorous evangelical social ethic as necessary for viable evangelical theology
in a culture that values taste over logic is welcome.

Conclusion

I would like to add one more characteristic of the overall thrust of
these essays without identifying it as necessarily "postconservative."
Without rejecting biblical exegesis, they all regard strong evangelical
theological methodology as more than merely biblical exegesis. In light
of certain recent proposals to the contrary, this is a powerful statement
made mostly by silence—silence about exegesis itself. Taken together,

these essays are saying that evangelical systematic theology already majors in exegesis and that its neglect of other aspects of the theological task is a weakness. Almost without doubt there will be a flurry of negative responses to these essays (or ones like them) because from a perspective obsessed with issues of epistemological rational certainty and doctrinal boundaries, they open a Pandora's box of options that expand the boundaries of evangelicalism and, in the words of one title, conduct theology "after the demise of foundationalism." I urge that these inevitable critical responses be included in the ongoing discussions within the evangelical theological community about the future of evangelicalism, theological methodology, and integrity. But I also urge that the naysayers not be allowed to control the switches and patrol the boundaries. The essays in this collection help make evangelical theological methodology interesting and vibrant without worshiping at the feet of a "goddess of novelty."

Subject Index

Scripture Index